Caroline

Books by Thea Holme

CAROLINE 1979

PRINNY'S DAUGHTER 1976

CHELSEA 1972

THE CARLYLES AT HOME 1966

CAROLINE

A Biography of
Caroline of Brunswick

THEA HOLME

ATHENEUM
NEW YORK
1980

To Rose,
with love

Library of Congress Cataloging in Publication Data

Holme, Thea Johnston
Caroline, a biography of Caroline of Brunswick.

Bibliography: p.
Includes index.
1. Caroline Amelia Elizabeth, consort of George IV,
1768-1821. 2. Great Britain—Queens—Biography.
I. Title.
DA538.A2H58 1980   941.07′4′0924 [B]   79-51398
ISBN 0-689-10999-7

Manufactured by Halliday Lithograph Corporation
West Hanover and Plympton, Massachusetts
First American Edition

Acknowledgements

I wish to thank Her Majesty the Queen for giving permission to reproduce the unpublished miniature by Philip Jean, painted of the Princess of Wales before her marriage in 1795, and now in the Royal Collection at Windsor.

The originals of the letters hitherto unpublished between Princess Caroline and Sir William Gell are in the possession of Mrs Philip Gell, O.B.E., of Hopton Hall, Winksworth, Derby and were bought at Sotheby's by her late husband, Lieutenant-Colonel Philip Gell, the vendor being Sir Eardley Holland. Sir Eardley had a typescript made of the letters prior to the sale and, after his death, these copies were given to Miss Edith Clay by Lady Holland who has since died. These typescript letters have been used for this book, and Mrs Gell and Miss Clay have given their permission for publication of this correspondence. The letters are of particular interest for their betrayal of Caroline's odd character, her originality and wit.

Miss Edith Clay has been most helpful, lending me her notes on Sir William Gell and Princess Caroline and her entourage.

I must also thank my cousin, Mrs Jeannette Wynne, for scouring Hampshire for the owner of original material. I offer my respectful thanks to Mr C. A. L. Richards for his scholarly translating and deciphering of letters.

I am especially grateful to Mr R. S. Hownam-Meek for so generously lending his collection of letters and diaries of his great-great-grandfather, Joseph Hownam, a protégé of Caroline who became her Private Secretary. Mr Hownam-Meek also lent me the Princess's sketch-book, in which she claimed that some of the drawings and water-colours were her own work.

As always, thanks are due to the staff of the many libraries who have helped me, especially those of the Wiltshire Library and Museum Service, Greenwich Local History Library, the London Library and the Bodleian Library.

Illustrations

FOLLOWING PAGE 54

1a The Duke of Brunswick. Contemporary engraving
1b The Duchess of Brunswick. Engraving after the painting by Joshua Reynolds
1c George, Prince of Wales. Engraving after a drawing by R. Corbould
1d Caroline of Brunswick. Miniature by Philip Jean, 1795
2a First Earl of Malmesbury. Engraving after a painting by Joshua Reynolds
2b Mrs Fitzherbert. Painting by Thomas Gainsborough
2c Lady Jersey. Engraving after a painting by D. Gardiner
3a Carlton House, north front. Drawing by W. Westall
3b Montague House at Blackheath. Aquatint by Paul Sandby
4a Lady Charlotte Douglas. Engraving after a drawing by A. Buck
4b Caroline, Princess of Wales. Painting by James Lonsdale
4c Princess Charlotte. Watercolour by Richard Woodman
4d Sir William Gell

FOLLOWING PAGE 150

5a Bartolomeo Pergami, lithograph by G. Engelmann
5b Countess Oldi. Engraving after sketch by A. Wivell
5c The Villa d'Este
6a William Austin
6b Lieutenant Flynn RN. Engraving after sketch by A. Wivell
6c Alderman Wood. Engraving by R. Page
6d Theodore Majocchi. Engraving after sketch by A. Wivell
7a A caricature of Caroline eating 'Pergami Pears'. 'I do love these Pears! but I hate the Windsor Pears.'
7b Patriotic Poster
8a Brandenburg House

Chapter One

UNTIL THE French Revolution cast fear and gloom over the courts of Europe, many young Englishmen completed their education by travelling abroad. In 1781, John Stanley* was taken away from his school at Greenwich and sent with a tutor, Mr Six, and a bundle of introductions, to Brunswick. Young Stanley was a lively boy and ready to enjoy himself. The Court of Brunswick, he wrote home, was just then particularly brilliant and imposing, with all the ducal family assembled for the marriage of the Duke's elder daughter, Princess Charlotte Augusta.

That winter the weather was exceptionally cold, but there were splendid entertainments. The great theatre was open for balls and masquerades; there were skating parties and sledge-drives through the frozen snow. Young Stanley paints a brightly coloured picture of the scene. 'The sledge-driving of the Court and gentry in the streets was brilliant, from the fantastic shapes of the sledges, the dresses of the ladies, the caparison of the horses;' while his ears were filled with 'the "hoch! hoch! hoch!" of the gentlemen drivers, and the sound of horses' bells'.[1]

In summer, the Court was held out of doors, which gave it a less formal air, and in the gardens the young Englishman and his companions rambled at will, or rode out into the country to Wolfenbüttel, coming back 'by moonlight through forests filled with nightingales singing their hearts out'.

Such happiness is rare and delightful: the Court of Brunswick did not strike other people as such a happy place. But John Stanley, now nearly sixteen, had fallen in love—with the Duke's younger daughter. 'I saw her ... three or four times a week, but as a star out of my reach.' Perhaps she blossomed in the light of his innocent admiration: to the lovesick boy she seemed a perfect creature, a fairy princess.

When he met her again, twenty-eight years later, 'I could not find a feature or look reminding me of former times. I saw her as a stranger ... Only once, when she smiled at something that had pleased her, I could have fancied she had been the ... lively pretty Caroline, the girl my eyes had so

* Created Lord Stanley of Alderley in 1839.

often rested on, with light and powdered hair hanging in curls on her neck, the lips from which only sweet words seemed as if they could flow, with looks animated, and always simply and modestly dressed. How well I remember her in a pale blue gown, with scarcely a trick of ornament . . .'[2]

As she grew up, the glimpses we get of Caroline are disconcerting. She was an odd girl, precocious, pert, with a freakish and rather cruel sense of humour. The great Frenchman Mirabeau, visiting Brunswick, was invited by the Duke, his host, to give his definitions of time and space. Before he could answer, the Princess pointed to a particularly ugly old woman courtier. '*L'espace se trouve dans la bouche de Mme X*,' she cried, '*et le temps dans le visage*.' This may have been considered amusing, but it was not endearing. Nor was her behaviour when forbidden, at the age of sixteen, to go to a Court ball. She was evidently a good actress, and succeeded in causing consternation by going to bed and screaming that she was pregnant and about to give birth. Her parents were summoned and sent for a midwife; the music stopped, the guests scattered. But Caroline, having succeeded in her plan to upset the entertainment, jumped up, wiped the white paint from her face, and screamed with laughter. 'Now, madam,' she demanded of her mother, 'will you forbid me to go to a ball again?'

She was brought up without religion, her parents having decided that when she married she would accept the beliefs—Protestant or Catholic—of her husband. Meanwhile, there was a pagan wildness about her which defied discipline. She could be kind, generous, confiding; but the kindness, the generosity, the confidingness, were on the spur of the moment. She saw herself in many guises, and in her time was to play many parts; but each part had its origin in some facet of her own personality. She believed implicitly in what, for the moment, she wanted to believe; and as Lady Charlotte Bury wrote of her later, her conversation was a mixture of truth and falsehood: she lied, not out of cowardice, but because she wished to make an effect. This, for a princess who was required above all things to practise discretion, was an unfortunate propensity.

The only person who could inspire anything like awe in her was her father, Prince Charles William Ferdinand, a distinguished soldier who had inherited his father's dukedom and his debts in 1780. The Brunswick Court was then known as Little Versailles, a gay and delightful place. The new Duke was anxious to preserve the jollity and good cheer of his father's Court, but he was obliged to economize; also, he himself was not a jolly man, and in time his brooding personality made itself felt by his courtiers as well as his family.

The city of Brunswick was circular and enclosed by high ramparts where people rode and walked. Above the dark ancient town with its narrow streets and overhanging eaves stood the Duke's palace, large, draughty and inconvenient. There were in fact three courts. The Dowager Duchess, the Duke's mother, had her own. Sister to Frederick the Great, she was an alarming person, formal and remote; refusing to conform to her son's economies, she drove daily through the small town in a coach drawn by eight Hanoverian creams.

His wife, the reigning Duchess, was English, the elder sister of George III and like him in appearance, with the same popping eyes and loose-lipped mouth, the same retreating chin, unexpectedly dimpled.

'*A la verité, elle est toute Anglaise*,' said Mirabeau, '*par les goûts, par les principes, et par les manières*,' and he found her simple directness a striking contrast with the strict etiquette of the German courts. 'A fair, well-looking woman,' one English visitor wrote, '. . . and I think when young must have been handsome. She is now a great deal too large.'[3] She took no exercise, and suffered cruelly from the cold, confiding in this fellow Englishwoman that she had the sleeves of her dresses 'entirely lined' with woollen stockings.

This Duchess, Caroline's mother, also had her own court, and her palace, three miles outside Brunswick, which she called, nostalgically, Little Richmond. She and her ladies could be found there, 'employed in knotting, netting, embroidery, and even the homely occupation of knitting stockings; while the idlers, who had no regular work, were given the wherewithal to make lint for the hospital'. This is not exactly a lively picture, but the poor Duchess led a dull life. She would chatter unceasingly to a confidante, and avidly seized upon any visitors from England. 'I think you will love me at last,' she told one of these ladies after begging her to call again—a pathetic assurance.

Her life was not particularly blissful, and although in the early days of her marriage she had written to her brother the King of England, 'My husband . . . is monstrously fond of me and I am a happy woman,' these were not her true feelings, and she knew that she had been a failure. The Duke took very little notice of her. 'Only private persons can be happily married,' he told Massenbach, 'because they can choose their mates.' He found the Princess Augusta stupid and dull, and spent all his spare time with his reigning mistress, Mlle Hertzfeldt, who had her own suite of rooms in the Ducal palace, where her lover dined in state once a week. 'She was the beautifullest creature and the cleverest,' Caroline said of her later. Much of this cleverness was devoted to cheering up the melancholy Duke, and keeping on the best of terms with the Duchess. The two women are said to have joined forces whenever the Duke was contemplating taking a new mistress, and to have been successful between them in queering the rival's pitch.

The Duke was impressive-looking but probably looked at his best on a horse, which would account for contradictory reports of his height. He had a fine head and a slight stoop. When he spoke, it was a very slow, emphatic French, and his elaborate politeness increased the alarm which he inspired. He held all civilians in contempt, particularly his own courtiers and his wife. He was a Freemason.

One shrewd observer said of Caroline, 'She fears her father too much and her mother too little.' She herself complained in later life: 'When I was civil to one I was scolded by the other; and I was very tired of being shuttle-cocked between them.' (It is significant that this description of the young girl torn between jarring parents might equally have applied to Caroline's daughter, Charlotte, who, till her mother left England, was perpetually 'shuttlecocked', and, being a more sensitive and affectionate character, suffered far more than her mother ever did.)

It was an ill-starred family. The Crown Prince Charles, though described as 'fat and greasy as a barrel of oil', fancied himself as an amorist, neglected his Dutch wife, and died before he was thirty. The second son, Prince George, was weak in the head; and his younger brother, Prince Augustus, was almost blind. Neither lived to succeed to the dukedom. The youngest and most normal of the family, Prince Frederick William, became Duke in 1806, though the title was all that Napoleon allowed him to inherit. Nine years later he was killed at Quatre Bras.

Caroline had one sister, Charlotte Augusta, whose death was a tragic mystery. It is known that when she was barely eighteen this beautiful flaxen-haired girl was married to the Prince of Wurtemberg and went with him to Russia, where he served in Catherine the Great's army. The couple had two sons and a daughter, and in the course of time the Prince returned home to Germany, taking the children with him. He left his wife behind. She had been unfaithful, and according to one version her lover was the Empress Catherine's son (another says Catherine's cast-off lover). In either case, it was a tactless choice. Left in the dubious protection of the Empress, who had no scruples about getting rid of unwanted offenders, the unhappy Charlotte Augusta was banished from St Petersburg and eventually imprisoned in a remote Baltic stronghold, Castle Lode. After two years of silence, the news reached her father and her husband that she had died. No details were given, and when the Duke demanded that her body be brought back to Brunswick, this was refused. It was never known how she died, or even, for certain, where. But 'years after,' wrote Miss Rigby in *Letters from the Baltic*, the Prince of Oldenberg, nearly related to the deceased, came expressly to Castle Lode. Here, in the cellars, a body was found, 'in a state of preservation (owing to the quality of the atmosphere) which left no doubt of identity'.[4]

Caroline was twenty when the news came of her sister's death. Though it must have shocked her at the time, she soon began to appreciate the dramatic possibilities of the 'horrid' mystery, which would probably never be solved, and which appealed to her lively imagination. 'She amused us very much,' wrote her lady-in-waiting, Lady Charlotte Bury, 'by telling us the history of her sister . . .' To have found this tragedy 'amusing' seems incredible. More and more details were added, including a theory that the Princess was still alive and had been seen at the opera in Leghorn, or other unlikely places. But like a heroine of Gothic romance, the Princess Charlotte Augusta seems a little unreal, and it is a shock to meet her eldest son, Prince Paul of Wurtemberg, getting drunk at Ascot Races in 1814.

Princess Caroline was, as we have seen, resilient: it was not in her nature to suffer for long. 'Gone is gone,' she said. 'That which is gone will never return, and that which is to come will come of itself.' She developed a fearlessness which, though not one of the more endearing virtues, was to become her chief support.

'*Ein Braunschweiger darf alles*,' she asserted. '*Furcht ist ein Wort den ein Braunschweiger kennt nicht*.'[5]*

Her first biographer, Huish, suggests that she had a strong masculine streak, and this, if true, would account for her hoydenish behaviour, as well as for her precocity: she was no fool, but she did not possess the feminine graces of gentleness and modesty. At twenty-six she was still unmarried. Eligible princes, though they may have found her amusing *pour passer le temps*, took themselves off when it came to a question of marriage. Among the small German courts disquieting rumours spread about the Princess's morals.

Although there is no positive evidence that Caroline had a love affair, it seems unlikely that a young woman of her temperament, with opportunities of meeting men of all ages and types, did not have her adventures, and perhaps even a serious affair. Huish states delicately—perhaps too delicately—that she did. She sometimes cast herself in the role of Lady Bountiful, patting apple-cheeked peasant children on the head and calling at cottages to offer help to the needy. 'Slanderous reports', said Huish, 'reached at length the ears of her mother,' that while ostensibly visiting the poor, she

* A Brunswicker dares do anything. Fear is a word which a Brunswicker doesn't know.

was keeping assignations with her lover. The Duchess 'saw in it nothing more than the mere babble of the antiquated maids and the sexagenarian bachelors of the Court'; but doctors took a graver view, and Caroline was ordered 'a temporary retirement from the bustle and turmoil of the Court'. How long she spent in retirement is not disclosed; but Huish, who clearly wishes to present a romantic view, alleges that on her return 'she was received at her father's Court with every demonstration of joy. She, however, looked around her and found a blank—one was wanting . . .' Her lover had gone to join the army. Who he was, we shall never know: Caroline herself, later on, insisted that the great love of her life was Prince Louis Ferdinand of Prussia, who, she said, was in love with her all his life, and—courting death in battle—was finally killed at Jena. But as she was inclined to tell romantic fables about her own youth, no one can be sure how much was true.

Nevertheless, the existence of this affair would explain a sudden upsurge of watchfulness by her father, and a scandalous report which travelled round the courts of Europe and this time reached the Queen of England.

Queen Charlotte wrote off in some agitation to her brother the Duke of Mechlenburg-Strelitz, who was looking for a wife: 'There, dear brother, is a woman I do not recommend at all.' The Princess Caroline of Brunswick, she said, was spoken of with very little respect. 'They say her passions are so strong that the Duke of Brunswick himself said that she was not to be allowed even to go from one room to another without her Governess, and that when she dances this Lady is obliged to follow her for the whole of the dance to prevent her from making indecent conversations with men . . .'[6]

The thought of Caroline being followed through the gavottes and quadrilles by a solitary dancing governess is bizarre, and must have put a damper on her partner's mirth at what she probably said on purpose to shock. But it seems unlikely that this, or the 'indecent conduct' of which her father also complained, would be cured by such methods. Nevertheless, the report was alarming, and Queen Charlotte's brother hastily transferred his interest to another princess.

It must have been a considerable blow to the Queen when, a year later, in 1794, George, Prince of Wales paid a visit to his parents who were on holiday at Weymouth, and announced that he had decided to marry the Princess Caroline of Brunswick.

Chapter Two

To the King the idea seemed an excellent one, and he took it up with enthusiasm. He wrote to his Plenipotentiary, James Harris, first Earl of Malmesbury, at that time completing a special mission to Berlin, and commanded him to proceed at once to Brunswick and request, on behalf of the Prince of Wales, the hand of the Princess Caroline, and bring her forthwith to England. The King had never set eyes on his niece; nor had the Prince. The Queen—though, as we know she had heard disquieting things—was schooled by thirty years of submission to her husband's will, and remained silent.* It seemed an oddly haphazard way of choosing a wife for the heir to the throne.

The King's abrupt command left Malmesbury no alternative but to do what he was told: to gain the Princess's consent, and to escort her through a part of Europe which was becoming overrun by Napoleon's armies and across the sea to England, and the arms of her Prince. The fact that Malmesbury knew the Prince well and guessed the reason for his sudden decision to marry, did not make his task any easier. A man of high principles, but also a practised diplomatist, he could only brace himself to the problems that lay ahead and rely upon his ability, when the time came, to solve them.

At Brunswick, the news was received rapturously by the Duchess, who thought that to be chosen Princess of Wales was an extraordinary piece of luck for her daughter. At twenty-six, Caroline was beginning to lose her bloom, and the Prince—the First Gentleman in Europe—was a great catch; indeed, all the young German princesses had been learning English in the hopes of marrying him. But she had never considered the choice falling upon Caroline: for one thing, the King of England, her brother, had so often expressed his dislike of the marriage of cousins.

The Duke was hesitant. He had once hoped to marry his daughter to the

* Prince Ernest, Duke of Cumberland, told the Prince 'that she had resolved never to talk, no never to open her lips about your marriage, so that no one should say she had any hand in anything'.[1]

Crown Prince of Prussia, thereby allying himself with his powerful and dangerous neighbour. Now, with the outbreak of war with France, his mind was even more fixed upon this alliance and the 'very serious consequences' that might follow to himself and his family if he were to irritate the King of Prussia. He had been invited to take command of the Austrian army in defence of Holland, and this proposition, and its effect upon the King of Prussia, filled his mind. During his first audience with his host, Malmesbury soon realized that it was quite impossible to interest him in the subject of his daughter's marriage. The Duke was obsessed by his dilemma. 'He took a paper out of his pocket,' wrote Malmesbury, 'which he said he wished to read to me, that I might be au fait with the situation.' After sitting up till three in the morning listening to the Duke's problems, Malmesbury decided that the question of Princess Caroline's marriage must wait, at least till he received his full powers from England.

He had, immediately on his arrival, been presented to the Princess, who was, he wrote, 'much embarrassed'—a surprising description of one usually so cocksure. Malmesbury himself would have been completely at his ease: a handsome, well-bred and much travelled Englishman; a fluent linguist and a diplomat familiar with all the courts of Europe.

His keen eyes were well practised in appraisal; and that night he jotted down his impressions.

'Pretty face—not expressive of softness—her figure not graceful—fine eyes—good hand—tolerable teeth but going—fair hair and light eyebrows, good bust—short, with what the French call "des épaules impertinentes".'[2]

It is not a very attractive portrait; Malmesbury can hardly have felt, even at this first brief meeting, that such a connoisseur of women as the Prince of Wales would be bowled over at the sight of Princess Caroline; but perhaps he still hoped that those 'impertinent shoulders'—and other, hidden, charms—would play their part in captivating his master.

While the Duke retired to cogitate about the King of Prussia, Malmesbury was entertained enthusiastically by the Duchess, who regaled him with old recollections of the English royal family, spiced with abuse of Queen Charlotte, her sister-in-law, whom she had always detested—'an envious and intriguing spirit'. After a little she turned to the subject of Princess Caroline. 'She . . . acquainted me,' said Malmesbury, 'with all the injunctions and advice she had given her, which were very excellent.' No doubt they would have been very excellent if Caroline had bothered to listen, but she never did to her mother.

The Duchess told Malmesbury that nothing would induce her to go to England herself: she had too many unhappy memories of jealousy and suspicion when she lived there, and of her own marriage there in 1764, when she and the Duke were most shabbily treated by the King and Queen, everything being done on the cheap, no cavalry escort for the Duke, not even the customary new liveries for the servants. The Duke, she said, was a great military hero, and the English people cheered him in the streets, but at Court he was snubbed. She and the Duke were glad to take their leave, and though she was sorry to bid farewell to the King and would probably never see him again, she would never go back.

For the first few days of his visit, Malmesbury saw little of Princess Caroline. He attended a number of vast dinners and suppers, met all the members of the Duke's family, including Caroline's aunt, the Abbess of Gandersheim. This lady reminded him coyly that they were already old friends, and soon became 'altogether too familiar', so that he was obliged to avoid her. He was also seized upon by the Duke's mistress, Mlle de Hertzfeldt—he had met her years ago in Berlin, and noted that she was 'at first rather ashamed' that he should be aware of her present position, 'but soon got over it'. She interested herself deeply in all the Duke's problems, and told Malmesbury 'the Duke has been cruelly used'; she 'always thought the King of Prussia a bête, and not a bonne bête'.[3]

In the evenings the Duchess invited Malmesbury to play at ombre with her, and during the game murmured a continuation of her long saga, which consisted chiefly of ancient grudges. Queen Charlotte, she said, was very much hurt at the very fine diamond ring which the King gave her as a '*bague de mariage*'. The Queen wanted it back 'and was quite peevish about it', but the Duchess would not give it to her. It was selfish of the Queen, for 'this ring', she assured Malmesbury, and a pair of bracelets were the only diamonds she brought from England.[4] Every time the Duchess saw Malmesbury she enquired whether or no his credentials had arrived: and showed great disappointment to learn that they had not. At last, on 1 December, an emissary, Major Hislop, arrived from England bringing the Prince's picture for Caroline and a letter from him to Malmesbury, urging him to set out for England with the Princess immediately.

Malmesbury was in a dilemma. He was obliged to obey the King and follow the plans for the journey that slowly issued from Windsor. The Prince, in London, was busily making different plans, with advice from his brother the Duke of York, who as Commander-in-Chief of the army at Arnheim, was in a position to report upon the safety of the route.

'I can easily conceive how anxious you must be for the arrival of the Princess,' wrote the Duke of York, 'and do not see any reason why she may not travel with perfect safety through Holland.'[5]

The Prince was in a fever of impatience, and wrote urging Malmesbury 'to fix your plan *immediately, and so immediately put it into execution*'.

Malmesbury sympathized with the Prince's impatience, but 'I am here under the King's immediate command,' he wrote to the Duke of Portland, 'and cannot act but by his special order,'—adding 'Everybody will, I am confident, feel this but the Prince, and nobody but the Prince would have placed me in the predicament I now stand . . .' He begged Portland to justify him, repeating, 'I cannot stir from hence but by the King's order.'[6]

It was a difficult situation. The Princess was 'in a hurry' to be off; and 'We are already pack'd up to go,' the Duchess wrote: but it looked as if they would have to wait some time for starter's orders. Malmesbury, well trained in patience, determined to make good use of the delay by trying to groom the Princess. Already he had noted that 'Princess Caroline improves on acquaintance, is gay and cheerful, with good sense'. Her reception of the Prince's picture was all that could be desired. She immediately sent for a ribbon and hung the miniature on her bosom like an order. Here, displayed proudly in its frame, lay the pink, self-indulgent, still handsome face with its tendency to puffiness, that belonged to the man she was about to marry. People looked at it and congratulated her: she was the centre of interest, the heroine of a romance. 'Caroline is so happy with your picture,' wrote the Duchess to her nephew, adding that her daughter's pleasure in her marriage quite lulled her own feelings of regret at losing her. It is doubtful whether she had ever experienced these feelings, but it rounded off the sentence and the King would be pleased. The Prince had asked for portraits of his future parents-in-law, to which she now replied, 'The Duke and me will obey your orders and send our old faces; I have taken the liberty to send a sett of China with views of all the Duke's houses and my picture on the cups, the [that?] my dear daughter should not forget Bronswic.'[7]

Just before she invested herself with the Prince's portrait, Caroline was formally betrothed to him in ancient traditional ceremony at which Malmesbury acted as his deputy. It was an emotional scene and the Duchess wept. Princess Caroline, according to Malmesbury, was 'much affected', but replied distinctly and well. The Duke, 'rather embarrassed' by the whole thing, gave his answers in a loud angry voice, and when it was over all the English at Court were formally presented to Caroline, now to be called Princess of Wales. For Malmesbury everything was proceeding well: the Treaty of Marriage, drawn up in English and Latin, was signed, executed and completed. He had accomplished what was expected of him, and all that remained was to get the girl to England. He was not happy about her: after the better impression which he had received, he began to notice many unfortunate habits which must somehow be eradicated before she could pass muster in London. Observing her closely he grew more and more apprehensive: she was far too easy in her manners, chattered and giggled with other girls, calling them *ma chère*, *mon cœur* and other familiar names—and he may have thought of the impeccable royal dignity of the six English princesses who would be her sisters-in-law.

The Duke of Brunswick, he found, was well aware of Caroline's faults, and in military fashion had drawn up for her a list of instructions and warnings. '*Elle n'est pas bête*,' he told Malmesbury, 'but she lacks judgement; she has been brought up strictly—and,' he added ominously, 'it has been necessary.' She must be told not to *ask questions*, 'and above all, not to be free in giving opinions of persons and things aloud'. And here the Duke hinted 'delicately but very pointedly' that Caroline's indiscretion was inherited from her mother, who, as he put it, was apt to forget her audience.

That night, seated at supper between Caroline and her mother, Malmesbury gave the first of his pieces of advice: 'I recommend perfect silence on *all* subjects for six months after her arrival.' He cannot have known Caroline very well.

Two days later the Duke—'this very clever but cautious, suspicious and cunning man', as Malmesbury now called him—once again set aside his preoccupation with Prussia and the war to appear in the character of anxious and loving father. He told Malmesbury that he had been with Caroline for two hours that morning, pointing out to her the tremendous responsibilities of her future position; that her life would not simply be one of amusement, but had its duties—and those perhaps difficult—to fulfil. Malmesbury found that the Duke was well aware of the Prince of Wales's character and of the difficulties that might lie ahead for Caroline. She would be bound to meet with 'inconveniences' either from the Prince liking her too little or liking her too much. The name of the Prince's current inamorate, Lady Jersey, now began to crop up in their conversation. Gossip from England had reached Brunswick, and it was reported that Lady Jersey was 'very well with the Queen, went frequently to Windsor, and appeared as a sort of favourite'. 'This, if true,' wrote Malmesbury, '. . . bodes no good.' The only advice he could give Caroline at this point was 'to be very attentive and respectful to the Queen; to endeavour, at all events, to be well with her'.[8]

Caroline had heard of Lady Jersey, but apparently not of her relationship with the Prince, and Malmesbury did not enlighten her. She confessed that she was afraid of the Queen, a surprising admission for one who professed to be fearless; but she was sure, she said, that the Queen would be jealous of her and try to harm her if she became popular with the people. She wanted to be popular, and she was determinded never to appear jealous. 'I know the Prince is *léger*, and am prepared on this point.' Malmesbury replied carefully that he did not believe she would have any occasion to exercise this very wise resolution.[9]

Mlle Hertzfeldt, the Duke's mistress, found an opportunity to draw Malmesbury aside and give him a word of warning. She was a clever and worldly woman, experienced in the ways of courts. 'I speak to you as an old friend,' she told the Ambassador. 'I am attached body and soul to the Duke. I am devoted to him . . . and all I want is the welfare of his family. He will be the most unhappy of men if this daughter's marriage fails as her sister's did.'

She believed it to be of vital importance that Caroline—at least in the early stages of her marriage—should lead a very quiet life. 'If she finds herself suddenly in the world, without a single restriction, she will be thrown off balance. She hasn't a bad heart,' said Mlle Hertzfeldt, 'she has never done any serious wrong—but with her the word always runs ahead of the thought: she gives herself unreservedly to those with whom she talks, and from there it follows—even in this little court—that people attribute to her feelings and intentions which have never belonged to her.' (In this rather cryptic sentence Mlle Hertzfeldt was perhaps trying to explain away the reports of Caroline's 'indecent' language and behaviour which had so disquieted Queen Charlotte.)

She begged Malmesbury to watch and advise the Princess in England. 'I fear the Queen,' she said. 'The Duchess here . . . does not like the Queen, and she has talked about it too much to her daughter. But Caroline's happiness depends on being well with the Queen, and for God's sake remind her always of this. She will listen to you. She finds that you give wise advice in a light-hearted manner, and so you make a bigger impression on her than her father, whom she fears too much, or her mother, whom she doesn't fear at all.'[10]

This conversation must have added to Malmesbury's anxiety: try as he would, he could not feel sanguine. 'She has no depths, no fixed character, a light and flighty mind,' he wrote in his diary. Nevertheless, he went on doggedly with his course of instruction. 'My eternal theme: *to think before she speaks.*'[11]

'I wish to be loved by the people,' Caroline said, disarmingly. But it was infinitely more important, her instructor assured her, to be respected, 'never going below the high rank in which a princess is placed, either in language or manners'.

These admirable precepts were passed on delightedly by Caroline to her parents. Though profoundly grateful, they feared that Malmesbury might fall foul of the Prince by presuming to lecture his future wife. The diplomat had no fears on this score. 'I replied, that I luckily was in a situation not to want the Prince's favour, and that it was of infinitely more consequence to the public . . . that the Princes of Wales should honour . . . her high situation . . . than that I should have the advantages and emoluments of a favourite at Carlton House.'[12]

It was now nearly a month since Malmesbury's arrival in Brunswick, and still no instructions had arrived for the journey. The delay began to tell on everyone's nerves. Caroline was upset by an interview with her aunt the Abbess, who exhorted her on no account to put her trust *in men*: they were never to be relied upon. The Prince of Wales, she assured her niece, would certainly deceive her; and having succeeded in making the girl thoroughly uneasy she added for good measure that she was sure that Caroline would not be happy.

'All the nonsense of an envious and desiring old maid,' commented Malmesbury, who had already had trouble with the Abbess. His advice to Caroline was brisk. 'Imagine,' he said, 'that you were to offer to change places with your aunt—to take the Abbey of Gandersheim, and give her the Prince of Wales. Would she then think *men* such monsters?' This advice completely reassured the Princess, and soon after, 'unusually at her ease', she started to quiz Malmesbury about the Abbess who, she said, had warned her against him—'*un homme dangereux*'. 'I tried,' said Malmesbury, 'to get rid of this sort of conversation,' but Caroline showed her want of tact by persisting. 'It was in vain to attempt to turn the subject—she went on during the whole supper—was in high spirits, and laughed unmercifully at her aunt, and her supposed partiality for me.'[13]

A few days later there was an unpleasant shock for the family in the shape of an anonymous letter from England containing virulent abuse of the Prince and reviling Lady Jersey—'the worst and most dangerous of profligate women'. It was addressed to the Duchess, who, 'with her usual indiscretion' said Malmesbury, 'showed it to the Princess and talked about it everywhere. I was quite angry with her.' The Duke examined the letter, which he decided was written in the guise of a man familiar with the daily society of Carlton House. Later on, Malmesbury had a look, and dismissed the letter contemptuously as 'evidently written by some disappointed milliner or angry maidservant, and deserving no attention'.[14]

In its crude way it had enlightened Caroline as to the position of Lady Jersey, if she was not already aware of it. But the writer's object, in Malmesbury's view, was to frighten the Princess with the idea that Lady Jersey would encourage her to have an affair on her own account. This, he noticed, did *not* frighten the Princess, although it did the Duke and Duchess, haunted perhaps by the ghost of Caroline's elder sister. Malmesbury evidently thought that it was time to give Caroline a shock. 'I told her Lady Jersey would be more cautious than to risk such an audacious measure; and it was *death* to presume to approach a Princess of Wales—no man would be daring enough to think of it. She asked me whether I was in earnest. I said such was our law; that anybody who presumed to love her was guilty of *high treason*, and punished with *death*, if she was weak enough to listen to him: so also was she. This,' wrote Malmesbury, 'startled her.'

Chapter Three

AT LAST, in the small hours of 26 December 1794, an envoy arrived with orders to Malmesbury to set out at once. In the same postbag was a letter from the Prince—'well satisfied and approves what I have done', wrote Malmesbury. Only one contretemps marred the general feeling of relief: the Prince of Wales firmly refused to allow Caroline's secretary, Mlle Rosenweit, to accompany her to England. This refusal was a blow to the Duke, who confessed to Malmesbury that 'the only reason why he wished her to be with the Princess was that his daughter writes very ill and spells ill, and he was desirous this should not appear'.[1] Though he pretended to shrug off this setback, the Duke, said Malmesbury, 'was at the bottom hurt and angry, and as usual it was the Queen who was blamed for the snub'.

Three days later the party set out on the first stage of the journey. The Duke did not accompany his daughter, but bade her an emotional farewell, and implored Malmesbury to be 'a second father' to her and to write to him. The Duchess was persuaded to go with Caroline as far as the coast: for one who never moved outside Brunswick, this must have been a great effort.

As the cavalcade drove off, the streets of Brunswick were lined with loyal citizens, and guns boomed from the ramparts as the royal carriages with their escort of Black Brunswickers rolled out through the city gates and away westwards over the frozen snow. In the little towns on the way to Hanover, people were gathered in spite of the bitter cold to greet the Princess; a band played *God Save the King*; at Vieuburg there was a triumphal arch; and at Diepholz there were illuminations. For Caroline the whole thing was the beginning of magic adventure, and she begged Malmesbury to sit in the same coach with her and share her delight. 'I resisted it as impossible,' wrote Malmesbury, 'from its being improper.'

The happiness was short-lived. On New Year's Day the party arrived at Osnabruck, where a courier brought the news that Napoleon's army had crossed the Dutch border and was established at Zuil: 'our journey retarded —great uneasiness'. Two hours later, however, another dispatch announced that the French had been driven back. There were rejoicings, but by this time Malmesbury had determined to remain in Osnabruck and await further news. The frost was reported to be very severe all along the Dutch coast, and it was likely that the English ships would be prevented from getting near enough to Helvoetsluys or any Dutch port to take the Princess on board. Thus marooned, and with French troops pouring into Holland, the position there of the royal party might become uncomfortable. He determined not to move till further news arrived.

While they waited, Malmesbury found opportunities for further education of the Princess. His first lesson was on charity. Osnabruck was filled with starving refugees.

'I persuade the Princess Caroline to be munificent . . . I tell her, liberality and generosity is an enjoyment, not a severe virtue.' Caroline was surprised and impressed. The next day, said Malmesbury, 'a French emigré, with a pretty child, draws near the table: the Princess Caroline *immediately*, of her own accord, puts ten louis in a paper, and gives it to the child.' This was excellent: Malmesbury felt that he was making progress. But the Duchess was not so easily taught as her daughter. Seeing the child take the paper, she asked in her inquisitive way what it was. 'I tell her a *demand on her purse*,' wrote Malmesbury. The Duchess became extremely embarrassed. '*Je n'ai que mes beaux doubles louis de Brunswick*,' she complained. 'I answer that they will become more beautiful in the hands of that child than in her pocket. She ashamed, and gives three of them.'[2] Apparently Caroline had never been taught to bestow money on the deserving poor, or indeed on anyone. Nor had she the least idea of the use or value of money. When Malmesbury admired the design of the Brunswick coins, she immediately offered him '*very seriously*', a small pile of double louis. 'It doesn't matter,' she cried, pressing them into his hand, 'I don't care about them, please take them.' Malmesbury was not pleased: the lesson had gone awry. 'I took an opportunity at supper of defining to her what real benevolence was, and I recommended it to her as a quality that would . . . give her more true satisfaction than any that human nature could possess. The idea was, I was sorry to see, new to her . . .'

Malmesbury was having a wretched time. He was concerned about the journey: the decisions he was forced to make, the dangers—travelling through what was virtually a seat of war—and the arctic conditions. He was also deeply concerned about Princess Caroline. The more he studied her, the more certain he became that she was totally unsuited to the position of Princess of Wales. He had hoped that he might succeed in polishing her up, as he would a raw diplomat, in order that she would pass muster at Court; but there were times when he decided that no amount of polishing would alter the Princess Caroline. She was eccentric, gauche, tactless, and unteachable.

And yet he felt impelled to go on teaching her; and whenever he noted some good point in her erratic character he held on to it like a rare jewel. After two days' journey out of Osnabruck, he received letters from Lord St Helens, advising him to turn back.* 'I mentioned this to the Princesses,' he went on, 'and I must in justice say that the Princess Caroline bore this disappointment with more good temper, good humour and patience than could be expected, particularly as she felt it very much.'[3]

He found the Duchess very trying. She was upset by the cold, and after six days announced that she wished to go back to Brunswick. She was frightened of being captured by the French. 'If I am taken,' she said, 'I am sure the King will be angry.' 'He will be very sorry,' replied the diplomatic Malmesbury, 'but your Royal Highness must *not* leave her daughter till she is in the hands of her attendants.' 'She argues,' Malmesbury wrote, 'but I will not give way, and *she* does.'[4]

Now they were obliged to turn round and go back to Osnabruck, breaking the journey at Delden, where they slept at an inn. Malmesbury caught a courier and dispatched letters to Lord St Helens at the Hague, to Commodore Payne, whom he believed to be in command of the fleet off the Dutch coast, and to the Prince of Wales in London. To each he gave his reasons for turning back. To the Prince he wrote that he had given orders for the party to remain at Osnabruck 'till I know His Majesty's pleasure'. 'I hope,' he continued, 'your Royal Highness will not disapprove my having come to this resolution. Nothing short of a miracle can save Holland; it will either be conquered or capitulate, and in either case, it would be impossible to think of exposing the Pss to pass through it . . .

'It is impossible for me to describe to your R.H. how much I am hurt and vexed at these very unpleasant delays; but it is a great alleviation to my feelings to observe the great good-humour with which the Pss submits to them . . .'[5]

That night Malmesbury was woken by heavy gunfire 'at no great distance', and felt justified in his decision; but Caroline, in the morning, 'seemed sorry not to go on. I mentioned this cannonade. "That doesn't matter," she said, "I'm not afraid of guns." ' But in spite of this setback, by the time they arrived at Osnabruck she had recovered her good humour, and won a good mark. 'At supper Princess Caroline very cheerful, and pleasantly so—understands a joke and can make one.'[6]

* 'The French', he said, 'had crossed the river Waal and were near Baren: there had been fighting all day. He recommends our turning back.'

The Duchess was still being tiresome. She received a letter from her husband who had a cold, professed to be uneasy about him, and had '*a hankering* to leave her daughter and return to Brunswick'. Malmesbury once again refused to entertain the idea. At supper the Duchess took a violent fancy to the Countess Walmoden, their hostess—'a clever talkative woman'. Malmesbury sat between them and was obliged to listen to a string of anecdotes which became increasingly lewd as the meal wore on. 'The Duchess,' said Malmesbury, 'told me that when they were quite children she and her brother the King slept in the same bed, that he was as disagreeable a bedfellow as any royal or plebeian infant could be, but that her father (the late Prince of Wales) cured him of his fault by making him wear the blue ribbon with a piece of china attached to it, which was *not* the George.' Malmesbury did not find this chamber-pot humour amusing—or proper from a royal lady.

'Things in Holland very bad,' wrote Malmesbury. '*Notre histoire est finie*', wrote the Governor of Amsterdam; while the Duke of Brunswick wrote 'very nervously' to his wife and daughter, infecting them both with his own alarm. 'I endeavoured to quiet them,' said Malmesbury, but admitted that it was difficult as he could find no convincing argument. It was an uncomfortable and miserable time. Caroline had toothache and was obliged to lose a tooth, which she sent to Malmesbury by her page. 'Nasty and indelicate,' he wrote crossly. The following day the party set out for Hanover.

The thermometer was 17 degrees below zero—'the cold greater than I ever felt out of Russia,' said Malmesbury. The wretched servants travelling outside the coaches barely survived: even the Duchess, inside hers and endeavouring to play at ombre, was numb and stupid. On arrival at Neustadt she went straight to bed.

The indefatigable Malmesbury chose this time for a 'long and serious' conversation with the Princess. They would be in Hanover the following day: she should use her arrival there as a sort of dress rehearsal, for the impression that she made there would be that on which she would be received by the King and Queen in England. He assured her (perhaps not quite sincerely) that 'proper, princely behaviour' was natural to her, and that the delays in their journey had the advantage of giving her time to practise it (he hoped). Caroline, after the trials of the journey, was in a docile mood, humble and confiding: Malmesbury with his mixture of encouragement and sharp criticism gave her the lesson she needed. 'I confess,' she said, 'I could not hear it from anyone but you.'

By now the Duchess had given up trying to curb her discontent. Everything was wrong. She complained when Caroline as Princess of Wales was given precedence over her mother. She was 'troublesome about choosing her apartment', disagreeable about the cold, 'peevish and ill-mannered': certainly no example to her daughter in how a royal princess should behave. By contrast, Caroline was at least good-humoured and cheerful; though this, too, had its drawbacks. 'Princess too childish, over merry at supper,' he recorded. He was clearly discouraged.

Life at Hanover was shot with anxiety: envoys arrived bringing disastrous news from Holland. Letters from the Duke of Brunswick to Malmesbury grew increasingly hysterical. 'He urges me in the strongest way possible to go to Berlin—spared no flattery or pains to make me feel the *impossibility* of any thing being done without Prussia.' But Malmesbury remained cautious. 'He, *perhaps*, may be right, but I cannot consent . . .'[7]

At last, on 6 March, nearly ten weeks since their journey had begun, Malmesbury received letters from England directing him to set out immediately for Stade; there the Hanoverian fleet would meet the Princess and escort her to the mouth of the Elbe, where the Royal Navy ships would be anchored.

The relief must have been enormous. Even the weather began to improve, and Caroline forgot the trials of the journey and prepared to enjoy herself. Some of her pleasure was spoilt by the arrival from England of a lady-in-waiting, Mrs Harcourt, who had been employed in English royal circles for some time and to whom—as it seemed quite unreasonably—Caroline took an instant dislike. The Duchess, on the other hand, settled down happily for a nice gossip, which went on, said Malmesbury, for the whole morning.

The arrival of Mrs Harcourt with her air of knowing how to behave at Court, may perhaps have prompted Malmesbury to make one further effort at improving the Princess. Although it would seem that Mrs Harcourt's first impressions were favourable—'I am sure the Prince will love her, she is so affectionate . . . her desire to please is very engaging . . . She is all openness of heart, and has not a shadow of pride'[8]—Malmesbury decided to take the lady into his confidence. The Princess was careless in attention to her appearance; and here, in his diary, he picked his way delicately round the subject of cleanliness. The Princess liked to boast of the speed with which she dressed herself. This lack of care must have been only too obvious: he hardly knew how to explain the appalling mistake she was making. 'I endeavoured, as far as was possible for a *man*, to inculcate the necessity of great and nice attention to every part of dress, as well as to what was hid, as to what was seen.'[9] He had made discreet enquiries of her female attendants.

'I knew she wore coarse petticoats, coarse shifts, and thread stockings, and these never well washed or changed often enough . . .' It was really dreadful, and he marvelled how her education could, on this point, have been so neglected. Her mother, an Englishwoman, should have known better. He determined to have a word with her dresser, Mme Busche, asking her to explain that the Prince was extremely fastidious and would expect from his wife a long and very careful toilette, which at present she neglected sadly—'and is offensive from this neglect'.[10]

He thought that he had won his point when next day Caroline appeared, as he put it, 'well washed *all over*'. She must have told him. This time, she had accepted his advice; but for how long? And he may have thought of the exquisitely dressed and scented beauties of the Prince's court, and the hours spent on achieving such a state of elaborate perfection.

On 24 March the party left Hanover. The Duchess was 'very much afflicted' at the imminent parting with her daughter. At Walsrode, on the way to Stade, the Duke met them, eager for a long discussion with Malmesbury, whose opinions he respected, on the state of the war. 'He . . . wished I would return to Berlin . . . said every possible flattering thing to me he could.' Caroline, at the very thought of Malmesbury's obtaining leave to remain in Germany instead of escorting her to London, burst into tears and showed genuine affection which Malmesbury found quite touching.

The Duke implored him to keep an eye on her in London. 'All his domestic happiness,' he said, 'depended on her doing well.'

At Stade, the party divided. While the Duke and Duchess turned back, Caroline and her entourage embarked on the Schwinde in Hanoverian boats. Commodore Payne, the naval officer commanding the expedition, met them: from now, the journey would be in his hands. At seven o'clock on 28 March, at Cuxhaven, the party boarded the frigate *Jupiter*, a Royal Naval vessel of 50 guns. 'Royal salute', wrote Malmesbury, 'from the Jupiter, returned by the Fleet. Very fine evening, and fine sight.'[11] For Caroline, who—as far as we know—had never before seen the sea, this sight must have been memorable. The love of travel which she manifested in middle age, may perhaps have stemmed from this moment. She had parted from her parents and from Brunswick with hardly a tear: she was excited and happy, the naval officers were 'greatly pleased with her manners and good humour',[12] and under their admiration, as was the way with her, she blossomed.

At last, it seemed to Malmesbury, things were going well, and he allowed himself a little relaxation, chatting with Jack Payne about the Prince and Lady Jersey ('he against her—and her behaviour, by his account, very far from proper'). Caroline, he now decided, was behaving very well indeed.

'Impossible to be more cheerful, more *accomodante*, more everything that is pleasant, than the Princess—no difficulty, no childish fears—all good humour.'[13]

The sea was calm, and the only contretemps was the sighting of three French privateers, which happily made off, disappearing into the fog now descending. The next day, 1 April, was still foggy, and became more so as the *Jupiter* and her escort approached the English coast. At Yarmouth the ships cast anchor, unable to proceed. The sea which had been calm began to roll and people to disappear to their cabins. Malmesbury was obliged to correct his pupil: never, he said, should she talk of being *sick*; it was not the thing in England to use such coarse language. She may have acquiesced, but she was obliged to make for her cabin.

On Saturday, 4 April, in fair weather, the ships set sail early, and entered the Thames. Both shores of the estuary were lined with people. 'The whole prospect', said Malmesbury, 'most beautiful.' It seemed an auspicious arrival as the *Jupiter*, with the wind behind her, sailed up the great river with her escort, the *Andromeda*, the *Leda*, the *Venus*, the *King's Fisher*, and the *Ranger*.

Early the following morning, the Princess disembarked from the *Jupiter* and stepped into the Royal yacht, *Augusta*, in which she was to sail upstream to Greenwich. 'Pleasant and prosperous sail,' noted Malmesbury, and at midday they arrived: the long, exhausting, difficult and dangerous journey was at an end, and the Princess of Wales set foot on English soil. It was, for Malmesbury, a triumphant moment: his mission was accomplished.

But alas, the King's coaches ordered to meet the Princess and her party were not there.

The party sent to meet the Princess and drive with her from Greenwich to St James's consisted of the Earl of Clermont, a polished courtier and close friend of the Prince, the Hon. Fulke Greville, and her two Ladies of the Bedchamber, Mrs Hervey Aston and Lady Jersey. It was this lady who made the party late in starting by simply not being ready. So secure did she believe herself in the Prince's favour that she thought nothing of keeping his bride waiting for over an hour, not to mention the rest of the London party and their mounted escort of a detachment of the Prince of Wales's Light Dragoons.

At Greenwich the Earl of Malmesbury waited, impatient at the delay, and the Governor, Admiral Sir Hugh Palliser, and his sisters tried nervously to entertain the Princess. The situation can hardly have been eased when

Caroline, observing the number of wounded pensioners about the place, attempted a tactless joke. 'Have all the English only one arm or one leg?' she cried. It is to be hoped that Malmesbury did not hear her.

When at last the coaches arrived, and presentations had been made, Lady Jersey expressed herself dissatisfied with the Princess's appearance. She had brought her a dress from London, she announced, and demanded a room where the change might be made. Caroline had been dressed by Mrs Harcourt, in a white muslin gown with a blue satin under-skirt and a large black beaver hat with blue and black feathers. In spite of angry protests from Malmesbury, Lady Jersey insisted that these clothes should be exchanged for a white satin dress and white turban topped by ostrich plumes.

The Princess submitted to being buttoned into the elegant white dress, but evidently drew the line at the turban and plumes, for when she got into her carriage she was wearing the black beaver hat.[14] She must have looked a little odd, poor girl, short as she was, wearing over her dress a green satin mantle trimmed with gold, 'with loops and tassels à la Brandenburg'. It looked as if Lady Jersey had won the first round.

Her Ladyship now proceeded to make a fuss about her place in Caroline's coach. She could not sit with her back to the horses, she told Malmesbury, it made her feel ill: she hoped that she might be allowed to sit *forward*. Malmesbury, who by now had had quite enough of Lady Jersey, refused. He suggested that she could, if she preferred, travel with him and Lord Clermont, and Mrs Aston could sit opposite the Princess, which was the correct place for a Lady of the Bedchamber. 'This, of course, settled the business,' he wrote. Her Ladyship was obliged to sit backward, and lump it.

'There was very little crowd . . . on the road to London,' he noted—perhaps on account of the long delay. At half-past two the coaches drew up outside the Duke of Cumberland's apartments in St James's, where, it had been arranged, the Princess would be presented to her future husband. She was waiting with Malmesbury when the Prince appeared, and—as she had been taught—Caroline attempted to kneel to him on being presented.

The exact significance of the rest of the scene, as recorded by Malmesbury, will never be known; but the Prince was evidently in a tumult of mind which made it impossible for him to proceed. After he had lifted the Princess to her feet and given her a formal peck, the exquisite manners attributed to him vanished, and he behaved like an oaf. Did he feel an instant loathing for the awkward, dumpy German girl? Or was he painfully and overwhelmingly regretting his decision to leave the woman he had secretly married and still loved, Mrs Fitzherbert? Without doubt he was overcome by a violent emotion which led him to break away sharply and walk to the furthest part of the room, calling Malmesbury. 'Harris, I am not well; pray get me a glass of brandy.' The famous words have gone down in history, together with Malmesbury's cryptic rejoinder, 'Sir, had you not better have a glass of water?' The Prince turned on him and swore. 'No! I will go directly to the Queen,' and he went.

Caroline neither wilted nor wept. She was, said Malmesbury, astonished; and, as was her nature, she fought back. '*Mon dieu*!' she exclaimed, 'Is the Prince always like that? I find him very fat, and nothing like as handsome as his portrait.'[15]

This was unanswerable, and even Malmesbury was almost floored. He could only murmur that His Royal Highness had naturally been 'a good deal affected and flurried at this first interview'. Caroline would find him quite different, he assured her, at dinner. Fortunately, at this point, Malmesbury was summoned to an audience with the King, and thankfully bowed himself out.

It would be easy at this moment to find sympathy for Caroline. Unfortunately she was never capable of keeping it. 'Fate cast her,' wrote Max Beerbohm, 'in a tragic role; but she insisted upon playing it in tights.' 'Is she good-humoured?' the King asked Malmesbury, who answered that 'in very trying moments' he had never seen her otherwise. This was true: she *was* good-humoured, but she could not control her tongue or her mischievous mind. To raise a laugh was her object, and she did not care what sort of joke raised it.

Malmesbury was horrified by her behaviour at dinner that day: 'it was flippant, rattling, affecting raillery and wit, and throwing out coarse vulgar hints about Lady Jersey, who was present, and though mute, *le diable n'en perdait rien*.' She could not have chosen a more disastrous line of talk. All the warnings she had received—from her father, from Mlle Hertzfeldt, most of all from Malmesbury: to think before she spoke, to listen but not to ask questions, never, never to give out her views on persons or things—all were thrown to the winds. She was at her worst, an *enfant terrible*. The Prince, said Malmesbury, was 'evidently disgusted, and this unfortunate dinner must have fixed his dislike . . .'[16]

In three days they would be married. There was no escape from this event, which was bound up in protocol; planned, ordered, organized, and in which the Prince was irrevocably involved.

Chapter Four

KING GEORGE III had strict notions about the marriage of royalties. He himself, at the age of twenty-one, had stifled a passionate devotion to Lady Sarah Lennox and married a plain and virtuous young woman, Princess Charlotte of Mecklenburg-Strelitz. She bore him fifteen children and gave him the quiet domestic life (till illness intervened) that he desired. He thought that his sons should follow his example. He did not wish his daughters to marry at all; he liked to have them about him: but for his sons he laid down certain rules, which were embodied in the Royal Marriages Act of 1772.

By this, no member of the royal family might marry without the King's consent, and as the King held strong Protestant views, only respectable German royalties could be considered: Roman Catholics were out, and so were the English aristocracy. It will be seen that this Act was extremely limiting to the King's seven sons, who decided to a man that their only hope of happiness was a secret marriage or a steady mistress.

The Prince of Wales, after a succession of mistresses, some of them expensive to part with, had fallen wildly in love with Maria Fitzherbert, twice widowed and a Roman Catholic, whom he had married, as he could have her in no other way, in 1785. The wedding took place at Mrs Fitzherbert's house in Park Street, Mayfair, in the deepest secrecy. A young and ambitious curate, the Rev. Robert Burt, agreed to conduct the service in return for £500 down and the promise of future preferment. The bride was given away by her uncle, Henry Errington, and he and her brother John Smythe were witnesses, signing a marriage certificate made out by the Prince himself. Orlando Bridgman, one of the Prince's close friends, was on guard outside the door.

The form of ceremony was that recognized by the Church of Rome as valid in the case of marriage to a Protestant; and for better, for worse, Maria Fitzherbert became the Prince of Wales's wedded wife, in the eyes of the church, if not in the eyes of the law.

At first the secret was well kept; the pair continued to live in separate houses; but they were seen everywhere together and soon tongues began to wag. Lady Jerningham, a Roman Catholic, told her daughter: 'Mrs Fitzherbert has, I believe, been married to the Prince. But it is a very hazardous undertaking, as there are two acts of Parliament against the validity of such an alliance . . . God knows how it may turn out.'

The Prince's intimate friends were certain that a marriage had taken place; but to Charles James Fox the Prince denied it categorically, causing pain to the lady and bitter resentment in Fox, who never forgave the lie.

Maria Fitzherbert was stately rather than beautiful: her nose was too long and her mouth was spoiled by badly fitting false teeth; but she was a woman of tact and intelligence, and she knew how to manage the Prince's bouts of hysteria, when to sympathize and when to be firm. She loved him and believed that she understood him; and though she herself had a hot temper, she succeeded at this stage in keeping it under control. The Prince adored her.

The only flaw in their happiness was the disastrous state of his finances. In April 1786 a statement of his debts revealed that he owed £269,878 6s 7½d. His father was not prepared to help him.

'The Prince of Wales has nothing to expect from me till I see reason to expect that the attempt to relieve him may be effectual, instead of probably only serving to involve him still deeper.'[1]

The Prince had a good idea. With his flawless instinct for drama he dismissed his servants 'with great reluctance', pawned his jewellery, sold his racing stud, his carriages and horses, closed up Carlton House and retired to Brighton (with Mrs Fitzherbert) in a hired chaise.

The gesture had its effect. After a few months' silence the King spoke: he was prepared to reinstate the Prince of Wales in the position belonging to him if he would—to put it shortly—turn over a number of new leaves and never again let his jewellers run up bills amounting to £17,000, and other tradesmen to proportionately high amounts. He would have to alter his way of life. The Prince tried to draw up a plan for simple living; but failed. 'He is sorry,' he wrote, 'to observe that the result of it only confirms him in his former opinion of the *utter impossibility of resuming* his establishment without the risk of incurring new debts.' In fact, he had to have more money.[2]

The King was generous. Every detail of the lavish alterations and furnishings of Carlton House was submitted to him, together with every pension or annual donation owing, from 'Perdita' Robinson, who had been the Prince's mistress (£500) to Mr Humphreys the rat-catcher (£31 10s). Regular amounts were owing to hairdressers, physicians, librarians, to countless indoor and outdoor servants, and also to coach-makers, makers of liveries, gardeners and stablemen—the list is lengthy. And as well as these legitimate expenses, there were the Prince's gambling and betting losses. When all the accounts had been passed by the King, it was settled that the Prince's debts should be paid in full, and that he should receive an extra £10,000 a year from the Civil List.

In the course of their correspondence the King touched on the subject of marriage. 'H.M. thinks proper to add that while the Prince of Wales continues unmarried, he does not conceive any increase of income can be necessary to enable him to support an establishment suited to his rank and station.'[3] He repeated this four days later . . . 'His Majesty cannot approve of any increase of income while the Prince continues unmarried, as the accounts hitherto produced can confirm His Majesty in the opinion that the Prince's present income is sufficient, under proper management, for every expense suited to his rank and station.'[4]

Unhappily, during the next seven years the Prince ran up a whole new set of debts: in 1792 they amounted to £400,000. This time his father refused to help him. He had spent thousands on magnificent additions and alterations to Carlton House, on exquisite pieces of furniture made by French cabinet-makers, he had begun to indulge a passion for Chinoiserie, and this was followed by the rebuilding in oriental magnificence of his Brighton Pavilion. His flair for buying works of art, recognized gratefully by posterity, was not appreciated by a nation impoverished by war. Indeed, his extravagance won him the hatred of a populace rioting for bread.

He was bankrupt. And this time he could only think of one way out: to marry. Lulled by Lady Jersey, he was able to dismiss the marriage with Maria Fitzherbert as irrelevant—and invalid by the Royal Marriages Act. He was able to satisfy his conscience with the thought that he would be sacrificing himself. Before, he had shed his worldly goods in order to please his father and Parliament; now he would give up his dearest Maria (who was, in any case, becoming rather tiresome and jealous), marry a German princess and beget an heir to the throne.

Mrs Fitzherbert had been ready to forgive much in her ten years' association with the Prince; but she found it impossible to forgive his treachery. She was shocked beyond words. He wrapped the pill in sugar, and in a letter excusing himself from joining her, wrote from Brighton on 23 June: 'My dearest love, I have just received a letter from my sister . . . desiring me to come to Windsor, which . . . I mean to comply with, and set out tomorrow morning early . . . Adieu, my dear love, excuse haste. Ever thine.'[5]

At the bottom of this letter is written in Mrs Fitzherbert's hand: 'This letter I received the morning of the day the Prince sent me word he would never enter my house.' The terse, cruel note which followed his letter had been handed her that evening. She endorsed it with her bitter comment: 'Lady Jersey's influence.'

Mrs Fitzherbert was well aware, then, of this dangerous rival and her influence, not only over the Prince but over his mother, who described her as 'bewitching'—a surprisingly eulogistic epithet from anyone as critical and strait-laced as Queen Charlotte. It was she who—pressed by the Prince of Wales—appointed Lady Jersey as Lady of the Bedchamber to the Princess Caroline, a choice as cruel as it was ill-judged.

Of course, Lady Jersey put up a very good show of respectability. She was the daughter of a bishop (an Irish one), and had been known as 'the beautiful Miss Twysden' before her marriage to the 4th Earl of Jersey, Master of Buckhounds to the King, and later Master of the Horse to the Prince. Unhappily he was not always master of his wife. (It is not known whether or no he was aware of her relationship with the Prince, or if he simply accepted it with a shrug. It was spoken of in the Prince's circle as a known fact, even though Lady Jersey herself indignantly denied it. The affair had its ups and downs, but at the time of Caroline's arrival Lady Jersey's power was immense, and she took full advantage of it. 'How very sorry I feel,' wrote Lord Hugh Seymour to Commodore Payne, 'that the P. is so thoroughly under the influence of Ly. J[ersey] who will certainly not fail to compleat his ruin.'[6] Prince Ernest, the fourth of the Prince's brothers, although well aware of the intended marriage, continued to end his letters to the Prince of Wales with 'My best compliments to Ly. Jersey', a greeting which was evidently accepted as being quite the thing.)

Lady Jersey was well over forty, and a grandmother, but her beauty had not faded and she was naturally elegant. Wraxall speaks of her 'irresistible seduction and fascination'; and Lady Bessborough, who had plenty of opportunities for judging her, talks of her wit, and her love of teasing, but does not disguise her dislike of Lady Jersey, who had few women friends. 'Lord Harcourt', wrote Lady Stafford, 'has lay'd his commands upon his wife to give up all intercourse with Lady Jersey, who is, as he says, the vilest, most artful of women.'[7]

It was particularly bad luck for Caroline that the Prince happened to be in Lady Jersey's toils when she arrived. It was a situation in which a little kindness on the part of the mistress and a little tact and patience on the part of the bride might have worked wonders, but neither lady possessed those qualities. As it was, Caroline played into Lady Jersey's hands, as Lady Jersey had intended that she should. Her rudeness and brash behaviour set the seal on her failure with the Prince, and after this bad start she was never able to redeem herself in his eyes. It would have been better if she had gone straight home. But poor girl, how could she? Here in England the arrangements for her wedding had been going on for months.

As far back as the end of October the Queen had been busy buying 'linnen and petticoats', choosing silks and ordering muslin dresses to be made up. On 18 November she had received 'the pattern of the Princess's nightdress which is very elegant and pritty' and a week later she was arranging to meet the dressmakers, Mrs Beauvey and Mrs Spilsbury, at Buckingham House, 'with a doll' (or dummy, which was presumably cut and stuffed to the Princess Caroline's measurements). In due course, the materials were all made up, and a box of English dresses—smarter than anything to be found in Brunswick—arrived in the Duchy for the Princess. 'It is amazing,' wrote Malmesbury to the Prince, 'how well they become her.'

Everything, down to the smallest detail, had to be approved and passed by the King, which made the preparations interminably slow, and the Prince had chafed. Queen Charlotte, to calm her firstborn, tried to hurry things up, but it was impossible. A glove and a shoe arrived from Brunswick as models for the English glover and shoemaker, but there was a muddle about the shoes, and Princess Sophia of Gloucester, a good-natured and competent girl, was called in to help. In the end the Prince had to be asked to bespeak a set of shoes to be made by his own shoemaker, Taylor.

The bridesmaids were chosen: there were to be four, not six as originally thought, since four was the number at the last marriage of a Prince of Wales.* But their dresses could not be made till it was settled what the bride would wear. The Queen went to the King, who said that the Princess might be married either in Court dress or royal robes. 'I own I should prefer her being married in robes,' said the Prince, and the Queen sent a messenger immediately for the dressmakers. This was a step forward.

Unfortunately, by this time the bad news about the delayed journey was reaching England. The Prince's creditors were becoming more and more insistent (by this time he owed £630,000), and he was in a frenzy of impatience for the arrival of his bride. The King's deliberate manner of arranging things with the Admiralty was infuriating, particularly when the appalling weather was making it impossible to approach any Dutch port. He felt certain that if he had been allowed to organize the Princess's journey, she would have been in England by the beginning of December. To add to his troubles, Lady Jersey was plaguing him with questions about the party sailing out to meet the Princess, of which she was one. Originally the idea had been for them to go in yachts to board the fifty-gun battleship in which

* This was Frederick, Prince of Wales, the father of George III, who married Augusta, Princess of Saxe-Gotha.

the Princess would be sailing. Lady Jersey was afraid that she might become unwell in a yacht on a rough sea. She also wished to know what the ladies were to wear; and Princess Elizabeth wrote on behalf of the Queen: 'About the ladies' dress, mama orders me to say that if they receive the Princess on board it had better be undress [i.e. informal dress] but in the case of their being unwell and forced to go on shore, she advises them to take a Court dress.'

Lady Jersey now became nervous in case the little squadron of yachts should be in danger of attack by the French. Accordingly the Duke of York ordered a fast sailing-vessel—a cutter—to join the yachts and 'in case of any accident' to rescue the ladies.

The weather continued to be frightful, but on Christmas Day the Prince took matters into his own hands, borrowed £200 and set off in a blizzard for Margate. There he hoped to find Commodore Payne, who was to command the frigate *Jupiter* in which Princess Caroline was to sail, and who was in charge of the whole operation. The Commodore was laid up with gout.

'I cannot express to you,' wrote the Prince to his mother, 'the vexations and plagues that have successively followed each other since first this business came upon the tapis. Had my wishes been followed, the Princess would have been at latest here six *weeks ago*.'[8]

The Prince suddenly lost interest in the whole thing and went to Rochester, where he was joined by Lady Jersey. He was full of self-pity: he had done his best to arrange things, and now everything had gone wrong. 'I cannot help railing at my ill-fated stars,' he cried to his mother, and then wrote imploring his father's permission to serve with the army abroad, like his brothers. First, he asked what he had always wanted—promotion to a higher rank than that of colonel.

'The boon for which I venture to look towards your Majesty's goodness is the rank of General,' he wrote. 'That rank would, if the country be invaded, afford the opportunity of my being employed in a real and important trust . . .'[9]

There was no answer, and the Prince wrote again; but still the King maintained his impenetrable silence. On 24 March, in a short, urgent note, the Prince of Wales implored his father 'to be pleased to relieve [*sic*] me from the agitating suspense which has tortured me for the last fortnight'.[10]

The King waited to reply till Caroline had arrived in England. He then wrote, refusing his son's request.

'. . . I cannot depart from what I have uniformly thought right. My younger sons can have no other situations . . . but what arise from the military lines they have been placed in. You are born to a more military one, and which I shall be most happy if I find you seriously turn your thoughts to.'[11] He added, 'May the Princess Caroline's character prove so pleasing to you that your mind may be engrossed with domestic felicity . . . and that a numerous progeny may be the result of this union, which will be a comfort to me in the decline of my years.'

This was not the answer which the Prince had hoped for. Once again, asking for 'a real and important trust' he found himself refused. He was fobbed off with a domestic bliss which he did not want; and expected to beget 'a numerous progeny' to please the King and ensure the succession. After his first encounters with Caroline of Brunswick he knew that neither prospect pleased him. During the three days that intervened before the wedding the Prince was observed to be restless and strained: he was drinking more than usual; and on the eve of his marriage he called for his horse to be saddled, rode to Richmond and galloped wildly past Mrs Fitzherbert's house. It is said that she saw him but made no sign: if he could not save himself, she could do nothing to help him. She had told her friend Lady Rose Seymour that she dreaded 'his being without a friend to turn him from the mischief and numberless difficulties which his present connection exposes him to'.

And apparently, up to the very last moment, she never lost hope that the marriage that she knew to be bigamous would not take place. Then, on the evening of 8 April, she received a visit from Lord Bradford who, as Orlando Bridgman, had guarded the door when she was wedded to the Prince, and who now came to break the news that the royal marriage had taken place. Mrs Fitzherbert fainted. A few days later she went abroad.

The ceremony was held at the Chapel Royal, St James's, in the evening. The King and Queen were there, and all six princesses in their old-fashioned hooped Court dresses. Of the Prince of Wales's brothers, only two were in England: the Duke of York, who had been recalled from his military duties after some mistakes in the Dutch campaign, and the Duke of Clarence, who happened to be unemployed and living at Richmond. The other four were abroad, either with their regiments or on account of bad health; and the King, for reasons of his own, wished them to remain abroad. They had all hoped that they would be allowed to return home for the wedding. Prince Edward (later Duke of Kent) was in Halifax, Nova Scotia, and, writing to congratulate the Prince of Wales, added, 'Allow me, dearest George, to seize this opportunity to beg your strenuous exertions in my favour to obtain his Majesty's consent for my immediate return home.'[12] Prince Adolphus wrote from Elst, 'I . . . seize the earliest opportunity I have for to thank you for your goodness in asking the King that we may come over for your marryage [*sic*]. I only hope that he will allow it.' While from Arnheim Prince Ernest wrote more urgently, 'How anxiously do I long and wish to come over to England. Pray for God's sake try and get me leave to be at yr wedding.' Only Prince Augustus, who was in Rome and had himself made an unfortunate marriage, showed no inclination to return, but wrote offering his brother 'a most beautiful chimney-piece' for Carlton House. He indicated delicately that the price was £300.

The Chapel Royal was crammed, and very hot; the ceremony was fraught with nervous tension: indeed, from the accounts of witnesses only Princess Caroline seemed calm and cheerful, chattering with the Duke of Clarence while they awaited the Prince's arrival. He arrived late, deathly pale and supported by his friend Lord Moira. The historian Wraxall supplies us with the impressions of three eye-witnesses, the Duke and Duchess of Dorset and the Duchess of Rutland.

It seemed that the Archbishop of Canterbury, Dr Moore, was clearly aware that all was not quite well. 'For when he came to the words "any person knowing of a lawful impediment" he laid down the book and looked earnestly for a second or two at the King as well as at the Royal bridegroom.' It must have been a tense moment. The Prince, we are told, 'was much affected and shed tears'. As the ceremony proceeded he became noticeably restless, turned continually to look at Lady Jersey, and at one point rose from his knees and started to move away from the altar. He had to be persuaded by the King to return to his place beside the bride.

When at last the service was over and the couple, arm in arm, moved out of the chapel, the Duke of Leeds, walking immediately behind them, noticed 'how little conversation passed between them during the procession, and the coolness and indifference apparent in the Prince towards his amiable bride'.[13]

After the ceremony the King and Queen held a Drawing Room, for which the guests who were not invited to the marriage had been waiting for some hours. Lady Maria Stuart, who was among them, was all agog. She wrote to her friend Charlotte Jerningham that while she waited an equerry told her that before the ceremony the Prince had been '*très morne*', hardly spoke to his bride, and twice spoke crossly. She had been all impatience to see for herself. 'The Prince looked like death and full of confusion,' she wrote, 'as if he wished to hide himself from the looks of the whole world. I think he is much to be pitied . . .'[14]

When the Drawing Room was over the royal family went to Buckingham House for supper, where, Huish reports, the Queen had ordered a magnificent wedding feast. At midnight the Princess of Wales and her husband retired to Carlton House, where they were to sleep. Outside, interested spectators waited below for the lights to be dimmed: which windows belonged to the nuptial chamber? And conjectures were made—as already they had been made among the more privileged at the Queen's Drawing Room. 'Most persons gave us to understand *all* the ceremony was not over,' wrote Lady Maria Stuart, 'accompanying their words, to those who understood them, with very significant smiles.' But Lady Maria added primly that she had no relish for 'conversation so grossière'.

The Prince of Wales had never been popular with the public, but a wedding was something to celebrate and London rejoiced accordingly. Guns boomed in the Park and at the Tower, church bells rang out; there were illuminations in the streets and squares—'the flashing of a million tapers, fantastically shining in all shapes and dimensions' over the metropolis. People danced and sang and shouted for joy, and no doubt many expressed their happiness by getting drunk.

The next day, when Lady Maria and her chaperone called at Carlton House to enquire, as was the custom, after the bride, they were told emphatically that 'her Royal Highness is *very well*, and at dinner'. Lady Maria herself had been eating wedding cake. 'They send a large piece, with their Royal Highnesses' compliments, and sealed with his seal, to all their attendants,' of which there must have been many, for a whole coach-full of cake had been sent out from Carlton House. 'The Queen,' wrote Lady Maria, breakfasted with the bride and bridegroom, after which the Prince 'took a solitary ride'. This, she decided, was odd the day after his wedding. But then, she added, 'what an odd wedding!'

Indeed, it was: not only odd, but tragic. According to Huish, the marriage was celebrated all over the country with 'the most enthusiastic effusions of loyalty and joy'. But there was little joy within the walls of Carlton House. No one will ever know what took place during that unhappy consummation, but it seems almost certain that Princess Charlotte was conceived, for it is highly improbable that the couple ever slept together again. That it was equally a nightmare experience for both seems likely, from Caroline's own version which some years later she retailed to her lady-in-waiting, Lady Charlotte Campbell.

' "Judge," said she, "what it was to have a drunken husband on one's wedding day, and one who passed the greatest part of his bridal-night under the grate, where he fell, and where I left him." '

Chapter Five

THREE DAYS after their wedding the couple went to Windsor, where the public hoped to get a good look at them when the royal family paraded on the terrace after church. They were disappointed. According to one onlooker, Mrs Selina Wilson, 'The Prince did not escort his bride to St George's, or yet on the Terrace after, but the King made up this deficiency by handing her everywhere himself & looking at her with so much delight as must impart pleasure of itself to all who wish him well.'

Mrs Wilson said that her husband approved of the Princess's appearance. 'He thinks her genteel, & her face, exclusive of her exquisitely fine complexion, he thought very pretty.' And she added reassuringly, 'She looked happy.'[1]

Caroline was putting a good face on things: the Prince, by not appearing, was only postponing what had to be done sooner or later. Two lay figures, two dummies with blank smiling faces, must in due course be shown to the world—the Prince and Princess of Wales. The people must be satisfied that 'they look happy'. As yet, there was only one smiling face, demonstrating her Brunswick courage. But she was rewarded: the King beamed his approval, and though it has often been said that the Queen and Princesses treated her with hostility, this did not manifest itself yet.

It is impossible at this stage in the marriage not to feel pity for both parties. Indeed, during the whole course of their tragic story one is torn between the two, just as later on their daughter was torn. 'My mother was wicked,' wrote Princess Charlotte, 'but she would not have turned so wicked had not my father been much more wicked still.' But was wicked the word to use? Certainly in the opening of her relationship with the Prince, Caroline's behaviour was not wicked, it was plain silly. She was neither vicious nor stupid, but she could not shut up; and if she thought she was being criticized she answered back like a pert schoolgirl.

Very little is known about her early life with the Prince, but in those brief glimpses one may see how lamentably she misunderstood him.

'One of the civil things his Royal Highness did,' she told Lady Charlotte

Bury, '. . . was to find fault with my shoes; and as I was very young and lively in those days, I told him to make me a better pair, and bring them to me.' This feeble joke in Brunswick would have produced a roar of sycophantic laughter, but at Carlton House it could only have caused embarrassment. It was as if some demon prompted her to say and do just what would irritate her husband; and indeed it has been suggested that such a demon existed in the person of Lady Jersey, whose game it now was to humiliate the Princess. Lord Albemarle in his memoirs asserts, 'From the day that this poor princess landed in England she became fully aware that she was beset by persons of her own sex who looked upon her as a rival, and who endeavoured to make her an object of disgust to her husband . . . One of these ladies told her that the Prince is a great admirer of a fine head of hair . . . "We Germans, [Caroline told Albermarle's grandmother] we Germans are very proud of this ornament, so the moment the Prince and I were alone, I took out a comb and let my hair fly over my shoulders, but my dear," she added with a loud laugh, "I only wish you could have seen the poor man's face." '[2]

She evidently saw, nearly twenty years later when she told the story, that to let her hair down before the First Gentleman was not the way to capture his admiration, but she does not seem to have realized, ever, just how foolish and gauche she made herself appear. It may be true that Lady Jersey amused herself by making a fool of Caroline, but her ladyship should not be blamed entirely for the failure of the marriage.

The Prince was fastidious, vain and sensitive. He was not deliberately cruel, and if Caroline had behaved with more dignity, had accepted the situation quietly and set about trying to make the best of things, it is just possible that she might have succeeded in building up a place for herself in the royal family. If she had had the ability to win his pity she might in the end have won his affection; for his sister Elizabeth said that he was '*all heart* . . . A more generous creature never existed, and had his talents been properly called out he would have been very different from what he was.'[3] This same sister about eight weeks after the marriage wrote of her sister-in-law's 'open character' and 'perfect good temper'. 'I flatter myself,' she told the Prince, 'that you will have her turn out a very comfortable little wife.'[4]

Unfortunately Lady Jersey was always about, present at every dinner party given by the Prince and Princess, standing close as a limpet to Caroline at her first Drawing Room, in constant attendance when the couple went to stay in the country after their marriage. Here, in the Prince's hired house, Kempshot Park near Basingstoke, the company consisted of a number of his male friends (invited possibly to shield him from tête-a-tête encounters with his wife)—and Lady Jersey. Two years later the Princess told Lord Minto that the men were constantly drunk—'sleeping and snoring in boots on the sofas'. The scene, she said, 'was more like the Prince of Wales at Eastcheap in Shakespeare than like any notions she had acquired before of a Prince or a gentleman'.[5] Lord Minto, who had only met her twice, was startled at her disclosures.

She alleged that the Prince had made her smoke a pipe—a story which could have originated in one of the desperate moments when jealousy ran away with her. Seeing the Prince drink lovingly from Lady Jersey's glass, it was said that she seized a pipe from her neighbour at table and blew smoke over the two of them. However much, in her loneliness and misery, Caroline may have exaggerated and invented, and however foolish and indiscreet she may have been in her revelations to Lord Minto and others, there is little doubt that the Kempshot 'honeymoon' was a mockery, and in early summer the Prince and Princess moved to Brighton.

By this time the Princess was pregnant. She could not believe it. 'I no more believed it than anything for a long time,' she said later to Lady Charlotte Bury, suggesting with significant hums and haws that she had thought her husband incapable—an insult which he never forgave. She also made it clear that that unforgettable night after their marriage was the only occasion when the Prince had honoured her bed. She was amazed, she said, when she knew that the doctors were right and she was, as she put it, wid child.

At Brighton she began to revive in spirits. The Prince always felt at his best there, in the strong sea air, enjoying his Oriental splendour and the popularity which he never received in London. His money affairs were settled at last, though the sum which Pitt finally extracted from Parliament for the payment of his debts was inadequate, and the income which he was to share with his wife was less than the £73,000 that he had received when he was single. But he was grateful to his father for championing him. 'The very kind and affectionate conduct which your Majesty has held towards me through the whole of this very unpleasant business . . . claims every feeling which gratitude and attachment can create.'[6]

To his mother he wrote asking 'what sum of money I ought to allow the Princess as pin-money during the time that I am obliged to live upon the reduced income to which the *liberal arrangement of the Minister* and the Parliament have condemned me, as I shall be totally guided by you in this respect'. And he added, 'She is extremely delighted with this place [Brighton] which seems to agree with her most perfectly, as she is in the best health &

spirits possible, excepting at moments a little degree of sickness which is the necessary attendant upon her situation.'[7]

'I am extreamly glad,' wrote the Queen, 'to hear that the sea air agreed so well with the Princess, & that she goes on so well in her present situation. I beg my compliments to her & hope that she will take all possible care of herself.'[8]

The Prince was evidently making an effort now to play the part of a conscientious husband, and his mother responded affectionately. She thought that £4,000 a year would have to be found for the Princess's pin-money—'as that must serve for cloathing, menu plaisir, charities, & many unavoidable expences in her present situation'.[9] But the Prince went one better. 'The Princess's five thousand pounds specified by Parliament as intended for her, I have settled entirely upon her & put into the hands of Trustees . . . for her pin-money, & have given her between seven & eight thousand more to pay the rest of the Establishment which I think she ought to retain to support her rank.' But he was compelled by what he called '*the infamous deceit of Pitt*' to cut down somewhere, and decided that the Princess would have to do without her Maids of Honour, 'the most useless' part of her establishment. She was left with a Mistress of the Robes and three Ladies of the Bedchamber, one of whom she would gladly have dispensed with.

The King and Queen both approved of this economy, but his sister Elizabeth feared that dismissing the Maids of Honour was a bad move in the eyes of the world, and would lose him popularity.* That he should be popular with the nation, which he had never been yet, was the constant theme of his mother and sisters. 'All I wish,' wrote Princess Elizabeth, 'is to have the world love you as I do. At this moment I would give worlds to be Argus. I would then distribute my eyes round the world & then you would be loved & esteemed as you ought.'[10]

Now that she was pregnant Caroline was becoming a person of some importance. Her state of health was enquired after and reported among the family. Princess Elizabeth, as usual speaking for all six sisters, wrote 'I am commissioned with loves, loves, loves, from all sides to you as well as to the Princess to whom I hope to be very kindly remembered . . .' The Duke of Clarence, who had already had two children by the actress Mrs Jordan (and was to have eight more) wrote knowledgeably, 'I sincerely hope the Princess will take care of herself, for I am afraid the weather is against ladies in her way.'[11]

Now that her son was, so to speak, a householder, some domestic details appear in the Queen's letters. A bad harvest was expected that year, stores

* In the end the Maids of Honour were not dismissed.

of wheat were low, and bread was dear and scarce. There were riots. The Queen found her own solution to the shortage: 'I take the liberty,' she wrote, 'of sending you a receipt for making potato bread which proves remarcably good, & we have had it baked with much success at Windsor.'[12] It is to be hoped that the royal kitchens at Brighton were equally successful.

She also, at the Prince's request, sent some sucking pigs to augment the Princess's diet. 'They are to be refreshed upon the road with milk so that they will be fit for killing immediately, and I hope they will prove to the Princess's taste.'[13]

About this time the Duke of Brunswick wrote to the Prince, saying how happy he was that Caroline was so happy (she had evidently written telling him so). Outwardly, then the marriage was a success. The child was expected in January, and the Queen began to busy herself with arrangements for its arrival.

Just before the family left for their annual holiday at Weymouth, the Queen succeeded in making an appointment to see the fashionable male midwife Dr Underwood. ('Impossible to be done sooner as he had so much business all the other days.') During the course of a long conversation, Dr Underwood outlined a regimen for the Princess. If she should 'feel too full', he said, a little bleeding might prove beneficial, but only on the advice of a physician. This must have been taken: 'The Princess continues perfectly well,' wrote her husband in an impatient postscript, 'and finds the advantage of being blooded.' After this he lost interest: his letters contained no mention of the Princess. The Dutch Stadtholder was staying at the Pavilion, and Caroline was well enough to enjoy all the gaieties provided for 'old Stadt'. Perhaps it was the Brighton air, or perhaps the Prince's lavish entertainment was too much for him, for he constantly fell asleep, and—according to *The Times*—'rather disturbed the harmony of the Band with the loudness of his snoring' at the Prince's Birthday Ball. And according to the same authority, even the charms of the Princess of Wales 'could not keep his Serene Highness awake' at the theatre 'for he fell fast asleep the moment he was seated in the box, and continued so till the conclusion of the performance.'[14]

Perhaps it was a good thing that the couple were obliged to live so much in public, and Caroline with her bright eyes and pink cheeks and naturally vivacious manner gave the impression of happiness—despite the alien presence of Lady Jersey, who was always in the background, listening, appraising, and storing up pieces of Caroline's conversation to report to the Prince. Like a festering sore, she could not be ignored and it is significant that Prince Ernest, writing to his eldest brother, still sends his 'complts to Lady J'.

On 8 September the Prince went alone to Weymouth, where he spent five days with his parents and sisters at Gloucester Lodge. On his return to Brighton, he wrote to his mother, 'Quant à nous, we go on tolerably well . . . as wicked, as slanderous, as lying as ever.' ('*aussi méchante*, *aussi mêdisante et aussi menteuse que jamais*'). Presumably he is referring to Caroline.

It must be remembered that the Queen was fond of Lady Jersey, and had never favoured the Brunswick marriage. It seems as if there had been some sort of *éclaircissement* between the Prince and his mother during those few days at Weymouth. Yet on 30 October Princess Elizabeth wrote that 'Mama . . . is very happy to hear that you are all so comfortably settled at Brighton & that the Princess is going on so well.'[15] Evidently whatever the Prince may have confided to his mother, she had kept to herself. This is borne out after the birth of the baby, when the cries of delight and happiness of the royal aunts betray no knowledge of the impending break-up of the marriage.

Whatever the Queen thought of her daughter-in-law, she was determined that the Prince's heir should be prepared for and received with all the pomp that its birth deserved.

On the return to London she became extremely busy, interviewing and engaging, on her son's behalf, the nursery establishment. Lady Dashwood, who had been Lady of the Bedchamber to the Queen's daughters, was appointed head governess. 'I never saw anybody,' Princess Elizabeth told her brother, 'more truly anxious to fulfil conscientiously the situation in which you have been so very very good as to place her.' That important personage the wet-nurse, whose occupation it would be to suckle the royal infant, was carefully chosen from ladies recommended by the *accoucheur*, Mr Underwood. Every detail of the applicant's background and state of health was examined. 'I saw Mr Underwood,' wrote the Queen, 'who tells me that besides Mrs Bower he has seen another lady who is the wife of a chymist, herself of very reputable parents, well brought up, & a very proper person for the honor she aspires to.'[16] He had also recommended a Mrs Smith, whose own child was expected by mid-December, but though he 'likes her person much' he was uneasy about her second child 'which he says is fourteen months old, very large-headed, & so fat that it cannot walk.'[17] Apparently this did not worry the Queen, who rather favoured Mrs Smith on account of her youth ('the youngest milk is always the best'): but in the end for one reason and another it was Mrs Bower from Brighton who by her radiant health and cheerful disposition won the job.

The Queen now turned her attention from nurses to what she called 'childbed linnin'. The Princess, she said, must order this at once, and she sent a list. 'It takes a great deal of trouble to make such a quantity in a short time,' she said.

Indeed it must have, when one considers the tiny stitches that went into nightgowns of finest lawn and cambric, trimmed with row upon row of fine lace; the beribboned nightcaps, the frilled bed-jackets. We know that the Princess of Wales had not been brought up with an appreciation of exquisite underwear, but now she was being taught. Her Mistress of the Wardrobe Lady Townshend, said the Queen, 'knows as well as anybody what is wanted'.

'The time draws near,' wrote the Queen on 5 November. In point of fact there were still two months to go, but the all-important Dr Underwood had said that the Princess should be brought to London sooner than the Prince of Wales had planned. 'It is a reasonable request, I must own,' wrote the Queen, as it was the first child; and she wondered if the Lord Chamberlain had ordered the cradle. 'Tell him I, as an experienced woman in such matters, say it shd be without rockers to it.' One wonders why, but fifteen cradles must have taught her.

Three weeks later, on 24 November, the Prince and Princess drove back to Carlton House. 'I have never seen the Princess look so well as she did today,' declared Princess Elizabeth. 'God grant that she may go on as well in her present situation & that you may be as happy as you deserve.'

Happiness for either party 'in their present situation' was out of the question, and for both this final month must have dragged intolerably. The child arrived at ten past nine on the morning of 7 January 1796, which was, as the *Morning Chronicle* took pains to discover, 'exactly nine calendar months wanting one day' from the date of the Prince and Princess's marriage. It was a girl.

'The Princess,' wrote her husband, 'after a terrible hard labour for above twelve hours, is this instant brought to bed of an *immense girl*.' In those words, which he underlined, he expressed his disgust and irritation with Caroline; but to his mother he went on, 'I assure you that notwithstanding we might have wished for a boy, I receive her with all the affection possible, & bow with due defference & resignation to the decrees of Providence.'

He was worn out. He had been up all night for two nights on end and no doubt Caroline's uninhibited screams during the last twelve hours must have been very trying to his nerves. By the time he had written announcing the news to his father, he was thankful to retire to bed.

When the news arrived at Windsor (carried by Lord Jersey) the King was out with his harriers in Windsor Park, and as he passed through Englefield Green on his way home to dinner, he was greeted by Mr Brown, a surgeon of Egham, who 'had the very singular gratification of giving his Majesty the first intelligence of the birth of a Princess'—a moment which must have remained with Mr Brown for the rest of his life.

'Indeed, indeed, this does look something like growing old,' said the King on receiving the congratulations of his wife and daughters. In his eyes the infant princess was his first grandchild, since he ignored the Duke of Clarence's bastards. 'May she present you with a boy for whom the nation must provide,' Clarence (who had to provide for his own) had written enviously.

The King was overjoyed. He could talk of nothing but his grandchild, wrote Princess Elizabeth, 'drank her health at dinner and went into the Equerries room and made them drink it in a bumper'.[18]

He wrote immediately to congratulate his son, assuring him that it was no disappointment that the child should be a girl. 'Indeed I always wished it should be of that sex.' And he ended by expressing his hope that 'this newcomer' would be a bond of union between her parents, who, he trusted, would have many more children. Unfortunately the excitement must have affected his digestion, for after writing this letter he was obliged to retire to bed with a bilious attack.

Thus it was that only the Queen and five princesses drove from Windsor to Carlton House next day to pay their respects to the baby and her mother; and the following morning a groom was sent from Windsor to ask for news of them both, and to bring a message that 'the King seemed less bilious last night'.[19]

The Prince was obliged to keep the groom waiting for three hours: the Princess was asleep and 'I was determined', he said, 'not to send you a hearsay account but such a one as might be depended upon, "having satisfied my own eyes first".' His account was, in the end, as impersonal as a hospital bulletin—'as well as she can possibly be (under her present circumstances)'. 'I have given every direction', he added, 'for her being kept as quiet as possible, & will certainly take the liberty of writing tomorrow morning an account, & will send it down by one of my own servants . . .'

He did no such thing. The next day he gave out that he was ill; and in a condition of misery and frustration which was with him akin to illness, he made his will, leaving everything of which he died possessed '*to my Maria Fitzherbert who is my wife in the eyes of God, & who is and ever will be such in mine*'.[20] In this lengthy document, clearly written under acute mental and emotional stress, he refers over and over again to '*my* Maria Fitzherbert', 'my wife', 'my second self', 'the beloved and adored wife of my heart and soul'. He seems to believe himself to be dying; or, assisted by his vivid imagination and sense of theatre, to be moving forward rapidly to the moment when he would be dying. It was not the first time that he had believed himself on the verge of death: indeed, he could work himself up into a frenzy of hysteria over a sprained ankle or simply a failure to get his own way. He was subject, it is true, to short bouts of illness, the cure for which was to be blooded; but now he did not send for a doctor, probably because he thought that he did not wish to live. He had nothing to live for. His marriage was an obscene mockery, and in what he persuaded himself were his last hours he decided to put on record his unalterable devotion to Maria Fitzherbert. He had deserted her because he had had no alternative; now he would show the world, after his death, that he had always loved her. He would leave her his all. Although he was unable to name any sum of money immediately available to anybody except his creditors, he left her Carlton House and everything in it; he also left her the Pavilion, Brighton, and 'every article of property that is mine'. And he went into details of his possessions worthy of an auctioneer's catalogue. 'Having now, I trust, made all the retribution that is in my power to *this most excellent woman*, there only remains for me to hope that . . . she will no longer withhold her forgiveness from me, accompanying it with *her blessing* . . .'

Having thus rewarded Mrs Fitzherbert, he turns his attention to his infant daughter, bequeathing 'the whole and sole management and care of her to the King, my father', and after the King's death to a trust composed of his mother, brothers and sisters till she should reach the age of twenty-one. 'The mother of this child,' he wrote, was to have no hand in her upbringing. 'The convincing and repeated proofs I have received of her entire want of judgment & of feeling, make me deem it incumbent upon me . . . to prevent by all means possible the child's falling into such improper and bad hands as hers.' He is unable to repress his loathing for Caroline. Having separated her from her child, he proceeds to divest her of her jewels which, 'having been bought with my own money', are to be taken from her and given to his daughter. He then adds the final thrust: 'to her who is call'd the Princess of Wales I leave one shilling'.[21]

Chapter Six

CARLTON HOUSE belonged to the Prince. It had been given to him by his father when he came of age, with the comment that all it needed was fresh paint and a few new pieces of furniture. So little did the King know his son that he expected this advice to be followed.

The Prince promptly engaged a fashionable young architect, Henry Holland, and gave him a free rein. In the course of time, and at enormous cost, the modest Queen Anne house was transformed into a palace, of which Horace Walpole wrote: 'There is an august simplicity that astonished me. You cannot call it magnificent: it is the taste and propriety that strike . . .' In the rebuilding and furnishing the Prince was able, for the first time, to use his considerable artistic gifts. But where, asked Walpole, was the money to come from? 'All the tin mines in Cornwall would not pay a quarter.'

Carlton House stood in its grounds where Waterloo Place now is, covering the present-day sites of the Athenaeum and United Services clubs; and its beautiful formal gardens, laid out by William Kent, sloped gently southwards to the Mall. On the north side of the house, where only a courtyard separated it from the street, Holland set up a Corinthian portico to screen the Prince's windows from the gaze of passers-by; but in 1827, when Carlton House was pulled down, this portico was moved to the other side of Trafalgar Square, where it formed the front of the National Gallery; and that is all that remains of the Prince's splendid house.

Inside, it was a triumphant blend of taste and skill. Superlative pieces of furniture, paintings and *objets d'art* filled the rooms, treasures which had graced French châteaux before the Revolution, together with masterpieces of cabinet-making made by exiled French craftsmen.

On the first floor was the Prince's bedroom, bow-windowed and facing south and west, with his dressing room and 'hot bathe' room leading out of it. In the same wing were his music room and drawing room, the latter hung with yellow silk and decorated *à la chinoise*.

It was as well, perhaps, that in their present predicament the Prince and Princess of Wales should be sharing this house, which was so spacious that they need never meet. The Princess had her own rooms and so had the Prince. Their daughter, surrounded by nurses and nursery maids, lived in yet another self-contained wing of the vast building, where servants scurried about their business and ladies- and gentlemen-in-waiting waited. It can hardly have been a happy home.

A set of rules for the royal nursery was drawn up with meticulous care by the Prince: this was the kind of thing he liked doing. At the top of the nursery hierarchy was Lady Dashwood, gentle, delicate and over-conscientious; and she was assisted by Miss Frances Garth, a rather colourless young woman chosen by the Queen: 'her appearance is neat and clean, not offensive in her manners, but modest and pleasing, not befeathered, nor any inclination to get into the great world'. Before she was engaged, Miss Garth was warned that she must never be 'familiar' with the servants, and must never on any account repeat anything outside the house that she had heard or seen inside it. Great care was taken to prevent the possibility of any gossip being carried *out*, or any infection being carried *into* the royal nursery, and when the baby was taken out into the garden for her 'airing', a page, Mr Howman,* must always be in attendance (perhaps to guard against possible kidnapping).

The nursery, the Prince insisted, must be run with 'order & regularity'. As for the baby's mother, he was obliged to add that she might see her child for a short time 'either before or after the airing, whichever her Royal Highness commands'.

On 11 February the royal baby was christened by the Archbishop of Canterbury—the same Archbishop who, with such grave misgivings, had married her parents. She was given the names Charlotte Augusta, after her two grandmothers, the Queen of England and the Duchess of Brunswick. The latter had written rather incoherently to the baby's father: 'As a mother most zealously attached to the dear Princess by every motive of gratitude, affection & duty to the King, give me leave, Sir, to congratulate on your having a daughter, an event on which no-one can be better adopted to insure every purpose of domestick and political happiness. I will intreat of your Royal Highness to be the interpreter of my sentiments of affn, and kindness for the dear dear Princess . . .'[1]

Poor Duchess, she had no inkling of the breach between the dear dear Princess and her husband: as we have seen, she did not enjoy her daughter's confidence.

But she was not alone in her innocence. As the baby was put back into her lace-trimmed cradle, she was the centre of a beaming circle of relations:

* See Chapter Eighteen.

the Princesses, her aunts, cooed at her delightedly, and the King could not hide his satisfaction with his daughter-in-law, who was also his niece, for her part in the production of his grandchild, who was also his godchild. There was no suggestion, at this happy moment, that the Prince and Princess would not be reunited by mutual delight in their daughter; indeed, it was expected.

But the moment passed. Alone with her ladies at Carlton House, Caroline was without a friend. 'I do not know,' she wrote to a German acquaintance, 'how I shall be able to bear the loneliness. The Queen seldom visits me, and my sisters-in-law show me the same sympathy . . .'[2]

In February the Prince gave a small dinner party, inviting his two greatly loved friends, the Duchess of Devonshire and her sister, Lady Bessborough, to meet his wife. Caroline was at her best: her manner to them was 'affectionate and almost coaxing', as if she longed for their friendship. She admired their dresses, and when they left, kissed the Duchess—'*Ma chère Duchesse*'—and hoped that they might meet again.[3]

But on the whole the Prince took pains not to meet his wife; he was away as much as possible, staying at country houses or at Brighton, where Lady Jersey was commanded to join him and was rewarded by finding her bed placed in his dressing-room. The mood in which, only a month or two ago, he had composed his will, had passed. He was not, after all, dying; his adored Maria, his only true wife, was still abroad; and while 't'other dear charmer' was at hand, he preferred to remain alive.

Caroline was solitary and bored: lonely in the midst of foreigners, like her doomed elder sister imprisoned in Castle Lode. She was only too ready to confide in any friendly person, but she did not know whom to trust. Her ladies were careful to keep on the right side of the Prince. She was not by nature a devoted mother, but she wished now to see more of her child, to visit the nursery and watch the infant being bathed and fed, to enjoy the little dramas and pleasures which were denied her. Hearing that Lady Dashwood was unwell, she decided to break the rules.

'I was upstairs', she wrote by way of apology, 'when my dear little Charlotte was undress'd and stay'd till she was in bed and the dear little Angel was remarcable well. I am much obliged to you for your great attention to her and hope you will not return at eight o'clock if it is not convenient to yourself as I am quite alone with my Ladys so I can go upstairs if anything should be the matter and then I will lett you know. Hope to have the pleasure of seeing you much better tomorrow.'[4]

'She is, I am afraid, a most unhappy woman,' wrote Maria Holroyd.*

* Later Lady Stanley of Alderley.

'Her lively spirits which she brought over with her are all gone, and they say the melancholy and anxiety in her countenance is quite affecting.' So Caroline had her sympathizers, who watched her with pity and concern; but as yet she was unaware of them. Some fourteen years later she told her lady-in-waiting, 'If anybody say to me at dis moment, "will you pass your life over again or be killed?" I would choose death . . . Sooner or later we must all die; but to live a life of wretchedness twice over—oh! mine God, no!'

This may have seemed exaggerated and melodramatic, but it confirms that in retrospect at least her misery was acute. Other women in her predicament would have wept: Caroline decided to fight. Indeed, it may be said that at this point she entered into the long series of campaigns, offensive and defensive—a twenty-five years' war—which only ended with her death.

She was denied at this time the wise and kind advice of Lord Malmesbury, her first ally. He was unable, as the Prince's friend, to cross the barrier which now lay between husband and wife: he could not help seeing the Prince's point of view. Caroline's brash behaviour horrified him, and when the Prince demanded 'How do you like such manners?' he could only reply, with truth, that he deplored them. But when the Prince asked why he had not, from Brunswick, warned him of the terrible mistake that they were making, the diplomat pointed out that he had been commanded by the King to escort the Princess Caroline to England, not to express an opinion as to her suitability.

Nevertheless, he was profoundly distressed when the Prince suggested the possibility of a separation. 'Let me humbly remind your Royal Highness that in your exalted situation it is not your private feelings alone . . . that you have to consult upon a measure of such magnitude; your interests and happiness are so closely united with those of the country at large that it is impossible for you to take any material step on which the public will not claim a right to form a judgment . . .'[5]

The Prince now assured him that there was no question of a separation. 'You are quite in an error, for pretty nearly the last words I made use of on our parting were, "that whilst things continued quiet & that the Princess did not attempt to give false impressions of me to the publick and to raise herself at my expense, I did not wish to expose her to the world".'

Caroline, he said, had lied about his ill-treatment of her. 'I can on my sacred oath affirm that I have neither used an expression nor acted in a manner that can even in the most distant point of view savour of the smallest degree of harshness.'[6]

It was a sorry state of affairs. He had begun to hate her, and the very thought of her made him feel ill. He refused to eat with her. 'I had rather see toads and vipers crawling over my victuals than sit at the same table with her.' And to his mother he spoke of 'her personal nastiness' that disgusted him as much as 'her want of all principle'. Alas, all Malmesbury's adjurations to the Princess to wash 'all over' had gone by the board: indeed, on this subject she was curiously obtuse, and consequently, she can hardly have realized fully the repulsion which she inspired in her husband. She was hurt and resentful at his treatment of her, but she did not hate him: her hatred was concentrated on Lady Jersey. By mid-April 1796 she felt that she could endure Lady Jersey's smiling presence no longer. She decided to write to the Prince.

'As I never have the good fortune to see you alone, I am obliged to have recourse to my pen to tell you what I wish in a few sentences.

'As I see only too well, my dear Prince, that it would cost you too much to bring yourself to dine again with me, I think you are not in a position to exact the same sacrifice from me, to dine alone with a person whom I can neither like nor esteem, and who is your mistress.'[7]

She begs him in her slipshod French to excuse her if her expressions are 'too strongly felt'; but she implores him 'to change my way of living at the moment, which can only be very disagreeable and as embarrassing as possible'. 'Also', she adds, 'for Lady Jerser [*sic*].' Towards the end she attempts drama. 'Think,' she cries, 'that it is the mother of your child who implores you on behalf of that darling child whom you love so well. For me, I will never forget this mark of your goodness, my dear Prince; my life will be devoted to you for the rest of my days, and I shall glory to name myself all my life *Voter fidelle et soumisse* Caroline.'[8]

The Prince replied coldly and in English. The letter was evidently composed with great care, in case the Princess might consider publication. (He was prepared for that.)

'Let me remind you, madam,' he wrote, 'that the intimacy of my friendship with Lady Jersey, underall the false colour which slander has given to it, was perfectly known to you before you accepted my hand, for you yourself told me so immediately on your arrival here, reciting the particulars of the anonymous letters which transmitted the information to Brunswick . . . I then took the opportunity of explaining to you that Lady Jersey was one of the oldest acquaintances I had in this country, and that the confidence resulting from so long a friendship had enabled her to offer advice which contributed not a little to decide me to marriage.'

After painting this idyllic picture of his relationship with the seductive Frances, the Prince goes on to remind his wife that she has seven ladies in attendance upon her as well as Lady Jersey, and any or all of these 'it is in your power to summon, either for dinner or company at any hour of the day . . . Let me therefore beg of you to make the best of a situation unfortunate *for us both*.'[9]

And that, he hoped, would end the matter. But Caroline persisted; 'Very unhappy,' she began her next protest. 'Very unhappy that you have interpreted my letter so badly; it came from the bottom of a deeply troubled heart . . .' She could not drop the sore subject of Lady Jersey, but dragged up old grievances, old wrangles at 'Breyten'* when he had told her that she ought to be very content to see him attached 'rather to an attraction of ancient date than to a young and beautiful woman'. But in case this broadside should offend him, she quickly added an apology for having referred to the lady as his mistress, 'which was at the end of my pen without thinking'.

This sort of thing could not be left unanswered, and the Prince felt himself obliged to hit back. So day by day the dreary quarrel dragged on, till at the end of April the Prince finally sounded the death-knell of the marriage.

'Our inclinations are not in our power, nor should either of us be held answerable to the other because nature has not made us suitable to each other. Tranquil and comfortable society is, however, in our power; let our intercourse be restricted to that . . . I shall now,' he added, 'finally close this disagreeable correspondence, trusting that as we have completely explained ourselves to each other, the rest of our lives will be passed in uninterrupted tranquillity.'[10]

Three weeks after receiving this letter, the Princess went to the opera, accompanied by two of her ladies and Colonel Thomas, the Prince's Vice-Chamberlain. She cannot have been prepared for the tumultuous reception which greeted her. According to *The Times*, 'the house seemed as if electrified by her presence, and before she could take her seat, every hand was lifted up to greet her with the loudest plaudits, gentlemen jumped on the benches and waved their hats, crying out "Huzza!" '

The Duke of Leeds, watching the Princess from his box, thought that she showed signs of alarm at the fervour of her reception, and went to join her. She told him that 'she supposed she should be guillotined for this', a remark not in the best of taste for a member of the royal family. As it was the newspaper account of her reception was bad enough.

The Prince believed that the demonstration was no spontaneous expression of loyalty to the Princess, but that the whole thing had been engineered against himself. He wrote to his mother giving the names of the ring-leaders

* Brighton.

—for the most part friends and supporters of Mrs Fitzherbert, or revolutionary Whigs—all, for one reason or another, harbouring a grudge against himself. Thus unwittingly Caroline found herself at the centre of an uproar which was directed more against the Prince than in her support. 'Think for a moment', he wrote to his mother, 'of the dangerous consequences of the Princess having thrown herself into such hands, & judge by what is passing the use they may make of her hereafter.'[11]

He became more and more worked up as he dwelt upon the dangers of the situation. The horrors of the French Revolution, never far from his mind, drove him to write urgent warnings to his parents: he was obsessed by fears for his own and their safety. In his wilder moments, he actually believed that Caroline was trying, by aligning herself with the extremist Whigs, to overthrow the monarchy. In a passionate appeal to his 'ever dearest, dearest, dearest mother', he cried hysterically, 'If the King does not now manage to throw some stigma & one very strong mark of disapprobation upon the Princess, this worthless wretch will prove the ruin of him, of you, of me, of every one of us. The King must be resolute and firm,' he continued, 'or everything is at an end. Let him recall to mind the want of firmness of Louis the Sixteenth.'[12] He was unable to separate the terrors of a revolution from his material miseries. '. . . Never for God's sake, dearest & best of mothers, propose to me to humiliate myself before the vilest wretch this world was ever curs'd with, who I cannot feel more disgust for from her personal nastiness than I do from her entire want of all principle. She is a very monster of iniquity.'[13]

Meanwhile, the Princess, having let things rest for a while, wrote a calm and carefully timed letter to the King, in which she declared that her only true happiness consisted in 'une parfaite reconciliation' with the Prince of Wales. At the same time, she pointed out that the only true means to a permanent reconciliation lay in the absolute withdrawal of Lady Jersey from her service and society.

By this time, the whole rumpus had been reported daintily by the press. *The Times* noted that 'for particular reasons' the Prince was not present at the King's Birthday celebrations, and had set out, incognito, for Hampshire. The Princess of Wales, it was pointed out, was at Court.

On the whole, the Princess was doing better than her spouse. While he travelled furtively from one country house to another, or lurked in Richmond with the Duke of Clarence, she was enjoying the sunshine of popularity when she drove abroad, and appearing boldly and alone at royal occasions. Whenever possible, she appeared in public with her daughter in her arms: this, she had learned, was a safe bet.

On 13 June, amidst scenes of tremendous excitement, Charles James Fox won the Westminster election, defeating the Tory candidate, Horne Tooke. *The Times* reported that when the results were announced a small army, wearing Fox's cockades in their hats, rushed to the hustings, where they chaired the successful Fox and paraded through the streets, accompanied by an ever-swelling crowd. 'As they passed by Carlton House, voices in the mob expressed a wish to see the infant princess.' For Caroline, caught up in the general excitement, this was an opportunity not to be missed. She ran upstairs, gave orders for a nursery window to be thrown open, and held up her daughter for the crowd to see. For the moment even Fox's popularity was eclipsed, and mother and child won ecstatic cheers. Not content with this, Caroline ordered her carriage and drove out through the crowds 'to pay her devoirs to Mr Fox'. This confirmed the Prince's suspicions of Caroline's revolutionary views. 'I think you will judge it right,' he wrote furiously to his mother, 'that the King should be told of the Pss's paying her court to Mr Fox and his mob . . . He will, I think, be convinced now of what her plots, plans and views are.'[14]

Then, suddenly, Lady Jersey resigned. In a letter of unconcealed venom, she told the Princess that she had wanted to resign long ago, but that the Prince had refused to allow her to expose herself to false scandal, invented and propagated 'by one person'. As carefully worded cruelty it was a masterpiece, but Caroline's joy at her enemy's departure outweighed any pain that the letter might have given her.

And now the King decided that the moment had come for him to take a firm hand in reuniting the couple. He had, he told his son, just received a letter from the Princess, 'which, now that I am fully possessed of your intentions, I flatter myself will enable me speedily to restore harmony into your house'.[15]

The Queen followed up with a tactful letter to her daughter-in-law, emphasizing that now that the Prince had agreed to Lady Jersey's resignation, Caroline ought to respond and welcome him home. To make the reconciliation complete, she added, both parties should abstain from reproaches or from confiding in others on the subject.

Unhappily, such a charming situation could not be envisaged by either party: the breach between them was too great. Hatred and misunderstanding held them apart, and neither was prepared to draw nearer.

Their daughter, Princess Charlotte, who the King had hoped would be a bond of union, became a sort of theatrical property to be held up and made use of for dramatic effect. The Prince tried to impress his father with his own concern for the 'poor little girl'. (Though in point of fact he seldom saw her, and showed little interest in her when he did.) 'As a father,' he wrote, 'I must feel the greatest anxiety to secure to her the advantages of an education suitable to her birth, and which, unfortunately, her mother has never known. Straitened as my income is,' he added, scoring his second point, 'I shall be happy to defray any expence.'[16]

Chapter Seven

THOUGH CAROLINE must have felt relief at the departure of Lady Jersey, she was disquieted to learn that the Prince had granted Lord Jersey possession of Conway House, which stood next to Carlton House in Pall Mall. *The Times* commented: 'We cannot believe the report that a certain Countess . . . has taken up her abode at the late Field Marshall Conway's house adjoining Carlton House. After having been dismissed from the household of the Princess of Wales, the public would not think it decorous that she should be again placed so near H.R.H.'[1]

It would not have been in Caroline's nature to let this affront go without comment; in reply the Prince felt obliged to defend himself elaborately and at length; and a new rumpus broke out, which was a pity, as the Queen had just extended an olive branch by inviting her daughter-in-law to a ball at Frogmore.

But this fresh outbreak of hostilities was halted by an event which came as a shock to both parties. On 6 October Caroline wrote to her husband: 'I find myself in the sad necessity of breaking to you a piece of news which I am sure will give you as much pain as it does me; it is the death of la bonne et l'aimable Lady Dashwood.'

She had been ill since July, when she had written anxiously to her assistant, Miss Garth, telling her the correct procedure for taking the baby to visit the Queen. The wet-nurse, Mrs Bower, would carry the Princess upstairs, she said; but Mrs Bower was not allowed into the Queen's presence, so 'In the first room above, you send in [word] that you are there with the Princess, and when her Majesty sends, you will carry her Royal Highness in your arms. And,' she added, 'I beg her Royal Highness may be covered up entirely as the wind on the staircase at the Queen's House is very great.'[2]

It was several months before a new governess was appointed; and in the meantime the Queen agreed to lend one of her own household, Miss Goldsworthy—affectionately known to the Princesses, whose governess she had been, as Gouly—to be in charge. Caroline, who was not consulted, quickly lost interest in the plans: she was more concerned about her own. She was bored. She had expected that as Princess of Wales she would lead a gay and interesting life; instead she found herself left to her own devices for days on end, allowed only to entertain dull elderly people approved by the King (no lady below the rank of Countess) and only to go to the theatre or opera if it was made certain in advance that there could be no repetition of the scenes of enthusiasm which had so enraged her husband before.

She decided that she needed a change of air, and without consulting anyone told her new lady-in-waiting to inform her sister Lady Cholmondeley that the Princess of Wales wished to visit her at Houghton for two or three days.

The Cholmondeleys were rather taken aback, but the Countess wrote agreeing a little nervously to the project. The Earl, who was Chamberlain to the Princess, decided that he had better write and tell the Prince.

Once again, the fat was in the fire. 'The idea', wrote the Prince to his mother, 'of a Princess of Wales travelling all over England to which this would be opening the door . . .' and he enlarged upon 'the dangerous consequences that may ensue . . . from her thus having an opportunity of *repeating her tricks* . . .'[3] In short, he was appalled at the very idea. Of course she could not go, and he wrote and told her so.

'Madam, I have this day received a letter from the Earl of Cholmondeley intimating your wishes of visiting him at Houghton; upon enquiry, not finding any precedent for a Princess of Wales making any such visit, I have written . . . to acquaint him with the impossibility of my complying with such a request.'[4]

He added, with surprising mildness, 'I am always sorry when I cannot with propriety give way to your wishes.' But the position was impossible—impossible for both of them. 'You must see,' he told his mother, 'that the Princess *will never* rest quiet.' And he pressed his father to agree to a legal separation.

But the King refused. 'You seem,' he said, 'to look on your disunion with the Princess as merely of a private nature, and totally put out of sight that as heir apparent of the Crown your marriage is a public act wherein the kingdom is concerned.'[5]

This was cold comfort; but the Prince was by now determined upon a separation, and Caroline's next move strengthened his determination. She sent him a note, demanding an interview. His Royal Highness was mounting his horse when a page hurried out wtih the message. He was too busy, he said, to see her now, but agreed to meet her later in the day in her apartments.

He decided to take Lord Cholmondeley with him; he always took someone with him if he anticipated an unpleasant scene. From the Prince's own account, as soon as they entered the Princess opened fire. 'Since I have been in this house,' she cried in French, 'you have treated me neither as your wife, nor as the mother of your child, nor as the Princess of Wales: and I tell you that from this moment I shall have nothing more to say and that I regard myself as being no longer subject to your orders—or to your *rules*'—the last word in English. She had worked herself into a state of strong emotion and her grievances choked her. The Prince asked if that was all she had to say. It was all that she could, for the moment, say: she was quite overcome. She nodded, 'Yes.' The Prince bowed, and withdrew. 'Thus,' he said, 'ended the interview.'[6] But it was not the end of his plans for separation. From an undated letter, addressed to Colonel McMahon, a factotum of the Prince's who later became his private secretary, it seems that Lady Jersey was at work behind the scenes. She was determined that a legal separation should be brought about, and on terms beneficial to the Prince: but at the same time she was astute enough to realize that the Prince must aim at an arrangement which showed him to the world in a gentle and generous light. At all costs, he must appear the kind and regretful partner—even if this meant offering better terms than those suggested by the Chancellor.

Altogether, she told McMahon, the Prince's terms were generous. 'So far from desiring her to live entirely in the country,' she wrote, 'he wishes her to make any use of Carlton House that will be conducive to her convenience, & is equally desirous that she should enjoy the amusements of the Opera, provided her going there is not made an instrument of insult to him.' Only towards the end does she show her true feelings. 'You know the reasons I have to abhor her,' she writes blandly, 'and you must be convinced that I can have no reason for wishing the Prince to be gentle and indulgent to her, but that he may appear in a true light and that *we* may still have the satisfaction of thinking that *we* have always acted generously by *her*.'[7]

This pair of Irish schemers wished only to please their master, and what became of Caroline was of no importance.

She certainly had her enemies. But she was also beginning to have her friends: society was divided between loyalty to the Prince and sympathy for the Princess. Rumours of her plight, discussed in detail and at length in London drawing rooms, brought her partisans. Stories of the Prince's cruelty were bandied about: how he had taken away the Princess's pearl bracelets—his present to her—and given them to Lady Jersey; how he had removed the best furniture from her rooms and replaced them with old, worn-out pieces; how he refused to eat with her. These stories, which grew in the telling, added to the Prince's vexations. He had, after all, some excuse for his harshness: he was frustrated, miserable and unable to find a way out of his troubles. Lady Jersey, far from soothing him as Maria Fitzherbert would have done, was beginning to irritate him by her continual machinations. He was growing tired of her. His marriage did not bear thinking about, and he could not rid himself of his wife: moreover, he knew now that his plan to get married and have his debts paid had been a ghastly mistake, for the arrangements planned by Parliament, far from making him better off, left him in as precarious a state as ever, and forced him to use the increased income which they had granted him to pay off his enormous debts.

At a ball at the Castle Hotel, Richmond, the Duke of Clarence summed up the situation to his partner, Mrs Sutton of Molesey. 'My brother,' he said, 'has behaved very foolishly. To be sure, he has married a very foolish, disagreeable person, but he should not have treated her as he has done, but made the best of a bad bargain, as my father has done. *He* married a disagreeable woman, but he has not behaved ill to her.'[8]

But the King was by nature a family man. He still hoped that the Prince's marriage would be saved by the procreation of 'a numerous progeny'. He did not know that his niece, far from feeling shame at her failure as a wife, went about recounting details of her wedding night, and holding her husband up to ridicule.

If he could have had his way, the Prince would never have seen her again. Meanwhile, he applied himself once again to the task of trying to persuade his father to grant him a higher rank in the army, and a chance to serve his country abroad. It was humiliating, he told his mother, that his brother the Duke of York should strut about in a Field-Marshal's uniform, and his cousin, Prince William of Gloucester—'such a dull, stupid boy'—should be a Major-General attended by two aides-de-camp, while he, the Prince of Wales, eldest son of the King, should remain a mere Colonel of Dragoons with no purpose in life beyond an occasional review.[9]

The Queen was sympathetic, but the King, once again, was adamant. His younger sons might serve their country in the army or navy, but the Prince of Wales was born to a more difficult task.

Meanwhile at Carlton House the problem of how to tame a shrew continued to torment him. Caroline, after one attempt at reconciliation, decided to change her tactices. She would let him know that she was not prepared to accept his terms or to behave meekly and submissively. She was particularly affronted by his attitude to her choice of guests. Several men displayed admiration for her, including George Canning, a brilliant young member of Pitt's administration. Naturally she wished to patronize people of this calibre. But the Prince made it clear (as Lady Jersey reported to Colonel

1*a* *The Duke of Brunswick. Contemporary engraving*

1*b* *The Duchess of Brunswick. Engraving after the painting by Joshua Reynolds*

1*c* *George, Prince of Wales. Engraving after a drawing by R. Corbould*

1*d* *Caroline of Brunswick. Miniature by Philip Jean, 1795*

2a First Earl of Malmesbury. Engraving after a painting by Joshua Reynolds

2b Mrs Fitzherbert. Painting by Thomas Gainsborough

2c Lady Jersey. Engraving after a painting by D. Gardiner

3a Carlton House, north front. Drawing by W. Westall

3b Montague House at Blackheath. Aquatint by Paul Sandby

4b *Caroline, Princess of Wales.*
Painting by James Lonsdale

4a *Lady Charlotte Douglas.*
Engraving after a drawing by A. Buck

4c *Princess Charlotte.*
Watercolour by Richard Woodman

4d *Sir William Gell*

McMahon) that although 'he will . . . allow his wife *any* new visitors to whom he has no personal objection', he considers it 'highly indecorous for a Princess of Wales to give dinners to men, excepting to the husbands of her Ladies'.

This edict was endorsed by the King, who, in answer to Caroline's protest, wrote that it was his opinion that she could not receive any society but such as the Prince approved of. This was the last straw. She felt hemmed in, imprisoned by 'rules', rules for her daughter as well as herself.

In January 1797, Martha, Countess of Elgin,* was appointed governess to the Princess Charlotte, who was just one year old. At the Prince's instigation a new set of nursery rules was drawn up, 'TO BE OBSERVED BY LADY ELGIN AND MISS GARTH AS GOVERNESS AND SUB-GOVERNESS'. These were virtually the same as before, but ended with the request that either Lady Elgin or Miss Garth 'will attend occasionally at her Royal Highness's dinner supper & undressing'—in other words, that the baby now needed some social life; but there is no mention of the baby's mother, and the rules were signed by the Prince.

Caroline had her own idea of entertainment for her daughter. When the weather was warm, she decided to take her out driving in an open carriage. There was no rule, as far as she knew, against this. The plan was an immediate success; the London public were enchanted at the sight of the blonde pink-cheeked Princess of Wales holding the little child in her arms. Caroline could hardly have thought of a better way of endearing herself to the people. Needless to say, the Prince was not in favour of this plan; but he had not put a stop to it when Miss Hayman, who succeeded Miss Garth as sub-governess, took up her duties.

Miss Hayman was described as 'rough in manner, right in principle, blunt in speech, tender in heart': from her we have several descriptions of the little Charlotte, and of the puzzling attitudes of the child's parents, though as yet she did not understand the bitterness that divided them. On the King's birthday she took Charlotte to see her grandparents at Buckingham House. 'The Prince of Wales was there,' she wrote, surprised by the absence of the baby's mother. But she was pleased by the King's fondness for the child, who, she said, 'played with grandpapa on the carpet a long while'. 'All seemed to dote on her,' wrote Miss Hayman, 'and even the Prince played with her.' He had not been near the nurseries since the arrival of the new sub-governess, nor had he sent for the child 'when dressing or at

* This elderly lady (she was sixty-four when she took up the post) was the widow of the 6th Earl of Elgin, and mother of Thomas, the 7th Earl, who brought the Elgin Marbles to England.

breakfast', which were his usual times for seeing her. The fact is that, although the Prince could be at his most delightful with children, he took precious little notice of his own daughter, particularly since her mother's exploiting of her. But to Miss Hayman his neglect was a great disappointment. 'I do not often know whether he is at home or abroad,' she wrote.

After the visit to Buckingham House, Miss Hayman and Charlotte drove back to Carlton House in an open carriage. 'We drove twice up and down the park,' she said, '... to show her to the crowd assembled there, and she huzzaed and kissed her hand the whole time, and the people looked extremely delighted, running with the coach the whole way. This evening,' she added, 'she has been doing the same from the window for a full hour to a great mob and all the procession of mail coaches.'

This and other similar exhibitions organized by the Princess of Wales, were frowned upon, not only by the Prince but by all the royal family, and the Princess Royal, newly married to the Hereditary Prince of Wurtemberg, wrote from Germany, 'I regret much the weakness of the mother, in making a plaything of the child, and not reflecting that she is a Princess, and not an actress.'[10]

The baby Charlotte was already showing democratic instincts inherited from her mother, instincts which, to the Prince and the royal family, were highly dangerous. It had to be remembered that the King on his way to open Parliament had been stoned by the mob, that the Prince could hardly drive out in an open carriage without rude shouts and boos (while lumps of mud were flung at Lady Jersey's coach). The horrors of the French Revolution were still too near for the monarchy to risk a closer relationship with the people. Caroline, by her crude attempts to gain popularity, was adopting a democratic attitude which, the Prince decided, must at all costs be stopped, at least while she lived under his roof.

Meanwhile, there was to be no more waving at Mr Canning from an upstairs window, with the child encouraged to imitate his salute by tearing off her muslin cap. And there were to be no more intimate chats with people employed by the Prince.

This referred to Miss Hayman, whose misfortune it had been to become too friendly with her royal mistress. The Princess had taken a fancy to her, offered her camphor julep to calm her nerves before a visit to Buckingham House, and asked if Miss Hayman might be allowed to look after her accounts in her spare time. This produced an explosion of fury from the Prince.

'The Sub-Governess is a person whose constant attendance must be such as will entirely preclude every other occupation ... And as the welfare of my child, from the affection I bear to her, & not for the sake of worldly applause' (a hit at the Princess's exhibitionism) 'will ever be the constant object of my most vigilant care, I never shall relax in the smallest degree from that attention to her which I feel to be the true duty of a parent.'[11]

Miss Hayman, after this *faux pas*, was obliged to resign—a sad loss to the nursery. As we have already noted, you could not be a friend of the Princess and work for the Prince.* But she became Caroline's Keeper of the Privy Purse, and shared her banishment when, in August 1797, the Princess left Carlton House and went to live at Charlton, near Blackheath.

* Lord Minto, one of Caroline's supporters, told his wife: 'Miss Hayman has just been dismissed by the Prince because, being uncommonly agreeable and sensible, the Princess liked her company.'

Chapter Eight

As Caroline drove through the gates of Carlton House and away south-eastwards towards Greenwich, she was making, in reverse, the journey which she made on her first day in England. Then she had looked forward to enviable glory as wife of the illustrious Prince of Wales and mother of his children. Now, leaving him, she did not know what to expect. At Charlton, alone with her ladies, Miss Garth, Miss Hayman and Mrs Harcourt, she would need both courage and philosophy in a situation which might have daunted other, less resilient, characters. In London, she had enjoyed her visits to the opera and theatre, her drives in the park, and the company of the friends and admirers that she was beginning to collect around her. Now, she was thrown back upon her own resources. She was evidently accustomed, from her Brunswick days, to find herself occupations, so now she thumped enthusiastically upon the pianoforte, practised her singing in a voice which, according to Lady Charlotte Campbell, was far from easy on the ear; she drew and painted, modelled portrait busts in clay, and stuck dried flowers in glass to make lampshades. Later on, after she had moved to Montague House, Blackheath, we find her hard at work in her flower garden. An admiring German gentleman, Herr Campe, was quite overcome by her industry, and Caroline was only too pleased to accept his admiration. After showing him 'her favourite spot, a small and extremely simple seat . . . overshadowed by two or three honeysuckles, the branches of which are bent in such a manner that one of the finest prospects which this place commands opens to the view as through a window, she invited me to survey the most important part of her grounds. I manifested some surprise,' he continued 'conceiving that I had seen everything. The lovely princess smiled, and conducted me to a considerable tract, covered with vegetables . . . "This," said she, "is my principal concern. Here I endeavour to acquire the honourable name of a farmer, and that, as you see, not merely in jest." ' She gave him to believe that her vegetables were 'carried to town and sold' for a handsome sum. The Caroline of Malmesbury's acquaintance, who had displayed such total ignorance of the use of money, was beginning to learn its value now that she was a householder.

She rented Montague House from the Duchess of Buccleuch—'a modest mansion', said Herr Campe, 'not so large as that of a petty German baron.' It had been built, towards the end of the seventeenth century, by Andrew Snape, sergeant-ferrier to King Charles II, outside the wall of Greenwich Park which was Crown property. It was suitable, perhaps, that Caroline should thus be placed outside the royal pale. But the house had dignity and the gardens were charming. She lived there, except when she went to Kensington Palace, for sixteen years.

She had one chance to move. In December 1798 the Prince—always unpredictable—invited her to spend the rest of the winter at Carlton House. If she had accepted, this might have changed the course of history: but Caroline refused.

'I told her she was wrong,' wrote Lord Minto, whom Caroline had taken into her confidence, 'and begged her to reflect very seriously on any step she might take if similar overtures were renewed, but she said she was a very determined person when once she had formed an opinion . . . that she knew I should think her a very wicked woman, but that I did not know and could not not imagine all the circumstances: I might otherwise agree with her . . .'[1]

She had lost her chance. The invitation was not renewed, and Caroline had no grounds, now, for considering herself the injured party. Perhaps, had she been less cocksure, had she learned discretion and the art of keeping silent, she might have managed to keep the marriage intact, and her own life would have been less disastrous. But she remained adamant. It had cost the Prince a great deal to make the offer: to refuse it cost her everything.

Now she was more determined than ever to make a life for herself at Montague House. Blackheath, a charming country village, had been made fashionable when the Earl of Chesterfield bought a villa there. It was within a two-hours' drive of London, so she would be able to entertain. The Arcadian existence observed by Herr Campe was only one facet of her life, and could never satisfy that longing for excitement—and for an audience—which was part of her nature. The parties which she began to give were, at first, crowded with distinguished guests, some not on the list of names approved by the King. 'She has a system of seeing all remarkable persons,' Lord Glenbervie wrote, happy to be himself within the Princess's circle. Soon she had a name for unconventionality: Lord Byron was among her guests; her parties were not quite suitable for young girls, however well chaperoned. One of these, Lady Caroline Stuart-Wortley, wrote to her mother, 'You will be glad to know that I am alive and *well* after yesterday.' She describes her feelings on arriving at Montague House. She had expected a small informal party, this was a vast royal reception—or so it seemed. 'O

Dio! anything like the first going in I never saw.' The Princess was standing at the further end of the room: a crowd of distinguished guests stood in a semi-circle round her, and Lady Caroline found herself obliged to walk through all these people and make her curtsey. Although the Princess, she said, was 'very goodhumoured, and took me by the hand, it was an ordeal. The dinner,' continued Lady Caroline, 'was very pleasant and there were a great many people I knew . . . After dinner it was not at all formal, and the Princess made me come and sit by her on a couch, and we grew quite intimate and had a great deal of fun with Lord Sackville.' The Princess was at her most kittenish, attacking the unfortunate Lore Sackville 'about never coming anywhere when he was asked to meet her, and when he begged her pardon, and tried to defend himself . . . she only laughed and said, "O I don't mind you, I don't believe *one word* you say, I know better than all that." And then she told him she was very much *afraid* of him, for she was sure he did not approve of her dissipation.'[2]

This sort of teasing was evidently her way with attractive young men. Sometimes she went too far. The Hon Amelia Murray writes disapprovingly of her brother's experience at Blackheath, where the party had evidently gone on all night, and breakfast was being served. Some of the guests were in the garden and 'there,' wrote she 'he saw the Princess, in a gorgeous dress, which was looped up to show her petticoat, covered with stars, with silver wings on her shoulders, sitting under a tree, with a pot of porter on her knee'.[3]

This was evidently a shock to the Hon Amelia Murray's brother, one of the young men who had gathered to cheer Caroline at the opera. But it is clear that descriptions of this kind were beginning to circulate, and she was already meeting with refusals to her invitations. She herself still received invitations to the Queen's Drawing Rooms, and almost invariably acccpted, in a spirit of bravado. She cannot have enjoyed herself, barely acknowledged by the Queen and Princesses, and carefully cut by the Prince.

The Prince's brothers, particularly Ernest, Duke of Cumberland and Edward, Duke of Kent, paid her visits and kept her in touch with Court gossip. And the King remained her friend. In February 1801 he became unwell, though the Queen hotly denied that it was anything worse than a cold. But she summoned his doctors, and though their reports confirmed that this was the case, it was hinted that all was not well and that worry, caused by the resignation of Pitt, was affecting the King's mind. However, in March he was said to be recovering; and in April he was well enough to ride in the manège at Buckingham House; 'but I hear,' said Glenbervie, 'he talks a great deal, that this is thought to do him harm, but that when those about him decline conversing with him, he becomes low-spirited and cries'.[4]

He was determined to visit Caroline. The first time of his being allowed to ride in his riding-house he rode out of it without giving any notice to any of his attendants, rode through the park, to the astonishment of the beholders, under the windows of the several public offices which look that way, out at Story's Gate and over Westminster Bridge, followed or rather pursued by equerries, grooms and life-guardsmen. They were 'totally ignorant of where he was going',[5] and had difficulty in keeping him in sight.

Caroline, who had been ill and was still suffering from a cough, was having breakfast in bed when the King was announced by a startled servant. She hastily threw on some clothes and ran downstairs. The King's wild appearance, said Glenbervie, terrified her. 'He insisted on seeing her alone, and ordered the Duke of Cumberland, who had caught up with him, to remain in another room.'

When they were alone, he assured her that 'he had thought a great deal about her during his illness' and that he had come to tell her that 'she would in future find the greatest kindness from all his family, with the exception, he was sorry to say, of one'. Caroline noticed that 'the King was very sedate in his manner and particularly never used the expression so habitual at other times of "What, what," at the end of every sentence'.[6]

On his return under escort to Buckingham House, he walked straight upstairs and into the presence of the Queen, the Princesses and the Duke of Gloucester. 'Guess where I have been!' he cried, like a schoolboy who has played truant. 'I have been to see the Princess of Wales, and I was determined none of you should know of it till I had been there.'[7]

Two days after this story was told, 'unpleasant reports' began to circulate about the state of the King's mind, and there were dreadful signs that the illness which had attacked him in 1788 was returning. The most modest and moral of men, he made violent advances upon his daughter-in-law. Finding himself alone with her at Montague House, he seized her in his arms, flung her down on a sofa, and would have ravished her had not the sofa been without a back, enabling her to escape on the other side.[8] This may have been one of Caroline's stories that grew in the telling; but there is no doubt that the King was behaving very oddly. The Queen, who had suffered untold agony of mind during his first illness, fought to silence the rumours. It must never be thought that the King was going mad. Madness was the word that she dreaded: a word used all too lightly by the King's sons, but now rejected.

Today nearly 200 years since the King's first attack, the researches of Drs MacAlpine and Hunter have led them to the conclusion that the King's malady was porphyria, a hereditary disease which they traced back as far as Mary, Queen of Scots. It takes several forms, and has painful and disturbing symptoms, mental and bodily. In the case of King George, his legs ached intolerably, his skin was dry and irritable. He grew flushed and excited, jabbering so fast that he was unintelligible, with bloodshot eyes—like black-currant jelly, said the Queen—bolting out of his head.

In 1788 he had been considered, by seven bewildered royal doctors, to be insane. They had reluctantly called in the Reverend Dr Francis Willis, who with his two sons kept a private lunatic asylum. 'A parson and a doctor too?' the King commented, observing Willis's clerical dress. 'Our Saviour, Sir, went about healing the sick.' 'Yes, yes,' said King George, 'but He didn't get £700 a year for doing it, hey?'

He had not lost his sense of humour. Nevertheless, he was strapped into a strait-jacket and given the brutal and humiliating treatment used at that time for mental patients. In spite of this, however, after five months he had recovered, and the whole nation rejoiced.

Now, thirteen years later, the old alarming symptoms began to manifest themselves. He told Willis's son, 'I do feel myself very ill, I am much weaker than I was, and I have prayed to God all night that I might die, or that he would spare my reason . . .' And he added, 'If it should be otherwise, for God's sake keep me from your father and a Regency.'[9]

His prayers were answered—at least in part. Ten days later he went into a coma: the Queen and the Prince of Wales were summoned to his bedside, for he was thought to be dying. But once again he displayed his extraordinary powers of recovery: by 11 March the country was told that he was out of danger; six days later he attended a Privy Council and gave audiences to his ministers. He was strong enough, he said, to attend to the business which had accumulated during his illness.

But the Queen watched him with growing alarm. He had always lived simply and frugally: now he made extravagant presents; he had sudden impulses to buy property—and he became increasingly fond of his daughter-in-law. This was soon a subject of gossip. 'Whenever he is in town on a Thursday, instead of dining at the Queen's House or going back to there, he constantly dines with the Princess at Blackheath and returns *late* in the evening across the country to Kew.'[10] On one of these visits, he made Caroline a Ranger of Greenwich, which gave her certain rights over property in Greenwich Park. Later he offered her Greenwich Park as a present: she refused, which was as well, since it belonged to the Queen.

The Queen was frightened of him. Whether at Windsor, Kew or Buckingham House, she made sure that there would be no question of their sleeping together, and locked the door against her husband. During the day, she commanded one of the Princesses to be present whenever she visited their father. These interviews were trying to both husband and wife: his mind became increasingly unbalanced, her temper became unbearable, and she bullied her daughters.

In this unhappy atmosphere the little Princess Charlotte appeared like a sunbeam. She was a beautiful child, lively and affectionate, and her grandfather doted on her. When she was two years old he gave her 'a very large rocking horse',[7] and her aunts wished that the Prince had been there 'to see her dear little countenance'. Before she was three we hear of her singing *God save the King*, and to her delighted grandpapa she gave a spirited rendering of *Heart of Oak*.

When she was five she presented the King with a cape string of plaited cord with tassels, which she had laboriously made for him. 'I wish it were better,' she wrote, 'but it is the first I have ever done.' She was working, she went on, 'at a footstool for my dear grandmamma & hope I shall see her soon & dear Aunts. Pray come back soon to Kew & send for Eggy and me.' And she signed herself 'Your dutiful child, Charlotte'.

Eggy was Lady Elgin, who had been Charlotte's governess for four and a half years. Her portrait by Allan Ramsey shows her to have been an elegant woman with beautiful dark eyes and an air of great dignity. When she came to Charlotte she was over sixty, but she took immense pains to tame her 'precious charge', taught her to read and write, to sing and sew, to distribute to the poor, keep accounts and say her prayers: in fact, to instil in her something of the prim virtue of the model child of the period, as taught by Ann and Jane Taylor:

> Not all the fine things that fine ladies possess
>   Should teach them the poor to despise;
> For 'tis in good manners, and not in good dress,
>   That the truest gentility lies.

What was most important, Lady Elgin won Charlotte's affection; and she tried conscientiously to teach the child to love both her parents. This cannot have been easy. Charlotte seldom saw her father, and Lady Elgin did not approve of the Princess of Wales or of the exciting effect she had upon the child. A day at Blackheath was apt to end in temper and tears, and once a week was, in Lady Elgin's view, quite enough.

Charlotte lived chiefly at Carlton House where she and her attendants were under her father's jurisdiction, but in the summer, as a concession to

Caroline's maternal feelings, the Prince arranged that Lady Elgin and Charlotte should spend a month or two at Shrewsbury House, Shooter's Hill, which was close to Blackheath. Their life there was quiet and regular (and probably a little dull) and Charlotte no doubt looked forward to the weekly visit to her mamma, and even more to the occasional summons to Kew or Windsor to see the King and Queen.

One Sunday morning in August 1804, the Princess of Wales drove up unexpectedly, 'in great spirits', wrote Lady Elgin, 'calling from her carriage that she had great news to tell us'. They were going to Kew, said Caroline, to see Their Majesties. 'The King', she told Charlotte, 'has wrote to me to desire I would tell you to come in order to take leave of you and me before he goes to Weymouth.'

Lady Elgin had no choice but to obey the Princess's commands. But she grew more and more uneasy. 'The singularity of the invitation worryd [*sic*] me,' she said. She had never taken Charlotte to see her grandparents without a written invitation from the Queen, or from one of the Princesses on her behalf: that the King should write himself to Charlotte's mother seemed odd. 'I felt quite awkward', she wrote 'at thoughts of presenting my precious love and myself without a little note or message from the Queen.'

The Princess wanted to take them in her carriage, but here Lady Elgin drew the line. Charlotte, she said, was already 'agitated from her joy', and must be kept quiet on the journey. But in the end it was Lady Elgin herself who needed to be calmed down. When they arrived she was horrified to find that the 'dear good King' was quite alone, and had come to Kew 'merely to see the Princess of Wales and the dear little girl' before he went to Weymouth. He embraced his granddaughter, and turning to her governess he said, 'The Prince has given up the child to me, but it is not settled.' Then, holding Charlotte by the hand he went to greet his daughter-in-law who had just arrived, and Lady Elgin was left, trembling with agitation at the appalling gaffe she had made in coming. She revived a little when the party sat down to their meal. 'The King ate heartily', she said, 'his pudding and dumplings', and insisted upon making the coffee himself; but the Princess of Wales 'seemed much on her guard'. All this was odd and disquieting: Lady Elgin felt that, unwittingly, she had become involved in some sort of plot. She knew the King had only lately recovered from another bout of his strange and frightening illness, and although he was 'so attentive to us all' at dinner, she did not like the look of him. 'I am afraid he over-exerted himself', she said, and added, 'I sincerely hope his Majesty will not suffer from his jaunt; *he is still weak*.'[11]

When she reached home she lost no time in writing a full account of the visit, first to Princess Elizabeth, who, she hoped, would take her part with the Queen; and second to the Prince of Wales, her employer. His reply was immediate. He had been trying to negotiate a reconciliation with his father—indeed, they were to meet before the King left for Weymouth—but now he forgot everything in the drama of the moment. Caroline, he believed, was trying to get the child away from him. 'The Prince of Wales', he wrote, 'feels himself under the necessity of laying his commands upon Lady Elgin not to part with her Royal Highness the Princess Charlotte on any account or under any pretence whatsoever . . .'[12]

He consulted Charles James Fox, who wrote a few days later of 'the desperate attempt that is making to take the Princess away from your Royal Highness', and advised the Prince to remove his daughter immediately from Woolwich to Carlton House. 'Where she is now,' he continued, 'she cannot be safe. For God's sake, Sir, let no-one persuade you that this is not a matter of the highest importance to you.'[13]

Lord Eldon, the Chancellor, intervened: he advised the Prince to wait till his father returned from Weymouth, and he warned him of the serious effect that any quarrel might have upon the King's mind. His odd behaviour at Kew had already reached the ears of Colonel McMahon, the Prince's busy little spy, who in a letter to the Duke of Northumberland marked Secret, reported that the King had received the Princess of Wales at Kew because at Windsor 'he knew that the Queen and Princesses would be rude to her'. There may have been some truth in this: the Queen was by now sick with worry over her husband's attitude towards her, which, after she had refused to sleep with him, became increasingly hostile. According to McMahon, he reverted to the idea which had possessed him in 1788, that his true Queen was the Countess of Pembroke.* She was now seventy-two, but according to Lady Bessborough, 'his pursuit of Lady Pembroke is renew'd . . . with so much ardour & such splendid offers that I tremble for her *Virtue*'.[14] He announced that he would like to live with her in the Great Lodge in Windsor Park, with his two youngest daughters. He would never go to London again, but the Queen should hold weekly Drawing Rooms, leaving him 'snug at the Lodge' with Lady Pembroke.

In the background of this crazy plan, reported with zest by McMahon, the King promised that 'apartments should be fitted up at Windsor' for Caroline, 'so as to make her comfortable & independent there whenever she came to visit him and her daughter' (for Charlotte would of course be living there too in her grandfather's charge).[15]

* Daughter of the 3rd Duke of Marlborough, who was deserted by her husband and became one of the Queen's Ladies of the Bedchamber 1783–1818.

At Weymouth, although he had to be restrained from riding his horse into church, and displayed other eccentricities such as insisting on appearing in a Hanoverian general's uniform, complete with gauntlets and enormous boots, the King presented his usual benign and friendly face, and on his return home seemed in excellent health. His ministers thought that the time had come to organize the long-delayed reconciliation between King and Prince.[16]

'I am indeed very happy,' wrote Caroline to her father-in-law, 'to hear of the reconciliation, which your Majesty is so very condescending to inform me of [*sic*].

'I am not able to expresse myself how much I feel penetrated with all the kindness and gracious goodness your Majesty show to my daughter and me, and both I hope will proof throught our whole lifes our gratitude and attachment and devotion.'[17]

For the time being, the storm died down: the King was back at work, displaying outward calm. No decision was reached as to Charlotte's future. Then in November 1804, Lady Elgin sent in her resignation. Perhaps the responsibility of being governess to this royal child was becoming too much for her; but the reasons she gave were gout and weak health. 'For eight years,' she wrote to the King, 'I have been honor'd with one of the most responsible and interesting offices in this country.' But there is a hint that she may have been asked to resign: Charlotte was now nearly nine years old and needed a more advanced education than Lady Elgin was able to give her. The Countess, bowing to the inevitable, begged for recognition of her services in the form of an English title, but had to be satisfied with a pension 'equal to her present salary'.

The King was now in charge; and it was his wish that the young Princess should live at Windsor, under his loving eye. But the Prince, still at odds with his father, wanted her in London where her mother could not interfere. In the end a compromise was reached: the child would divide her time between Lower Lodge, Windsor and Warwick House, a down-at-heel royal residence adjoining Carlton House.

The choice of persons who would in future surround her—headed by a bishop—was lengthy, and appointments were made by the King. As far as we know, Charlotte's mother was not consulted.

Chapter Nine

ALMOST EVERYTHING that Caroline chose to do now was by way of compensation. She had lost her husband, she had lost all chance of family life; but she wished it to be known that though she was estranged from the Prince, she was still attractive; and that though she was not allowed to share in the upbringing of her daughter, she would nonetheless provide herself with a family.

'I have nine children!' she declared, assuring her incredulous hearers that it was true—'true upon honour'. And so it was. In a small way she ran an orphanage, taking in carefully chosen specimens offered at her door by parents with woeful histories of sickness and unemployment. As will be seen later, her page, Thomas Stikeman, who had served her since she arrived in England, was in charge of these proceedings, and learned to sift the deserving cases from the rascals who thought that the Princess was a soft touch.

The children were boarded out, but came to Montague House during the day. The admiring German, Herr Campe, was dining with the Princess and her ladies when the nine well-scrubbed infants dressed in clean but humble garments, were shown in, suitably abashed by the presence of a stranger. 'Their dignified benefactress conversed with them in a lively, jocose, and truly maternal manner,' he wrote delightedly. One boy of five or six, he said, had an open sore on his face, but the Princess called him to her and embraced him, which Herr Campe thought deeply affecting, but which others, more squeamish, evidently found hard to stomach at dinner.

Caroline had worked out a plan. 'It is not my intention', she told Herr Campe, 'to raise these children into a rank superior to that in which they are placed; in that rank I mean them to remain, and to become useful, virtuous, and happy members of society.' In short, the boys were destined for the navy, the girls for domestic service. This plan on the face of it, seemed admirable, and though things did not turn out quite as Caroline hoped, she deserves credit for it, and for the quite genuine impulse which first inspired it—the same impulse discovered by Malmesbury when the French *émigrés* at Hanover awoke her pity, and she learned for the first time what money could do.

Now that she was established at Blackheath an income was allotted to her by Parliament: £12,000 from her husband and £5,000 'pin money' from the Exchequer. This seemed a generous allowance but, as it turned out, it was not enough. What she wanted was happiness, and she did not care how much she spent in search of it. She soon ran into debt.

She thought that her nine children would make her happy: her love for them was not quite normal, but it was a genuine instinct. She hated dogs and birds, she said, so she would keep children instead. And she ordered that her favourite child, William Austin, should be carried in by a footman at the end of dinner and suspended by his breeches over the table to grab anything he fancied from the dessert. 'Don't you think he is a nice boy?' Caroline cried delightedly to Mr Pitt, her guest of honour. 'I don't understand anything about children,' the Prime Minister replied carefully; 'Your Royal Highness had better ask his nurse.'

'It was unpardonable in the Princess', said Lady Hester Stanhope, 'to lavish her love upon such a little urchin of a boy, a little beggar, really no better.'[1]

She was restless, seeing herself in many guises—sculptress, gardener, musician, mother, authoress (she was writing a novel, she told Lady Charlotte Bury)—and she was 'always looking about for someone to pour out her heart to', said Lady Charlotte, who was obliged to listen to many of these outpourings.

'Oh, mine God, I could be the slave of the man I love!' cried Caroline. She longed to love and be loved: she read a great many novels, and in her preoccupation with romance she surrounded herself with a court which consisted almost entirely of men. 'I like Englishmen very well,' she announced, 'but I cannot say the same of Englishwomen. It is impossible to open one's heart, they are so cold.' (She made exceptions of three of her ladies—Lady Sheffield and Lady Glenbervie, who were present when she made the announcement, and Miss Hayman, her Privy Purse, whose outspokenness was shortly to cause her downfall.)

It was natural that after the bitter humiliations of her marriage she should try to show the world that she was not unattractive to men. After the shock of her rejection by the Prince, it was also natural that she should seek satisfaction elsewhere: though perhaps what she unconsciously asked for was kindness. Some of her so-called lovers were married, but she flatly refuted charges of immorality. 'Nobody can improve me in morality,' she declared. 'I have a system quite of my own.'[2] (If we knew what this system was, perhaps the question that hangs over her life might be answered.)

One of her first admirers was George Canning, a handsome and ambitious politician who became a regular visitor at Blackheath, and was flattered but embarrassed by the Princess's encouragement. 'What am I to do?' he wrote to his friend Granville Leveson-Gower. 'The thing is too clear to be doubted.' Fortunately, at this point, he fell deeply in love with someone else, and gently withdrew. 'I know not how I should have resisted', he wrote rather pompously, 'the abundant and overpowering temptations to the indulgence of a passion . . . which must have been dangerous, to her who was the cause of it, and to myself.'[3] The friendship was not broken, however, and Caroline stood godmother to his eldest child. Canning never wholly lost his regard for the Princess.

Not all her favourites were so scrupulous. In these affairs Caroline's object seems always to draw attention to herself, as if it were not so much what happened during the long private sessions which she arranged with her admirer of the moment, as the impression which she made upon other guests by her odd behaviour. She had a way of disappearing during the course of a party with the favourite in tow, leaving her guests like sheep without a shepherd. After a considerable interval the pair would rejoin the party, the gentleman trying to ignore lifted eyebrows and whispered disapproval. One admirer, Lord Henry FitzGerald, came back bearing, ostentatiously, an open book. 'I have been reading to the Princess,' he murmured. Perhaps he had. But what the Princess wanted was to make a little mystery, to start a little scandal, to set people talking. If she did not actually remove her inamorato from the room, she took him into a corner where she whispered and laughed with him in a manner which left no doubt as to their intimacy. The rest of the world, she seemed to say, might go hang. All this is easily connected with Caroline's Brunswick manners and the days of the dancing governess. At Blackheath there are times when, etiquette forgotten, a romping hoyden orders all the doors of Montague House to be thrown open, seizes a partner and invites the company to follow her in a wild gallop through the half-dark house and grounds.

The Princess's behaviour was becoming notorious. At last Miss Hayman, kind, brave and outspoken, decided to speak. At one of the big parties at Montague House the Princess, as usual, had taken some young man downstairs to the Blue Room which led through a conservatory into the grounds, and they remained away for some hours. 'On their returning, sandwiches were brought up . . .'[4]

The company, hungry and cross, grabbed their refreshments and took their leave. Next morning Miss Hayman delivered carefully considered words of advice to her mistress. English manners, she told her, were different from those of other countries, and what did not strike her Royal Highness as unbecoming behaviour would be thought so here, and give rise to unkind remarks. Caroline was furious. Her ladies, she said, were attendants, not counsellors, and had no business to criticize her actions.[5]

Miss Hayman, formerly a favourite, was never forgiven, and a month later was deprived of her suite of rooms at Montague House and told to find herself lodgings in town. Needless to say, this caused further scandal. The Princess of Wales would now have no lady actually sleeping in the house with her, which was both unheard of and improper. And about this time reports began to circulate that Caroline was four months pregnant. Some went so far as to say that the Prince 'had contrived to have a private interview' with her, and the child was his. Another rumour ran round Blackheath: the Prince had arrived drunk at Montague House, and asked for a bed. Caroline had replied that she had no bed to offer him, whereupon he had answered, 'I hope I may share yours.'

Speculations of this kind, once started, spread like fire. Caroline chose to live in an unconventional, democratic way: she behaved, as one of her ladies was to say, 'as any woman would who enjoys flirting'; and the goings-on at Montague House were talked about in London drawing rooms, dramatized and exaggerated. They reached the ears of the Prince who, surprisingly, took no notice. He might have been expected to pounce, as he generally did, upon any piece of evidence that added to his store of grievances against his wife; but at this moment, happily reunited to his Maria Fitzherbert, he only wished the subject of the Princess of Wales to be dropped. And so, for the present, it was.

As Malmesbury had begun to discover when he escorted her to England, one of Caroline's most tantalizing characteristics was her unpredictability. She was not always outrageous: she could be quite ladylike if she tried. It is a pleasant surprise, for instance, to find her sedately attending the village church at Lee, near Blackheath, in company with Miss Mary Berry. 'The parish of George Lock is a mile from here,' wrote the latter, 'a small country church in a charming situation. After church,' she added, 'we went into his house: the prettiest parsonage, with the gayest and most agreeable view.'[6]

The Rector of Lee, the Rev George Lock, was brother-in-law to John Julius Angerstein who had made a fortune as a marine underwriter, and became known as the Father of Lloyds. He had built himself a charming country house at Blackheath, which he named Woodlands,* and here he housed his superb collection of old masters.†

* Woodlands is still there. The Greenwich Borough Council bought it in 1967, and after careful restoration it was opened in 1972 as an Art Gallery and Local History Library.

† Bought by the nation in 1824 to form the nucleus of the National Gallery.

At Woodlands and at Lee, Caroline was made welcome. The gentle, artistic Locks and the opulent Angersteins befriended her—'the poor Princess' they called her, for she seemed dogged by disaster. It was to Amelia Angerstein at Woodlands that she hurried for help when a footman slammed the carriage door on her hand, nearly slicing off the top of her finger. She called for laudanum, which was brought—a pint of it. Against the doctor's order, she plunged her hand into the drug and instead of developing lockjaw, as he threatened, was soon eating a hearty meal.

On her way to visit old Mr and Mrs Lock at Norbury in Surrey, Caroline's carriage, driven too fast round a corner, overturned. The Princess and her two ladies, Miss Cholmondeley and Lady Sheffield, were flung violently into the road, and Miss Cholmondeley who fell on her head died almost immediately. The Princess herself was bruised and shaken, but Lady Sheffield was unhurt. Caroline decided that they must drive on. 'I am as well as the melancholy catastrophe will enable me to be,' she wrote to Amelia Angerstein. 'But oh! poor Miss Cholmondeley! . . . who has been the sufferer and martyr of this unfortunate journey. She will never be forgotten by her friends . . .' And she added a tribute to young Mrs Lock. 'The presence of mind of Mrs William Lock has most astonished me, and I admire her.'[7]

This was Elizabeth Lock whom the Princess called 'Zenzie', from her maiden name of Jennings. With her mass of auburn hair and enormous brown eyes, this lovely creature possessed the kind of beauty which artists love to paint. Her portrait by Thomas Lawrence appeared at the Royal Academy Exhibition of 1799, and 'caused great alarm amongst portrait painters'. The President, Benjamin West, considered that 'it made all the other portraits look like dowdies'.

Caroline decided that she too would be painted by Lawrence, and applied to her father-in-law for permission. Accordingly, in 1801 the King commissioned a painting of the Princess of Wales and her little daughter. Lawrence was invited to dine at Montague House, a number of sittings were arranged, and Caroline became friendly—in the end too friendly—with the handsome artist who had made love to one of Mrs Siddons's daughters and married the other. He was a man of enormous charm, and it was said of him that he could not write an answer to a dinner invitation without making it sound like a *billet-doux*. He knew how to please and flatter Caroline.

The finished portrait is a triumph of discretion. The Princess is depicted with one arm flung upwards as she tunes a vast harp, and the tall vertical line of the instrument gives an illusion of height to her stocky figure. The lighting is suitably dramatic, with a stormy sky seen through an archway behind the Princess; while at her feet the blonde, self-assured child Charlotte is holding up a sheet of music with a gesture which suggests that she finds the pose tiresome and wishes the sitting would end.

Lawrence had a shrewd eye for character, and later was to paint a less heroic but probably truer likeness of the Princess. Dressed from top to toe in scarlet velvet, she sits looking straight into the artist's eyes. Her expression is defiant, and her mouth seems about to break into a smile of triumph when she suddenly decides to fling the dart which she is holding in her hand. Her wilfulness, her unpredictable changes of mood, are clearly shown: she is a person to be reckoned with, a dangerous enemy.

Towards the end of 1801, Sir John and Lady Douglas took a house on Blackheath Common. They were a handsome couple. Sir John, after distinguished service as a lieutenant-colonel in the Marines, had been appointed Groom of the Bedchamber to the Duke of Sussex. 'The emoluments are small,' said this plump Prince, 'but one gives what one has, can one do more?' Apparently not, for Sir John remained unpaid. However, the Douglases were ambitious people who appreciated the value of a position in royal circles. And as they were hard up they were glad to let off part of their house to Rear-Admiral Sir Sidney Smith, who had successfully defended Acre against Napoleon. This gallant sailor had a roving eye, and it was rumoured that Lady Douglas was not averse to her lodger's advances.

But she was to have a rival, for he was invited to Montague House and soon became a regular visitor. The Princess begged him to advise her on redecorating one of her rooms 'in the Turkish style', which offered further opportunities for meeting. The Admiral gave her a drawing of the tent of the Murad Bey, and taught her to trace the arabesques designed for the ceiling.[8] As he lived so near, he was in and out at all hours, sometimes letting himself in with a key from the park into the conservatory which adjoined the Blue Room. The Turkish room was finished to his satisfaction and the Princess pronounced herself delighted. Her taste, on the whole, was bad, and so must his have been, to judge by Lady Charlotte Bury's description—'all glitter and glare and trick . . . tinsel and trumpery'.

But Caroline was delighted with the Admiral. She was also curious about his friends, the Douglases, and one November morning set off across the snow-covered heath to see where they lived. Miss Hayman, reinstated but not forgiven, went with her. Lady Douglas, who happened to be looking out of her parlour window, saw the Princess who (she said later) was dressed in a lilac satin pelisse, yellow half boots, and a small lilac satin cap trimmed with sable. With her short bulging figure she must have presented a striking appearance walking up and down in the snow, and stopping from time to time to look at the house. Lady Douglas caught her eye, and—not knowing quite what to do—curtsied hopefully. To her surprise the Princess returned her curtsy by a familiar nod. Thus encouraged, her Ladyship decided to go out to the gate. The Princess said, 'I believe you are Lady Douglas, and that you have a very beautiful child; I should like to see it.'

But Lady Douglas explained apologetically that she was only in Blackheath for an hour or two: she had left her child in London, where she and her husband were staying during the bad weather. Meanwhile, she held open the gate, and Caroline and Miss Hayman walked in, sat down in the parlour and stayed for above an hour.

This was the beginning of a violent friendship, made up of flattery on both sides and a common interest in indecency and scandal. Lady Douglas was a handsome young woman with hard, bold black eyes and a disregard for truth as total as Caroline's own. Their meeting was a disaster to both.

But at first, all was honey.

'In a short time', said Lady Douglas, 'the Princess became so extravagantly fond of me, that, however flattering it might be, it certainly was very troublesome.'

Caroline visited her new friend constantly. Leaving her attendants below, she would push past the servant who admitted her and rush upstairs to kiss and embrace her beloved Lady Douglas, assuring her that she was beautiful: 'your arms are fine beyond imagination, your bust is very good, and your eyes—all other women who have dark eyes look fierce, but yours are nothing but softness and sweetness, and yet quite dark.' In this manner —according to Lady Douglas—she went on perpetually, even when they were not alone. On one occasion the Duke of Kent was present: Caroline insisted that Lady Douglas should take off her hat, dragged it off herself when she refused, and told her to show the Duke her beautiful eyes. But the future father of Queen Victoria was not amused, and changed the subject.

After three months of this sort of thing, Lady Douglas was invited to come and spend a fortnight at Montague House, and to act as lady-in-waiting while Miss Garth was away. She would be given the round tower, said the Princess, where Miss Hayman used to live; and as it contained a suite of rooms, she could bring her youngest child and a maid, and Sir John would be able to visit her. From her own account, Lady Douglas was exceedingly coy about accepting this invitation; but apparently her husband encouraged her to go. Sir John Douglas, in all the events that followed, seems to have behaved honourably and discreetly; but he was clearly dominated by his ambitious wife.

Now the intimacy between the ladies grew even deeper: they had no secrets from each other, and there were little supper-parties in the tower, when, said Lady Douglas, Caroline would sometimes arrive dressed like a peasant, in a long red cloak with a silk handkerchief tied under her chin, and a pair of old, down-at-heel shoes, all of which must have been part of some fantasy which she was enacting.

The virtuous Lady Douglas was, according to herself, 'greatly surprised at the whole style of the Princess of Wales's conversation, which was constantly very loose, and such as I had not been accustomed to hear'.[9]

At the end of her fortnight's visit she went home to Sir John, still high in the Princess's favour. The friendship seemed as close as ever: and she had confided in her friend and patroness that she was expecting another child. Caroline was delighted. Then, with apparent reluctance, and urging the greatest secrecy, she announced that she too was with child. On her visits she insisted upon comparing notes, and the Princess's freakish cravings—for ale and fried onions or for tongue and chicken at breakfast—had to be described. 'After this,' Lady Douglas alleged, 'we often met . . . and one day as we were sitting together upon the sofa, she put her hand upon my stomach, and said laughingly, "Well, here we sit like Mary and Elizabeth in the Bible." '

They would go through this ordeal together, she said, and she insisted that when Lady Douglas's time came, she, Caroline, would be present. She had never seen an *accouchement* and would like to, and she would bring a bottle of wine and a tambourine to keep up her friend's spirits. But by this time, the friendship had begun to totter.

Caroline did nothing to confirm or deny the report of her pregnancy. It amused her to pretend that she was with child, to play a sort of game with Lady Douglas which both half-believed was true. She would give the Prince as the father, she said, as she had slept twice at Carlton House within the year. In answer to her ladyship's anxiety lest any of the royal family should notice her condition if she went to Court, Caroline said 'she knew how to manage her dress, and by continually increasing large cushions behind, no-one would observe—and she had no doubt of managing it all very well.'

By the time Lady Douglas's child had been born, Caroline was ready to demonstrate that she too, had been successfully delivered. 'Here is the little boy,' she announced on her ladyship's next visit, indicating a sleeping infant. 'Here is the little boy, I had him two days after I saw you last. Is it not a nice little child?'[10] In this rather ambiguous way she allowed her friend to think, if she wished, that the child was hers, while at the same time she let her know that it was not. The game had gone far enough. Then, sending her lady out of the room, she proceeded to outline the whole story of William Austin's origin. She had played her game, she had created a mystery, and now she would tell 'God's truth, upon my honour!' At this, the beautiful dark eyes of Lady Douglas might well have revealed a dangerous glitter. Caroline was obviously lying. But what was the truth? Who was this child?

Chapter Ten

ON 11 JULY 1802, at the Brownlow Street Hospital, Deptford, a woman named Austin was delivered of a male child. She already had two children, and her husband was an out-of-work dock labourer. When she left hospital there seemed little prospect that he would get a job; work was hard to come by and he was in wretched health. However, on the advice of a friend called Mrs Lasley, his wife persuaded him to write a petition to the Princess of Wales, who was evidently known in those parts as a charitable lady; indeed, a number of poor women went regularly to Montague House for left-overs from her lavish table.

Accordingly, Mrs Austin, with her baby in her arms, walked the two miles from Deptford to Blackheath, and presented her husband's petition to the page who opened the door, Thomas Stikeman. He gave her a shilling and asked how old the baby was. About three months, she said. He shook his head, and told her that if it had been about two weeks he could have got it taken care of. Then he 'turned up the child's clothes' (presumably to ascertain its sex) and seemed to change his mind. 'Give it to me', he said, and marched off into the house with the baby in his arms, dancing it up and down and talking to it as he went. He seems to have been a kind man.[1]

Mrs Austin was left at the gate for a long time, and was in tears when Mr Stikeman returned, thinking that her child had been taken from her for ever. The baby, he said, had been a very good boy, 'and he desired her to give him the shilling again, that he might make it up to half a guinea'. This, he said was a present from the ladies-in-waiting. The Princess had not been at home.

But the affair did not end there: after several visits from Stikeman to the Austins' lodgings in the house of a Deptford milkman called Bearblock, Mr Austin was given a job turning the mangle for Mrs Stikeman, who washed the Princess of Wales's linen. Mrs Austin made several journeys to Montague House, trudging to and fro through fog and rain, carrying the child and stumbling over the rough dangerous heath. Then the Princess's doctor, Thomas Edmeades of Greenwich, drove to Deptford to examine the child, and it was finally pronounced healthy, and handed over—'to be brought up and treated like a young prince'. So said one of the ladies; but Mrs Lloyd, the Princess's coffee woman, ordered to serve a cup to the tremulous mother, told her crossly, 'I don't suppose the child will be kept in the house; I don't know what we shall do with it here; we have enough to do to wait on her Royal Highness.' Mrs Lloyd supposed that the child would be put across the heath, where Her Royal Highness had some children at nurse.[2]

But she was wrong. William Austin, the dock labourer's son, would sleep in the Princess's bed. He would stay close to the Princess, far closer than her own daughter, for the rest of her life, a visible proof of the fantasy which she was beginning to create around herself.

Before the baby was a year old, Caroline decided to end her friendship with Lady Douglas. Her ladyship had been spreading malicious reports about the Princess's relations with several men, including Sir Sidney Smith and Captain Manby, RN, a regular visitor to Montague House whenever his ship, *Africaine*, was in dock. Lady Douglas's information, picked up from servants' gossip between the two houses, trickled back to Caroline's ears. She wrote and told Lady Douglas that she did not wish to see her again.

But Lady Douglas was not prepared to accept dismissal without a fight. While in favour she had kept her eyes open and she had learned a great deal about Caroline which would now, she believed, prove useful.

First, she made her husband write to the Princess, requesting an explanation for her banishment. There was no reply, or rather no direct reply. But a long anonymous letter reached Sir John by the twopenny post, followed by two indecent drawings, all informing him that his wife was an adulteress. The writer cited Sir Sidney Smith and the Duke of Sussex as Lady Douglas's lovers, and the drawings in the style of Gillray (the Princess was a clever artist) confirmed it.

'They were designed', said Sir John, 'not only to destroy the happiness of my family, but to produce such feelings as might impel myself and my friend [the Duke of Sussex] to cut each other's throats.'

The Duke of Sussex had no wish to cut anyone's throat, but he felt that steps must be taken to clear his name. He and his brother, Edward Duke of Kent, reported the matter to the Prince of Wales, who was tiresomely indifferent. After all, his brothers argued, it was his neglect of Caroline that drove her to this mischievous behaviour: by introducing this child she was endangering the succession, and even if the Prince of Wales did not choose to act, his brothers would.

The Duke of Kent summoned Sir John and Sir Sidney to an interview, and eventually, after some argument, Sir John reluctantly agreed, '*under existing circumstances* to remain *quiet*, if unmolested'.

'This result', wrote the Duke of Kent in his report, 'I communicated . . . the following day to the Princess, who seemed satisfied with it.'

And well she might. If the letter and drawnings were hers—and no one seems to have doubted this*—she had played with fire, and escaped having her fingers burned. Being Caroline, she dismissed the affair from her mind, and continued in her usual feckless way to take life as she found it. She was besotted with her wretched little child, her Willikin as she called him, and enjoyed the daily routine of his cleaning and feeding, uninhibited in her devotion to these not always attractive functions. Before the quarrel, Lady Douglas was invited to watch operations, and later expressed her disgust.

'The drawing-rooms at Montague House,' she said, 'were literally in the style of a common nursery. The tables were covered with spoons, plates, feeding-boats and clothes; round the fire, napkins were hung to air, and the marble hearths were strewed with napkins which were taken from the child . . .' She thought it peculiar that '*this* was a part of the ceremony her Royal Highness *was particularly tenacious of always performing herself*'.[4]

Willikin was her darling. She dressed him in grand clothes and encouraged her nine-year-old daughter to play with him, which Princess Charlotte did with the greatest reluctance. 'A sickly looking child with fair hair and blue eyes,' she later described him: she very naturally resented his position in her mother's house. Caroline could not have doted on him more if, as she liked to believe, she had really been his mother. 'Prove it, and he shall be your King!' she cried when someone referred to him as her son.[5] This was dangerous talk, and when the report of it reached the Prince, it decided him to take the situation more seriously. Caroline's behaviour was a perpetual source of irritation, but when she suggested that her brat was heir to the throne, something very like treason was in the air. In fact, the law would have to intervene.

He consulted the Lord Chancellor, Lord Thurlow, who took a serious view. 'Sir, if you were a common man, she might sleep with the Devil; I should say, let her alone and hold your tongue. But the Prince of Wales has no right to risk his Daughter's Crown and his Brothers' claims.'[6]

Accordingly, the Prime Minister informed the King, which till now everyone had been reluctant to do. His Majesty accepted the situation with

* The Prince put into the Solicitor-General's hands some letters from the Princess to himself, 'and', said Romilly, 'upon a comparison of the hands, no one of the 4 Lords had any doubt that the anonymous letter, the inscriptions upon the obscene drawings, and the directions upon the envelopes in which the drawings were enclosed, were all of the Princess's own handwriting'.[3]

melancholy calm. 'Two years ago,' he said, 'this would have surprised me, but not now.' Asked what his orders were, the King replied that 'if it had been one attachment, and even a child, he would have screened her if he could have done it with safety to the crown, but that there seemed so much levity and profligacy that she was not worth the screening.'[7]

He began at once to appoint a council to examine the witnesses in what became known as the Delicate Investigation.

This was conducted in private at number 10, Downing Street by the Prime Minister, Lord Grenville, and Lords Spencer, Ellenborough and Erskine, when statements made under oath by numerous witnesses were read and examined. After long deliberation, the learned lords drew up a report and submitted it to the King.

The first people to be examined were Sir John and Lady Douglas, who both 'positively swore' that the Princess had declared herself to be with child, and had shown them the infant, declaring to Lady Douglas that it was hers. To Sir John, however, she had told another story. 'Here, Sir John, this is the Deptford boy, I suppose you have heard I have taken a little child.'

Lady Douglas's statement contained some startling passages. Referring to herself as 'the daughter of an English Officer . . . educated in the highest respectful attachment to the Royal Family', she proceeded to tear the German Princess's character into small pieces. 'I found her a person without education or talents,' she said, 'and without any intention of improving herself.'

Some of Lady Douglas's statements have already been mentioned, when it seems that without actually lying she embroidered upon the truth for the sake of strengthening her case. She tries to represent herself as an innocent and virtuous female, helpless in the hands of this profligate foreigner. There is even a hint that there was something unnatural in the Princess's violent affection. 'She would . . . kiss me, take me in her arms, and tell me I was beautiful, saying she had never loved any woman so much.' She offered to choose Lady Douglas's clothes, 'for she delighted in setting off a pretty woman; and such high-flown compliments that women are never used to pay to each other'.[8]

Lady Douglas must have possessed extraordinary effrontery to have been able to repeat to the Prince some of the statements she attributed to his wife. Caroline's description of the Prince himself is hardly flattering. 'He lives in eternal warm water, and delights in it, if he can but have his slippers under any old Dowager's table, and sit there scribbling notes; that's his whole delight.'

From Lady Douglas's account, Caroline emerges as a woman determined to live her own life and totally without morals. In this the Prince encouraged her, she said. 'When I lived at Carlton House, he often asked me why I did not select some particular gentleman for my friend, and was surprised I did not.' But now, she is alleged to have told her confidante, 'Now I have a bedfellow whenever I like; nothing is more wholesome.'

Lady Douglas's statement, which Huish refers to as 'a farrago of gross ribaldry and consummate nonsense', was carefully studied by the noble lords, who then proceeded to call their witnesses. The servants' gossip which provided the bulk of the evidence was unreliable, trivial and sordid, and it is not difficult to understand why the Prince had been reluctant to authorize its release.

Captain Manby was mentioned by several servants as Caroline's lover. 'Delightful doings, always on shipboard, or the Captain at our house,' said one of them, Frances Lloyd, on returning with the Princess from Southend.[9] Manby seems always to turn up at the seaside, sometimes by boat. 'Not from his situation, birth or manners a person one could expect to meet in the society of the Princess of Wales,' said Glenbervie. But her page Robert Bidgood (who had been page to the Prince for twenty-three years and doubtless wished to remain in the Prince's good books) declared: 'I was waiting one day in the ante-room; Captain Manby had his hat in his hand, and appeared to be going away; he was a long time with the Princess, and as I stood on the steps, waiting, I looked into the room in which they were, and in the reflection in the looking-glass, I saw them salute each other—I mean that they kissed each other's lips.'

Manby denied the accusation as 'a vile and wicked invention', and solemnly swore that he had never slept, as had been suggested, in any house occupied by, or belonging to, the Princess of Wales. His naval uniform, at a time when the glory of Trafalgar still echoed in English ears, may have added authenticity to his defence.

Admiral Sir Sidney Smith, now safely at sea, made no attempt to reply to the accusations levelled against him. Indeed, some of the evidence was extremely fragile. One servant saw 'a man wrapped up in a great coat go across the park'; a lady-in-waiting 'met a man in the passages'. The page, Robert Bidgood, 'a deaf, quiet man', considered that the Princess was 'too familiar with Sir Sidney Smith', and went on to describe how in the course of locking up he 'found the blue room door locked, and heard a whispering within'. He cannot have been so very deaf.

In this case it was Sir Thomas Lawrence who was under suspicion. He had no difficulty in proving that art, not love, was the theme of his relationship with the Princess; he admitted freely that he had asked for a bed in the house, in order to get to work early in the morning: had not Sir William Beechey, PRA, done the same? And he added that during the late sittings—as far as he could recollect—two ladies, Miss Garth and Miss Hayman, had always been present.

'At that time', said Caroline 'Mr Lawrence did not dine with me; his dinner was served in his own room. After dinner he came down to the room where I and my ladies sat in an evening. Sometimes there was music, in which he joined, and sometimes he read poetry ... Sometimes he played chess with me.'

What could have been more innocent?

No servant was prepared outright to state that the Princess had committed adultery; yet all were ready with dreary little allegations of suspicious behaviour, or with sordid stories on 'What the Butler Saw' level. One servant, William Cole, gave evidence of a startling nature, which cannot have been wholly reliable. The Princess had dismissed him in 1802 but he continued to hang about the servants' quarters at Montague House. He was now able confidently to report the most damning evidence at fifth-hand: that 'Mr Bidgood's wife had lately told him, that Fanny Lloyd told her, that Mary Wilson had told Lloyd, that one day, when she went into the Princess's room, she found the Princess and Sir Sidney *in the fact*; whereupon this sensitive female turned to leave the room, and fell fainting at the door'.

It is odd, though, that when this same Mary Ann Wilson (housemaid) made her deposition, the incident was not mentioned. Indeed, she made no accusation against her royal mistress, and when the question of the Princess's being pregnant arose, she spoke up in her defence.

'I never had thought that the Princess was with child ... I think she could not have been with child, and gone on to her time without my knowing it ... I make the Princess's bed and have been in the habit of making it ever since I lived with her Royal Highness ... From what I observed I never had any reason to believe that two persons had slept in the bed ...'

According to the servants, Captain Manby seems to have been the chief suspect, with Sir Sidney Smith close at his heels. But when the serious point arose, of the Princess's having given birth to a child, it was Manby who was generally thought to have been the father. Three years after the Investigation, Glenbervie (not always reliable) was announcing authoritatively that Manby was the father of Willikin, while in 1815 Princess Charlotte aged nineteen, said that she had been brought up to believe the same thing.

But not one of the servants could be certain that their mistress had ever been pregnant: indeed, for the most part, their evidence was against it. Dr

Edmeades of Greenwich, the Princess's surgeon, was prepared to swear that he had never, while attending her, suspected for one moment that she was 'in the family way'; indeed, the whole evidence on this extremely serious allegation came from Lady Douglas, who was building on Caroline's own fantastic stories. So we, posterity, may read through every statement without reaching any sure conclusion.

The wearisome business dragged on through the summer and autumn of 1806. Finally, Sophia Austin was summoned to Downing Street and deposed that she was the mother of the child William, and had left him at Montague House in November 1802 when he was four months old. The Investigators now reached their conclusion, and a statement was sent to the King. The Princess was cleared of the charge of adultery; the child was not hers but the son of a dock labourer, as she had claimed.

But they added, in their careful legal language, that it was evident that the Princess had for some years been behaving in an unseemly and improper manner 'such as must, especially considering her exalted rank and station, necessarily give rise to very unfavourable interpretations'.

Caroline evidently felt that she had triumphed. With characteristic resilience she lost no time in writing to the King asking to be received once again into his presence. After careful thought and consultation with his ministers, the King wrote pointing out the seriousness of the situation, but adding '... his Majesty is advised that it is no longer necessary for him to decline receiving the Princess into his royal presence'. But, he went on, 'there have appeared circumstances of conduct on the part of the Princess which his Majesty could never regard but with serious concern'. And he ends with the hope that in future Caroline will behave herself in such a way 'as may fully justify those marks of paternal regard and affection as the King always wished to show to every part of his Royal Family'.[10]

Caroline, blind to criticism, now assumed that she was restored to favour, and wrote proposing a date in the following week 'when I hope again to have the happiness of throwing myself, in filial duty and affection, at your Majesty's feet'. She was sorry that the date could not be sooner, but she was recovering from measles, and could not venture upon the long drive to Windsor quite yet.

But the King was evasive: he would prefer to see her in London, and at a later date. It appeared that the Prince of Wales had 'several documents which he was putting into the hands of his lawyers'. Until the contents of these papers was known, the King regretted that he could not agree to meet his daughter-in-law.

Caroline was indignant. 'I received yesterday, and with inexpressible pain, your Majesty's last communication,' she wrote. 'The duty of stating, in a representation to your Majesty, the various grounds upon which I feel the hardship of my case . . . is a duty I owe to myself . . .'[11]

She went on to protest at length against the cruel prolongation of her banishment, when she had just been exonerated by the King's 'confidential and sworn servants'; had just been told by the King himself that there was no longer any reason for his declining to meet her. And now, she declared, her punishment was to be continued, pending the result of some new proceedings to be suggested by the lawyers of the Prince of Wales. This was not only cruel, it was unjust. 'It is impossible', she added, 'that I can fail to assert to your Majesty . . . that I am, in the consciousness of my innocence, and with a strong sense of my unmerited sufferings, Your Majesty's most dutiful and affectionate, but much injured subject and daughter-in-law.'

She sat down to await results: she was determined to fight the whole royal family if need be, in order to be reinstated.

She had her supporters and sympathizers, among them Lord Eldon, the ex-Lord Chancellor, and Spencer Perceval, who later became Tory Prime Minister. With their help and advice she proceeded to draw up a lengthy and detailed defence which set out to refute every charge made against her in the Delicate Investigation. It was written in the form of a letter to the King, but was intended for general consumption. The Prime Minister, Lord Grenville, thought it an artful piece of work but 'highly unsuited . . . to the station of the Princess in whose name it is drawn'—and he also criticized the flippant tone of some of its wording which seemed to come directly from Caroline herself. 'I trust Your Majesty will feel it the hardest thing imaginable that I should be called upon to account what corner of a sofa I sat upon four years ago, and how close Sir Sidney Smith was sitting to me.'[12]

This folio volume, 'of no small size and closely written', was printed under the title of *The Book*, and might well have become a best-seller had it not been hastily withdrawn from circulation (at a cost of £10,000) by royal command. Stray copies went for large sums of money, and the Princess's popularity was increased by the general feeling that she had been cruelly and unjustly used. 'If she is guilty she should be punished,' said Perceval, 'but if this cannot be prov'd by the Law of England, she is innocent, and should share her husband's honours.'[13]

Caroline was fully in agreement with this theory, and by exercising the same dauntless, blind determination to win as that displayed by her Brunswick forebears on the battlefield, succeeded at last in regaining her position as a member of the royal family. On 18 May 1807 she appeared at the opera, where she was greeted by tumultuous applause; and in June, after several appeals to her father-in-law, she went to Court to celebrate his birthday and, head held high, made her curtsy to a frigid Queen. The Prince of Wales was present, but it was observed that he managed always to have his back to the Princess. The King, suffering from rapidly increasing blindness, peered into her face, hoping for signs of remorse. But Caroline felt none: she felt that she had won.

Chapter Eleven

'ARE YOU not glad to see me with my head upon my rump?' Caroline enquired of a puzzled visitor. Her English was often odd, and apparently she meant that, with her head still attached to her torso, she was ready to start life afresh.

The year 1806 had been for her a trying one. During the Investigation she had not been allowed to see her daughter, and Princess Charlotte, now ten, was generally at Windsor under the supervision of her grandparents. The Prince of Wales sometimes caught sight of his daughter, but took little interest in her upbringing beyond insisting that Caroline should have no say in it.

After the resignation of Lady Elgin, the King decided that Charlotte's education must be taken seriously, and he began making lists. Her household, he decided, must be headed by a bishop. Only a bishop could provide the 'more extended education' that Charlotte, as heiress presumptive, needed. A bishop, also, would cure her of telling lies, an unfortunate habit which she had inherited from both her parents. Dr Fisher, Bishop of Exeter, was the King's choice. He was made Bishop of Salisbury, and given an assistant, also in Holy Orders, who would teach the Princess religion and Latin. The rest of the establishment consisted of a governess, a sub-governess and an assistant sub-governess; and the King then appointed teachers of history, geography, *belles lettres* both German and French; writing, drawing, music and dancing.

Compared with her mother, for whom one old governess was thought to be enough, Charlotte was to receive a magnificent education, and her days were planned so that not a moment was wasted. But in spite of the formidable array of instructors, she learned only what interested her, and listened only to what caught her fancy. She was quick-tempered, careless and impatient; but she was an affectionate child who responded eagerly when her feelings were touched.

Lady Elgin's successor as head governess was the Dowager Baroness de Clifford, 'a good natured commonplace person', said Lady Charlotte

Campbell. In her youth the Baroness had lived abroad, and had learned a certain grandeur of manner from associating with members of the French aristocracy. She wore rouge and took snuff, and was quite incapable of controlling Charlotte. Happily, one of her assistants, Mrs Alicia Campbell, a thin, humorous Scotswoman known as Tammy, was better equipped for this task, and Charlotte grew to love her. She had also some admiration for the Bishop's assistant, an erudite bachelor called Dr Nott, who worked hard to capture her interest, though she assured him that she disliked Latin more than anything in the world. Poor Dr Nott soon found that his post was no sinecure. Charlotte's writing was abominable, her spelling worse; she made mistakes, he declared, which 'a common servant would have blushed to have committed'. After a year he told her, 'It has given me extreme pain to observe how careless you have been of improvement and how insensible to reproof.' Shortly after this his health broke down.

Charlotte was plunged in grief and remorse. 'I must entreat the Almighty God, who is good and kind to those who pray to him, to forgive my former sins and to implore the forgiveness of Mr Nott.' Fortunately her prayer was answered: Dr Nott recovered.

'What should I have had to answer for,' she wrote, 'if you had been taken out of the world?' And she assured him that she would work hard, and that her only wish was to please him and make him happy. She would try her hardest not to tell lies. 'Oh, my God, my God,' she cried, 'enable me to do my duty in this world and in the world to come . . . Never shall another lie come out of me.'[1]

It was in this pious frame of mind that she decided, at the age of eleven, to make her will. By this, Mrs Campbell, her sub-governess, was to receive 'my three watches, and half of my jewels'. The remainder are to go to Lady de Clifford, 'except those that are most valuable, and those I beg my father and mother, the Prince and Princess of Wales, to take'. She leaves her prayer-book and Bible to the Bishop, and all her 'playthings' to his daughters. To Dr Nott she left 'all my best books, and all my books', begging him to distribute to the poor all the money he finds in her possession. 'I . . . trust that after I am dead a great deal may be done for Mr Nott. I hope the King will make him a Bishop.' Having arranged for her two maids, Mrs Gagarin and Mrs Louis, to be handsomely paid and set up in a house of their own, she ends with the ominous words, 'Nothing to Mrs Udney, for reasons.'

Mrs Udney was the second sub-governess; and what the 'reasons' were we shall never know, though there are grounds for believing that the lady was flirtatious and—from a later remark of Charlotte's—fond of drink. But when Dr Nott saw the will he insisted that Charlotte should remove this clause. He had not forbidden the making of the will: he believed it would encourage her to think of other people and their needs. Neither he nor Mrs Campbell knew that this harmless whim would cost them both their jobs. In the manner of most royal rows, it took a long time to come to a head; but in April 1809 charges were brought against Dr Nott and Mrs Campbell. She was accused of having encouraged Charlotte to make a will in her favour, while Dr Nott was charged with allowing Charlotte to indulge in gossip and attempting to influence the child's mind.

In spite of a vigorous defence by the Bishop, Dr Nott was removed from his appointment: Mrs Campbell resigned on the grounds of ill health. It is interesting to note that she wrote to Caroline.

'I have this day humbly solicited His Majesty and the Prince of Wales to be graciously pleased to allow me to retire from the honourable situation which I now hold in HRH the Princess Charlotte's establishment, the duties of which I feel I am no longer able to fulfil from the very bad state of my health. It is with feelings of sincere regret that I think of parting with HRH with whom it is impossible to have lived so long without feeling for her the strongest interest and attachment.'[2]

Charlotte was deeply grieved by the loss of these two friends. 'These few days,' she wrote to Dr Nott, 'may be our last days together. If we never meet again, keep for me your regard and affection . . . What you have taught me I never shall forget.' It is hard to believe that a child is writing. But to Mrs Campbell she strikes a different note.

'Good God my dear Mrs C.—I am sure papa would let you stay for five or six months in the country and then let you come back. Consider what I lose by your leaving, o consider . . . I cannot go on—think of me! I am ever your affectionate child Charlotte.'

The correspondence went on long after Mrs Campbell had gone away. 'Write to me long letters & grave ones & give me advice,' Charlotte begged her. There is no doubt that Caroline's daughter longed for affection and understanding, and it is fairly certain that her mother was unable to give her either. She had found the little precocious golden-haired child an asset when they drove out together, and particularly when they visited the King. But Caroline, who had a passion for babies, lost interest in her daughter as she grew into a girl, and a strong-willed girl who knew herself to be a person of importance. The Prince had sent orders that 'that nondescript of a boy', as he described William Austin, should no longer be allowed to associate with the young Princess, and Caroline was obliged to obey. Her Mistress of the Robes, Lady Townshend, begged her to send Willikin away for good. 'I do really think' she wrote, 'I do really think that His Majesty's returning affection has been entirely stopped by your keeping *that boy*.' But the Princess was adamant.

'After all that Scandal's Tongue has said I think that the more equal and the more uniform my conduct to that Child . . . would be the most natural in my Opinion . . . Besides, as I have never had the comfort to have my own Daughter under my care or roof, I always had poor Orphans or poor parents' children with me, of all ages and sizes . . . Everybody,' she cried 'must love something in this world.' And she added, 'It seems to me really too ludicrous that I should be the only person in the Kingdom who was not allowed to have a child or any person under my care, whom morality and principles were not shocked at.'[3] So Willikin stayed.

But for the Princess, misfortunes small or great were never far away. At home, after the Investigation, she was being subjected to minor annoyances. Three of the servants who had given evidence against her—'three traducers and slanderers of my honour'—were still in her household and behaving rudely and truculently. In this house without a master, the butler, Mr Bidgood, in particular, was trying by every means in his power to annoy her. Even in church, where, she said, she went constantly if she was well enough, Bidgood managed to insult her, sitting at the end of the servants' pew nearest to her own and staring at her in an impudent way. The Princess implored the Lord Chancellor to give her permission to discharge him and his fellow servants without further delay.

While she worried about domestic troubles, worse awaited her: the news from Germany was alarming. The Duke of Brunswick, her father, was preparing to support the King of Prussia and declare war on Napoleon.

On 14 October the fighting began, and the old Duke mounted his charger and rode at the head of his troops to meet the French under Davoust, at Auerstädt. At seventy-two, he had old-fashioned ideas about fighting, not recognizing the importance of infantry. He was 'much blamed for resisting the entreaty of all the Generals and refusing to march to attack the French'. It was a risk that should never have been taken: in the twin battles of Auerstädt and Jena which followed the two Prussian armies were routed, suffering appalling losses. Riding valiantly but disastrously at the head of his Black Brunswickers, the Duke was shot through the eyes, and was carried off the field. He died a few weeks later at Altona, attended by his aide-de-camp and his mistress—not Mlle de Hertzfeldt, but a temporary, wartime one. 'The Duke of Brunswick (very foolishly at his age)', wrote Malmesbury, 'kept a French actress. Montjoye, his aide-de-camp, procured her for him. She attended him to the camp.'[4]

A slow death, blind and mutilated, was a tragic end for this proud, melancholy man. His life had been filled with disappointments, to which his children, mad or bad, had contributed. He had never been able to inspire his daughter Caroline with any emotion other than fear; nevertheless he was deeply concerned for her future happiness. Only a few weeks before his death he wrote to Lord Grenville, the Prime Minister, begging for his help in speeding up the report of the commissioners in the Delicate Investigation. He evidently hoped that his daughter's name might be cleared, and her position in the royal family restored, before he went into battle.[5]

The news of the Duke's death did not reach England till 27 November, seventeen days after it took place. Lord Howick* wrote immediately to the Duke of Kent, begging him to break the news to the Princess of Wales 'in such a manner as may alleviate as much as possible so dreadful a shock'. He wrote himself to offer his condolences to the Prince who, however, received the news of his father-in-law's death calmly.

'I cannot help thinking,' he wrote, 'that had he survived, & had taken a review of his past political conduct, & of the very disgraceful proposals which he is supposed to have sent to the French tyrant after the complete rout of the Prussian forces under his command, he would & must have suffered most grievously indeed. I cannot therefore say that his death has occasioned me either surprize or much regret, for though we were in various ways related to one another, still I had no acquaintance with him, nor had the smallest intimacy at any time subsisted between us.'[6] But outwardly, at least, the Prince paid tribute to his father-in-law and put all his household into deepest mourning.

The Duke's aide-de-camp, Count Montjoye, was sent to England with letters for Caroline from her brother, now Duke Frederick William, and also to return to the King the late Duke's Order of the Garter. She agreed reluctantly to receive the Count. 'It will be a severe task', she wrote, 'for the Princess to see anybody at the present period which brings her such a melancholy and despondent tidings from her unfortunate & persecuted family; besides, the Princess's mental and bodily state is so much dejected from the frequent agitations that she can see nobody except her physician.'[7]

Brunswick was occupied by the French, and Napoleon planned to incorporate the Duchy into his puppet kingdom of Westphalia. The fate of the widowed Duchess of Brunswick began to cause alarm: King George feared for his sister's safety. It was rumoured that she had narrowly missed being taken prisoner by the French, but had managed to escape into Sweden and was trying to make her way to England. The King ordered the frigate *Clyde* to go to her aid; but speaking for the Admiralty, the Duke of Clarence,

* Later, Grey, 2nd Earl.

always cocksure, was 'inclined to think' that his aunt would not make the attempt. 'If I know the Duchess at all,' he told the Prince of Wales, 'she will be the least welcome visitor to her *wise* and *virtuous* daughter.' (The Delicate Investigation was still going on.) 'The Report of the Commissioners,' the Duke of Clarence insisted, 'will have a very severe effect on the Dutchess whenever she is in possession of it, and believe me, the *frail fair one* at Blackheath will shudder at the sight of her mother if she comes over.'[8]

He was wrong, however, for on 7 July 1807, the frail fair one wrote to her uncle, 'I take the earliest opportunity to inform your Majesty of the happy arrival of my mother. Since an hour I am so fortunate to possess her under my roof.' And she added that the Duchess was '"particularly anxious" to know where and when His Majesty would receive her'.

An awkward situation now arose. The King, and with less enthusiasm the Queen, would be happy to receive the Duchess at Windsor, as would any available Princes and Princesses. But if the Duchess were accompanied by her daughter, her reception could not be attended by the Prince of Wales.

This caused a fluttering in the Windsor dovecotes, and the Princesses, who were devoted to their eldest brother, became distracted with anxiety. The Queen ordered Princess Augusta (the eldest since the Princess Royal's marriage) to suggest to the Prince that he write to the Duchess of Brunswick explaining that he was obliged to go to Cheltenham for his health, which would delay their meeting. 'This,' said Princess Augusta 'appears the best and easiest method of arranging the business, *not omitting* at the same time that motives of delicacy prevent your visiting her at Blackheath till she is established *in her own house*.'[9]

The Prince joyfully accepted this rather dubious taradiddle, thankful for any excuse not to meet his wife; and the Court at Windsor—without the Prince—prepared to give a warm welcome to the Duchess who was accompanied by her daughter Caroline. 'The meeting', Princess Elizabeth told her eldest brother, 'went off to perfection.' Even the Queen, who had always detested her sister-in-law, managed to give her a cordial greeting, and 'they appeared mutually pleased with each other'.[10]

The Duchess had grown very large, and since her husband's death dressed entirely in white crêpe. She spoke slowly and loudly, feeling for her now unfamiliar mother-tongue.

The King was very much shaken by this reunion with the sister whom he had not met for thirty-six years. He wept, it was reported, because he was blind and could not see her. The Duchess, on the other hand, was 'in such health and spirits that little Princess Charlotte told her she was the merriest old woman she ever saw'.[11] She was delighted, she declared, to be in England again.

Everybody remarked on how like the King she was ('though much older', said one observer*), and Princess Elizabeth admired her hands and arms, 'as beautiful as a girl's of fifteen'.[12] 'She certainly is a fine old woman when she is sitting down,' added this niece, 'but you see when she walks or tries to get into her carriage she is very infirm.'

The Duchess was penniless. All that she had brought with her was her husband's collection of coins and antiques, which she hoped that her brother would sell for her.

The King undertook to provide a pension for his sister, and in due course found himself obliged to provide pensions for the rest of her exiled family, which consisted of her three sons—two unfortunately imbecile, and the youngest, Prince Frederick William, now Duke of Brunswick-Oels and an officer in his late father's army. He brought with him his wife, Maria of Baden, and their two sons aged six and four.

For the time being, the old Duchess was lodged at Montague House and Caroline moved out. She accepted—with a bad grace—the King's offer of rooms in Kensington Palace: she had hoped for St James's. She consoled herself with the thought that Kensington was, at least, a town residence where she could, as soon as she was out of mourning, entertain more easily than at Blackheath.

The Duke, her brother, was 'very near being handsome', according to Lady Charlotte Campbell, who considered that if he held up his head, 'he would be a noble looking person'.[13] He seems to have inherited his father's stoop. He evidently bore no likeness whatsoever to his sister Caroline. 'Sombre' is the word Lady Charlotte applies to his expression: 'indeed, the whole cast of his countenance is gloomy'. And on another meeting she calls him a misanthrope. But perhaps he was not at his ease with women, or, like Young Marlowe, with fine ladies.

The Duke was, first and foremost, a soldier in the Brunswick tradition of fearlessness: his talk was of war and politics. His English was not good: he was a fish out of water, a sober fish—at the Prince's birthday celebrations he was the only royal gentleman who did not drink himself under the table. His niece, Princess Charlotte, eleven when he arrived in England, grew very attached to him, and was disappointed when he shaved off his moustache and exchanged his military uniform for dull civilian clothes.

Like the rest of his family, the Duke was beset by misfortune. Only a few months after arriving in England his wife died, leaving the exiled duke

* Cornelia Knight: *Journal.*

alone with his two little boys, Charles and William. Their aunt Caroline dutifully visited the motherless children in their room at the top of the Duke's house in Vauxhall, but said afterwards that she really could not go again, the boys were so ugly—'frightful to look upon'.[14]

The arrival of the Brunswick family brought little comfort to Caroline. She had never liked her mother whom she considered both stupid and dull: there was no reason why she should like her better now. 'There is a hardness of manner in the Princess towards her mother,' said Lady Charlotte Campbell, . . . 'which sometimes revolts me.'[15]

Indeed, after the first rapture of her reception by the royal family, and the glamour of her escape from Napoleon, the old Duchess found herself left to her own devices. Gone were the delicious, dull days of Little Richmond, when she and her ladies dug up old scandals over their knitting. Alone now for hours with her lady-in-waiting, Mme de Haeckle, she felt neglected, and was not after all the merry old woman that her granddaughter had thought her. 'I have nothing to love; no-one loves me!' she exclaimed. The Prince of Wales had promised to call, but he never came. Efforts were made by the Queen and Princesses to visit her, but the Queen was anxious about the King's health and did not care to leave him. The Duchess's granddaughter, Princess Charlotte, was the most regular of her visitors, for the Queen, finding a convenient way of fulfilling her own obligations, ordered that Charlotte should dine with her Brunswick grandmamma every Saturday.

In 1810 the Duchess moved from Blackheath to Hanover Square, and hoped that now she was in London she would have more company. She was growing very infirm, and had to be carried upstairs on a cushion, so she remained for most of the day in one room. The house belonged to Lord Palmerston, but evidently no one had troubled to make it comfortable. 'The dirtiest room I ever beheld, empty and devoid of comfort. A few filthy lamps stood on a side board; common chairs were placed around very dingy walls; and, in the middle of this empty space sat the old Duchess, a melancholy spectacle of decayed royalty.'[16]

Between the lonely old woman and her granddaughter Charlotte a friendship grew up, though the Duchess's habit of saying whatever came into her head was sometimes hurtful. 'You are grown very fat and very much sunburnt,' she roared in her rough, abrupt way when Charlotte went to dine with her after a holiday in Bognor. The young Princess was beginning to be conscious of her appearance, and 'fat' was not a word she cared for. A year or two later, Lady Charlotte Campbell, always critical, considered that Charlotte was growing like her mother: 'Without much care and exercise she will shortly lose all beauty in fat and clumsiness.' The young Princess had only to look at her mother's uncontrolled figure—that exuberant bosom and globular stomach—to see what in time might be her fate. Perhaps her grandmother did well to warn her.

But the Duchess's lack of tact could have more painful effects. In her desire to be treated as one of the royal family she deliberately overlooked Caroline's anomalous position; and on several occasions she accepted the Queen's invitations pretending that she was not aware that Caroline had not been invited. Challenged by her daughter, 'They said nothing to me,' she protested, 'and I could say nothing.' 'It was very different,' she continued, 'when you and I lived under the same roof. I see nothing of you now, I know nothing about you or what you do, and I don't desire to know.'[17]

On one of Caroline's rare visits to Hanover Square, when the party was assembled the old lady suddenly boomed in tones of triumph, 'Madame de Haeckle, you may have a day to yourself on Wednesday next, for the Prince has invited me to dine at Carlton House.' The announcement was followed by a terrible silence. Even Caroline could think of nothing to say. If the Duchess was being deliberately cruel, she could hardly have been more successful. She made it clear that she intended to accept, and was astonished when, prompted by the Duke of Brunswick, Caroline wrote a letter carefully explaining why it would not do for her to go: that by appearing at Carlton House she would be accepting the Prince's treatment of Caroline, allowing him to be in the right.* Caroline's lady-in-waiting, Lady Glenbervie, spent two hours trying to persuade the Duchess, but she stuck to her guns. She had been invited, and she would go. 'I love my daughter above all things,' she announced . . . 'but I must go to Carlton House.' Caroline gave up. Two days later she received a letter from her mother: 'Far be it from me to do anything contrary to your interests; and hearing that there is a doubt upon the subject, I shall not go to Carlton House.'[18]

Caroline made an attempt to repay this gesture. A few months later Louis XVIII, Madame d'Angoulême, and all the exiled French court accepted an invitation to dine with her at Kensington Palace. She invited her mother to meet them, or, as she put it sardonically, 'My mother, and the Princess Sophia, and some old fogroms, male and female, will be there to enliven the party.' It was not Caroline's fault that only the old fogroms turned up, the exiled King and Duchess being obliged—probably at the Prince of Wales's request—to find excuses at the last moment. ('Louis the XVIIIth could only offer me the gout in one knee and in one toe, and

* 'It was so evidently a trap, that was set to inveigle the poor old Duchess into a tacit condemnation of *me*.'

Madame d'Angoulême a swelled face; so that I have not been blessed with a sight of these charming creatures,' wrote Caroline.)[19] Such disappointments were becoming part of her life, making her hurt and angry till she learned to shrug them off.

She was disappointed, too, in her hopes of a reunion with the King. His youngest and favourite daughter, the Princess Amelia, was slowly dying of tuberculosis, and a pall of grief hung over the family at Windsor. Caroline, summoned to pay one of her rare visits to the Queen, was affronted by her reception. She was never asked to sit down (Queen Charlotte had a way of keeping people standing) and when she asked after her 'poor dear uncle', was told, 'The King is quite well, but he will not see you.'[20] 'When I left the royal presence,' said Caroline, 'I thought to myself, "You shall not catch me here again in a hurry."'

On 2 November 1810, Princess Amelia died. The Duchess of Brunswick shed tears of sincere grief for her niece, but Caroline's chief emotion was annoyance that her entertainments would have to be given up during the period of mourning.

The King, crushed by grief, exhausted by the emotion of daily sessions at the sick-bed, was unable to acknowledge the muted cheers of his people on 25 October 1810—the fiftieth anniversary of his accession. A Jubilee feast was spread in his honour by the London merchants and bankers, the streets were filled with rejoicing subjects, and all London was illuminated. Although he made no public appearance at his Jubilee, at no period in his region was he more loved. He was seventy-two, and it was hoped that his reign would go on for many years. No one, not even the King himself, knew that it was virtually ended.

On the day of the Jubilee, the royal family dined quietly at Windsor, but it was noticed that the King was showing signs of unnatural excitement and began to speak rapidly and convulsively as he had done in his illnesses. A witness spoke of 'the dreadful excitement in his countenance'. After dinner he called each of his sons to him in turn. As he could not see, they were obliged to announce themselves one by one. He spoke to each in a curious despairing rush, as if he feared that he would never be able to speak freely again.

The next day the royal doctors were called, and a week later they reluctantly sent for Dr Simmons, the physician to St Luke's Hospital for lunatics. But by now the King's health was improving: he was calm. He asked to receive his ministers, and questioned them about the war, displaying an accurate memory, though it was noticed that his attention wandered and he could not listen for long to what they told him. He was, as one of his doctors put it, like a man walking in his sleep. He spent much of his time playing the harpsichord, or talking to his dead children.

Then, suddenly, he grew violent. He had to be held down, tied to his bed: the dreaded strait-jacket was brought back and the old, drastic remedies applied. 'We do not expect the King's recovery, but it is always possible,' announced the doctors, playing for time, and in time he did grow quiet. They were baffled by his illness: he was not insane, they maintained, but he was deranged. 'He is *quite lost*,' wrote his granddaughter, Princess Charlotte, 'and takes no notice of anything that goes on in his room and knows *no-one*.'[21] She believed him to be 'in great danger at present, & there is more to be feared than hoped for'.

The Queen visited him daily, always with a daughter at hand. 'The King is quiet and composed,' she reported; 'The dear King is comfortable in every sense.' But there were dreadful times when he cried out—'a sort of wailing, most horrible and heart-rending to hear'—and she must have known that there was no hope. King George was a head on a coin, a name in the prayer-book, and nothing more.

Chapter Twelve

On 6 February 1811 the Privy Council met at Carlton House, and the Prince of Wales (who arrived nearly an hour and a half late, attended by all his brothers) was sworn in as Regent. Outside in the courtyard the band of the Grenadier Guards played, rather confusingly, *God Save the King*, while Princess Charlotte, now fifteen, rode up and down in the gardens at the back, trying to follow the proceedings through the windows. As the Privy Councillors moved slowly past him, her father held out his hand to be kissed, sometimes bowing graciously and saying a few words, but occasionally turning his head away sharply like a child refusing food. He had his likes and dislikes.

'A new era is arrived,' the Prince announced to his brother the Duke of York; and though, for a year, his powers would be restricted, he felt himself to be virtually sovereign.

It had been expected that with the Regency there would be a change of government; but to the astonishment of the Tories—and the bitter disappointment of the Whigs, many of whom had been the Prince's personal friends—he announced that at present he would make no change; the Tory government under Spencer Perceval—Caroline's supporter—would be asked to remain in office. The Prince had long promised, and everyone had expected, that he would bring in his Whig friends: he had even had the bust of Charles James Fox placed in a prominent position when he was sworn in, to show where his feelings lay. But he was swayed by the pleas of his mother and sisters—that if the King should recover, he would be made ill again by the shock of finding the Whigs in power. The same argument was put forward by Sir Henry Halford, the royal doctor. Also, and more significantly, his new goddess, Lady Hertford, and her husband, were Tories. So was his brother, Ernest, Duke of Cumberland, recovering at Carlton House from near-assassination by his valet, and exercising a strong, almost hypnotic, influence over his eldest brother.

This strange character, Cumberland, was tall and lean, and would have been the best-looking of the Princes had he not been disfigured by a deep sabre-cut over one eye. His niece Princess Charlotte considered that 'he has *no heart nor honour*, but a *deep, dark vindictive malicious* minde'. He was 'very odious', she added, 'with his indecent jokes'.[1]

In allying himself with the Regent, Cumberland was playing a clever game. Always odd man out in the royal family, shunned by his brothers, disliked and feared by his mother and sisters (one of whom, Princess Sophia, had had a child by him), he now found himself in high favour at Carlton House and wielding a powerful influence over the Prince. According to Glenbervie, the sudden intimate friendship between the two brothers was 'matter of as general notoriety as the Prince's undisguised hatred of Cumberland had been before that time'.[2]

Caroline viewed the situation with dismay. Her brother-in-law Ernest had been her friend and ally: she had encouraged him to confide in her over his love affairs and behaved towards him with the particular blend of playful familiarity which she kept for her male intimates. The bawdy jokes which disgusted her daughter Charlotte were just what she enjoyed, and she relished the scandal which he brought from Carlton House and Windsor.

The breach had opened before Ernest's alliance with the Regent. Assuming the character of well-wisher, he had written begging Caroline to be more discreet in her behaviour towards Willikin. At least, he said, she should keep him more in the background and not slobber over the child in front of her guests. She was exposing herself, he told her, to all kinds of malicious gossip.[3]

The Princess was affronted, and—as always when criticized—became angry and rude. The friendship came to an abrupt end and Ernest was not seen again at Blackheath or Kensington; soon he was the Regent's 'right hand man', and seen with him everywhere.

Now that her mother had moved to lodgings in Hanover Square, Caroline made use of Montague House whenever she felt in need of good air, or, as she put it, 'to take in an additional stock of health & strength'. On returning there in February 1811, soon after the Prince had been made Regent, she found a large bust of the Duke of Cumberland which she had commissioned from the sculptor, Tonerelli, awaiting her. It had been placed on a bracket, out of reach of her short arms, but she seized a poker and set to work to batter the thing to bits. A servant came in, and she ordered him to take it down and place it upon a table, within her reach. She then grabbed the poker again, and smashed the sculpture into small pieces. Shaking with rage, she ordered Miss Hayman to throw the pieces out of the window. She was venting her hatred and frustration not just on Cumberland but on the Prince, her husband and enemy. She was beginning to realize the full extent of his power as Regent: with the removal from public life of the King she was left without an ally. The Prince, who hated her and whom she now began to hate bitterly, was supreme, and her whole way of life was threatened.

There were rumours that she was to be turned out of Kensington Palace: it was suggested in some of the papers that she might be sent abroad. Soon it became apparent that many of the people who had appeared at the Princess's dinner parties were no longer able to accept her invitations.

'The Princess', said Glenbervie, 'invited Perceval and the Attorney and Solicitor General to dinner for next Thursday.' They all sent excuses, pleading the House of Commons. They were all invited again for the following Sunday, when they could have no excuse, but 'I think', said Glenbervie, 'they will find one.'

The Prince was one of those who believed that any achievement should be celebrated by giving a party. He accordingly set about arranging for an enormous and splendid fête to be held at Carlton House in honour of his Regency. The fête was twice put off, as the King showed short-lived signs of recovery: in any case the Queen would not be there—this, she believed, was no time for rejoicing—which meant that the 'sisterhood' would not be there either, so Windsor may be said to have turned its back upon the event. Princess Charlotte hoped against hope that she would be invited, and wrote to Miss Hayman:

'My dear Hamy, ... Only to tell you that the Prince Regent gives a magnificent ball on the 5th June. I have not been invited, nor do I know if I shall be or not. If I should not, it will make a great noise in the world, as the friends I have seen have repeated over and over again it is my duty to go there; it is proper that I should. Really I do think it will be very hard if I am not asked ...'[4]

But alas, there was no question of her being asked, and at the beginning of June she was packed off to Windsor—'Heavens how dul,' she wrote, deeply hurt by being thus treated as a child.

Owing to the postponements, invitations were not sent out till the last minute, and then in so great a rush that several persons no longer alive were begged to attend. The King had relapsed into his former state and it was now considered that he would never recover. As his son the Duke of Clarence put it cruelly, 'We have turned the key on him, and he won't come out again.' The Carlton House fête was to proceed with the Prince's new inamorata, Lady Hertford, in the place of honour at his table.

The reign of Maria Fitzherbert had ended as finally as that of the King. On receiving her invitation, she had written to the Prince to ask at which table she was to sit. He replied that she might sit wherever she chose, except at his table where rank alone regulated the ceremonial. Hurt and angry, she told him that their relationship entitled her to the first place at his table; but she was too proud to press her claim: she preferred to stay away. And so the woman whom he had once called his only true and real wife withdrew herself from his life for ever.

The day of the Regent's fête found Caroline at Kensington Palace. Her ladies in waiting, Lady Charlotte Campbell, Lady Charlotte Lindsay and Lady Glenbervie, had all been bidden to the feast, and in her impetuous generosity she urged them to go, and invited the Misses Berry, Mary and Agnes, to come and keep her company.*

The long summer evening must have dragged intolerably, though the Berrys did their best—'without any hope of getting away', said Miss Berry, 'till Lady Glenbervie came back'. First, the ladies strolled out into the gardens, and then the Princess proposed going indoors, when she would play upon the piano. 'She played', said Miss Berry tactfully, 'a great deal' and 'in a manner to convince one that she had played very well, but had been out of the habit of playing.' From music the ladies turned to conversation, something that both Berrys were good at. They talked about their governesses, the Princess describing hers as 'various and anxious'—which, if we remember Caroline at Brunswick, was probably an apt description. Although she can hardly have enjoyed this quiet and exclusively feminine evening, Caroline responded to the Berrys' valiant efforts to keep her amused and divert her thoughts from the Prince's Babylonian fun.

At last at half-past twelve Lady Glenbervie returned and, encouraged by the Princess, kept the ladies up till nearly two while she described the magnificent scene at Carlton House. The decorations, she said, were stunning. Against a background of massed flowers, framed by hangings of crimson and gold, a fountain played, and gold and silver fish swam into a stream which ran through mossy banks down the centre of the immensely long table with the Prince at its head. The scene was lit by huge candelabra, and diamonds flashed and glittered: the heat was frightful. No wonder some of the gold and silver fish were dead and floated upside down on the surface.

The Prince, who had grown very large, was dressed in a Field-Marshal's uniform (one of his first acts, on becoming Regent, had been to promote himself to this rank) and surveyed the scene with satisfaction, Lady Hertford at his side. Caroline's opinion of his new liaison was contemptuous. Ambition

* Miss Mary Berry and her sister Agnes were jointly beloved by Horace Walpole in his old age. He called Mary 'an angel both inside and out, with a face that is formed for a sentimental novel'.

and vanity, not passion, she considered, had inspired the lady. She was confident that it would not last.

Naturally, the Regent's fête came in for gibes from his critics. 'What think you of babbling *brooks and mossy banks* at Carlton House?' demanded the poet Shelley. 'It is said that this entertainment will cost £120,000.'[5] Others echoed this criticism. The Prince's debts were over half a million pounds, and only the day before the fête he had given £5,000 for a Rembrandt. His taste in art was inspired, but his spending of the nation's money shameless. Nevertheless, the Regency had opened with a bang.

The Regent was proud of his treasures, which could hardly be called his possessions, and in a surprisingly democratic gesture, threw open Carlton House to the public for three days after the fête. The public responded enthusiastically, and on the last day the crowds were so great that women were trampled underfoot by eager sightseers determined upon a good look at their Prince Regent's home. As they gaped awestruck at the rich magnificence, and tried to assess the value of the furniture and plate, some may perhaps have wondered if his wife and daughter ever had any part in all this splendour.

His wife, as we have seen, was obliged to make a home for herself as best she could; and the new situation created by the Regency did not make her life any easier. It was no longer considered the thing to attend the dinner parties which she had been in the habit of giving, with guests of royal or political importance. The important people excused themselves and stayed away. Caroline, undeterred, invited people of less conventional significance, and her table was filled with artists, historians, philosophers, some of dubious morals. She chose peogle who would amuse and entertain her: she could not endure anyone boring. 'Mein Gott! dat is de dullest person Gott Almighty ever did born,' she cried.[6] Her dinners, in consequence, were lively: wit rather than respectability was the passport to her table. But 'unfortunately', said Lady Charlotte, 'the Princess prolonged her pleasures till they became pains': her parties went on and on, her guests being obliged to sit for five or six hours at table. She could not bring herself to let them go. 'To tell you God's truth, when I am happy and comfortable, I could sit on for ever.'[7]

On Saturdays Princess Charlotte dined with her mother, accompanied by a disapproving Lady de Clifford. No doubt at these dinners Charlotte heard many things discussed which she should not, at her age, have heard at all. But the scandalous gossip and loose talk shocked her far less than the conversations that she had with Sir William Drummond, who had written a book in which he tried to prove that certain parts of the Old Testament were allegorical. 'I can assure your Royal Highness there is nothing in it, it is all allegory and nothing more.' He was evidently struck by the young Princess's intelligence, and told her to study Oriental history—'far more amusing than the Scriptures'. The royalty and nobility of this country, he said, had always been educated by priests—'the most corrupt and contemptible of mankind'. For once, deeply perturbed, Charlotte found herself on the side of her much mocked preceptor, the Bishop of Salisbury. She extricated herself with difficulty from Sir William, saying that she would rather believe her catechism, and, safely back at Windsor, unburdened herself to the Bishop. In due course a decree came from the Regent: the Princess Charlotte was to meet no society whatsoever at her mother's house.

He would have put a ban on Sir William Drummond: but 'no society whatsoever' indicated that he was afraid that the influence of any of her mother's guests might corrupt his daughter's morals. In the brief glimpses that he had had of Charlotte lately he had observed that she was growing up fast. He did not like this: he wished her to remain a child, in the background. But already she was in mind and body a woman. He observed with disquiet those slightly prominent Hanoverian eyes, that 'full but finely shaped bosom' and 'voluptuous' figure. Charlotte would have to be watched.

Soon after the excitements of his fête had died down, the Prince became seriously ill. His brother the Duke of Kent brought the news to Caroline. He was suffering from 'sicknesses, swelled legs, etc.,' the etcetera suggesting troubles which could not be mentioned. At the same time Lord Glenbervie was announcing that the Prince had had 'three epileptic fits'—but this diagnosis was unconfirmed. It was known that he suffered from sudden, mysterious bouts of violent illness; in this case he was evidently in a highly nervous state, and had resorted to alcohol to give him strength in his difficult and exhausting job—far more difficult and exhausting than he had ever imagined—as head of state.

His taste in drink was bold. At one sitting he was seen to consume 'at least three bottles of wine, besides maraschino punch and Eau de Garouche'. This liqueur he drank in large quantities and he liked it 'excessively hot and strong'. The effect upon his liver must have been disastrous. In order to counteract any ill effects he resorted to opium, laudanum and other drugs: altogether, he made demands upon his body which the doctors observed with alarm.

Caroline received the news of her husband's illness calmly. 'I am not sanguine enough to flatter myself that the period to all my troubles and misfortunes is yet come. But one must hope for the best.'[8]

Till now she had always done that; but if she hoped that the new era was going to make her life happier, she was bitterly disappointed. At the beginning of 1812 the King was pronounced incurable. The Regent took over full powers: he was virtually King, and the future destinies of his wife and daughter were in his hands.

At forty-three, Caroline was a short, fat woman with a handsome face and a head too large for her body. She had practically no neck and accentuated this by wearing a variety of lace ruffs and frills, 'ill put on, and some not looking too clean'.[9] Alas, she had never cured herself of skimping her toilette; and Miss Berry noted that it was quite impossible to keep up with the speed with which she dressed for dinner.

She was constantly criticized—even when quite young—for wearing too much rouge. It seems possible, though, that she had by nature a very light colour, which would be likely with her blonde hair and white eyelashes: she evidently spent very little time on her appearance.

'Her temper is strangely altered,' Glenbervie noticed. She had quarrelled with the last of her gentlemen admirers, Lord Henry Fitzgerald—the only one who had really shown her something like love. Now she had lost much of her gaiety and recklessness: she was a bitter, disillusioned woman. 'All the day long,' Lady Charlotte complained, 'her Royal Highness continues to talk of wishing people dead . . . I have been an accomplice in murder many a time, if silence gives consent.'[10] Sometimes the Princess was simply bored. She compared herself with the Roman Empire—'in a state of decadence'. Kensington Palace was uncomfortable, 'desperately cold' and inconvenient: all those empty rooms seemed to emphasize her solitude. She longed for amusement: she banged on the piano and decided that she must practise her singing; then she engaged a family of Italian musicians, the Sapios, to play for her and accompany her when she sang. Enjoying herself, she sang loud duets with young Sapio, whose throbbing tenor won him the nickname of Chanticleer. Before long, her ladies observed with horror that the Sapio family were being treated by Caroline as her guests: and in the sunshine of her favour they began to take liberties. They were constantly turning up, and Caroline's household and guests began to dread the musical evenings to which they were now subjected. The father—known as the old Orang-outang—was quite at his ease in spite of the cold and contemptuous treatment he received from the ladies. The Italians were on to a good thing, and the 'music mania' reached fever pitch.

'In the intervals between singing and eating', as Lady Charlotte put it, Caroline relapsed into gloom, complaining unceasingly of her misfortunes; or she played a game in which she imagined the Regent dead, and herself travelling abroad 'with a court of her own making, of which the fiddler is to be King'. The music combined with the flashy good looks and flattering manners of Chanticleer to turn her head. She adored him. She bought a cottage in Bayswater, selling everything she could lay hands on to raise the money, and installed the family where they were within easy reach, and where she could join them in the evenings and shed etiquette.

Honest, outspoken Miss Hayman—in charge of Caroline's finances and always critical of her morals—could endure the situation no longer, and firmly tendered her resignation.

While Caroline killed dull care with this 'set of low persons', her daughter was virtually a prisoner at Windsor. Her correspondence was watched, and to her intense grief she was shut off from communicating with her friend and confidante, Mercer Elphinstone. Miss Mercer, as she was called, was eight years older than Charlotte and thoroughly sophisticated and worldly-wise. Charlotte admired and loved her, and tried to follow her advice in all things. They both interested themselves in politics, and both were enthusiastic Whigs.

On 11 May 1812 the Tory Prime Minister, Spencer Perceval, was assassinated by a half-crazy commercial traveller called Bellingham, whose business had been ruined by the war.

The assassin gave himself up, was tried and sentenced to be hanged. He made no attempt to defend himself, but the shock to the nation was considerable, and in the industrial towns riots broke out. For a time it seemed that Bellingham had given the signal for an English Revolution. 'Provisions cheaper—bread or blood!' the starving people cried, and the Prince—safe in Brighton—was alarmed by anonymous letters threatening his life.

Caroline was stricken by Perceval's death. 'I have lost my best friend,' she said, 'though even he was changed towards me since he had become a Minister.' And she remembered the empty chair at her dinner table, and the evasive refusals to her invitations. She believed that the Tories would stay in office. 'The Prince will never have sufficient energy to change his whole set of ministers . . . He will merely get Lord Wellesley, or some such person, to plaister up the rent this great man's death has made.'[11]

The prognosis was astute. The Regent, after taking advice from every side, invited Lord Liverpool to 'plaister up the rent', and, after a stormy start, the Tories came back to stay. Carlton House closed its doors to members of the Opposition, and Charlotte wept when she heard the news. She believed that her father had betrayed his friends, and she also knew that her friendship with Mercer, a staunch Whig, would be threatened. She was right: Miss Elphinstone was asked to cease her correspondence with Princess Charlotte.

Caroline was shocked by Miss Hayman's departure; but she could not bring herself to put an end to the Sapio affair. She realized that the Bayswater cottage was a folly, and tried to invent excuses for taking it: it would be just the thing for Lady Charlotte Campbell's children; Lady Charlotte was to have it when the Sapios left, she said—and she tried to excuse her freakish behaviour by saying that she was unhappy at being deprived of her daughter's company, and was concerned about Charlotte's treatment at Windsor.

Till now, Charlotte had been allowed to see her mother once a week. Then in June 1812 Caroline received a letter from Lord Eldon: 'The Lord Chancellor humbly begs leave to communicate to your Royal Highness the Princess of Wales that he has been commanded by the Prince Regent to inform your Royal Highness that it is his pleasure that the Princess Charlotte of Wales should at present reside at Windsor; and for the purpose of waiting upon your Royal Highness at Kensington, should come from Windsor once a fortnight . . .'[12]

The Regent was careful to add that the Princess Charlotte was on no account to receive visits at Windsor, as she 'is residing in a house appropriated for the use of the Prince Regent'.

Another door had closed. Caroline perceived that the war against her husband had moved into a new and more dangerous phase but she was determined to fight on.

At the end of one of her long dinner parties, a thunderstorm broke out just as the guests were leaving. Some waited, lingering in the drawing room, when the room was suddenly illuminated by a prolonged flash of brilliant light—'brighter than the beams of the sun'. This was followed immediately by a loud hissing noise, as what seemed to be a ball of fire fell just outside the window where they stood. Some of the gentlemen ran out to see what had happened, and found that the sentry at the door had been flung to the ground, and that the gravel path had been torn open. The servants and soldiers in residence were terrified: there was a feeling that it was an evil omen. 'This,' said Caroline, 'this forbodes my downfall.'[13]

Chapter Thirteen

THE PRINCE did not want his daughter at Carlton House, or at Brighton. He gave her instead two rather ramshackle houses, Warwick House which was near Carlton House, 'an old moderate-sized dwelling, at that time miserably out of repair',[1] and Lower Lodge, Windsor, which had once belonged to Nell Gwynne and was now damp, dark and sadly neglected. 'This infernal dwelling,' Charlotte called it, 'a perfect prison.'

By refusing Caroline permission to enter either of these houses, the Prince hoped that he was separating the mother and daughter as completely as he could without upsetting popular feeling. Charlotte, he announced, was to dine at her mother's house once a fortnight, always by her father's consent.

For a time this arrangement worked: then for one reason or another two meetings were cancelled, and Caroline took the law into her own hands. She went to Windsor. One of the lodges there had once been given her by the King; she had never made use of it, but now she decided to make it her headquarters. From there she sent a request that Lady de Clifford would bring Charlotte to see her. A note came, refusing; whereupon she demanded an audience of the Queen. This brought the Queen's Chamberlain with another refusal, and Caroline, clutching her two written rebuffs, drove back to Kensington to prepare for another attack.

'In the papers', wrote Charlotte in a smuggled letter to Mercer, 'you have seen . . . the unpleasant circumstances relating to the Princess *coming* here. All I can say is that *feeling* her *claim* is *just* she will *pursue* it till she gains her *point*.'

On the Princess's second visit to Windsor she was met by the Prime Minister, who politely but implacably refused her request. She asked for the refusal in writing with Liverpool's signature, then called for her carriage and swept out of the castle, once again without having seen her daughter or any member of the royal family. It was humiliating, but Caroline was used to humiliations. In any case, she had a plan. Always when there was a battle to fight her spirits rose, and gleefully she told Lady Charlotte Lindsay of the 'fun' she was having 'teazing and worrying the Royal Family'.

It is now that Henry Brougham makes his appearance. For some time the eminent and disgruntled Whig politicians, Brougham, Whitbread and Tierney, had been seen at the Princess's dinners, and now she began to realize the importance of an alliance with this powerful cabal, who were disposed to interest themselves in her problems. The Prince's failure, after the murder of Perceval, to assemble a coalition government left him no choice but to go on backing the Tories, and thus to continue to give his support to Wellington's campaign in the Peninsula. But inevitably this decision met with dislike and anger from the Opposition.

This was the time chosen by Caroline to launch her new offensive. Brougham, ambitious, eloquent lawyer and astute politician, seemed to be sent to her from heaven. She did not trust him; he was wary of her; but the alliance was valuable to both.

Caroline, since her first rejection by the Prince, had learned the importance of keeping records. She had by now amassed a tremendous quantity of written evidence—letters from the Prince, letters from the King, newspaper cuttings, copies of old letters—all of which she believed would, at some future time, come in useful. She insisted, when she invaded Windsor, upon getting the refusals to her requests in writing, and in due course these documents were shown to Brougham. From now on he would be obliged to read a quantity of similar papers, as the Princess's affairs became more and more complicated.

The present campaign, she said, was being fought for the liberation of Princess Charlotte.

Charlotte herself was a little dubious about the Princess's way of doing things. Although they had never been intimate, she knew her mother well enough to realize that she could not be trusted to act with discretion or even caution. She was grateful for Caroline's support, but her position as heiress presumptive made her wary of her mother, while by Mercer's advice she tried to keep on the right side of her father. It was a complicated situation.

'She is still my mother, whether acting right or wrong,' she told Mercer: she felt obliged to support her, though there were times when she must have been sadly disillusioned. Now she agreed to back her mother's claim that they should meet more frequently, even though she did not particularly enjoy these meetings. Her eyes were wide open to her mother's way of life. 'It is a distressing thing,' she wrote, after seeing young Sapio's horse outside the Princess's door, 'to entertain suspicions, but when things *have occurred* one cannot help having one's ideas upon some things.'[2]

Lady de Clifford now, unwittingly, entered the fray. After attending a *fête champêtre* held in the castle grounds in a downpour of rain, she developed 'inflamed eyes' and was obliged to retire to London to recover. This meant that Charlotte's visits to her mother were again cancelled. Caroline wrote to the Queen, asking her to appoint someone else to accompany Charlotte to Kensington, and accordingly Miss Cornelia Knight, at that time Lady Companion to the Queen, was sent, with strict orders not to let Princess Charlotte out of her sight for one moment. But even Miss Knight's vigilance could not prevent a parcel containing a pair of shoes being handed to Charlotte by her mother just before she left. The shoes were stuffed with papers; and Charlotte was able to read for herself what Brougham was proposing to do—and probably other news of particular interest to Charlotte.

The Queen, in her anxiety that Charlotte should not be left alone with her mother, had reason to fear that the young Princess might be drawn into some mischievous plot. She was developing a grudging admiration for the high-spirited girl, and had already defended her to the Prince, assuring him that Charlotte 'is blessed with an uncommon share of good sense; she has talents and facility to learn anything, is easily led to follow good advice when treated with gentleness, desirous to oblige when opportunity offers, and capable of very strong attachment . . .'[3]

What the Queen did not yet know was that Charlotte, at the age of sixteen, was in love. Lady de Clifford's inflamed eyes were the culmination of a quarrel with Charlotte which had caused the poor lady much heart-searching.

Charlotte was a fine horsewoman, and at Windsor her chief compensation for the boredom of that life—where everything moved as if by clockwork and the same things happened at the same times throughout every day and night—was in riding. She would have enjoyed it more if her four aunts* had not insisted upon riding with her, but at times she managed to throw them off and gallop happily with her cousin, Captain George FitzClarence,† as dashing a young officer as a girl could wish to see. The happiness was short-lived, for the Captain was obliged to join the Prince's Regiment at Brighton, and—to the relief of her aunts, who remembered similar clandestine gallopings when their dear dead sister Amelia was in love with Captain Fitzroy—Charlotte was once more obliged to ride sedately in their midst.

But not for long. She had made the acquaintance of another young officer, Lieutenant Hesse of the 18th Light Dragoons, rumoured to be the Duke of York's son by a German lady of rank. Hesse was handsome, if a little short of stature, but he looked well on a horse and had a confident air. Charlotte,

* Augusta, Elizabeth, Mary and Sophia.

† Eldest son of the Duke of Clarence by the actress Mrs Jordan.

driving in an open carriage with Hesse on horseback at her side, fell imperceptibly and delightfully in love.

For six weeks, Lady de Clifford sat day after day and twice a day in the carriage with her charge, pretending not to notice what was going on. Notes, tokens, rings were exchanged, and she tried not to hear what the two voices were murmuring gently to each other. It was a wartime romance, precarious and therefore thrilling: at any moment Hesse's regiment would be sent abroad, and Charlotte, like tens of thousands of other young women, would be left at home to mourn. Doggerel verse expressed the situation in various forms, framed in weeping willows on jugs and mugs.

Sweet, o sweet is that sensation
When two hearts in union meet;
But the pain of separation
Mingles bitter with the sweet.

Lady de Clifford suddenly came to her senses. The affair must be stopped, she must speak—and at once. Unfortunately, after more than seven years of Charlotte, the old Baroness had quite given up all hope of controlling her. They were good friends, indeed, there was a genuine affection between them, but Charlotte went her own way. When Lady de Clifford summoned up the courage to tell her that she must give up meeting Captain Hesse, the young Princess flew into a rage which ended in floods of tears. The quarrel took place as they drove to visit the Princess of Wales, and Lady de Clifford's heart must have sunk as they reached the gates of Kensington Palace. She knew that she would get no support there.

She was right. Caroline knew of the affair already, and thoroughly approved. At sixteen, a girl should take her first lessons in love. She was half in love with Captain Hesse herself she declared, and, without pausing to consider the consequences, hurled herself joyfully into battle. 'This will play the devil at Windsor,' she cried, 'but I will make amends for it.' She would make sure that the young couple had a good time. She would be the go-between for their letters: she would arrange meetings. Whenever Charlotte came to see her at Kensington, she would see that Hesse was there. Unknown to Lady de Clifford, she would let him into her own apartments through a door that opened into the gardens. Then, in her half-crazy, reckless way, she led the lovers to her bedroom, where she left them together, saying as she turned the key, '*A présent je vous laisse, amusez vous.*'[4]

She must have been mad—or at least unbelievably foolish. She cannot have paused for one moment to consider the possible consequences: all she thought of was the excitement and triumph of hoodwinking the Regent. Had Charlotte not kept her head, had Hesse not behaved with unexpected decorum, the affair might have ended in total disaster for both. What actually took place in that bizarre bower will never be known. Caroline's 'double headed Couch Bedstead' with its 'carved heads and Paws, finished in Burnished Gold' presented itself invitingly to the lovers' eyes—but in vain. From Charlotte's stammered confession to her father two years later, it seems certain that love-making, if it took place at all, was of a most decorous nature. 'God knows what would have become of me,' she said, 'if he had not behaved with so much respect to me.' To this the Prince, with tears, replied, 'My dear child, it is Providence alone that has saved you.'[5]

Providence saved Caroline also: her mischievous plot was not discovered. It was as well, perhaps, that the 18th Light Dragoons were ordered to Portsmouth, on their way to France, and Lieutenant Charles Hesse was removed from temptation. Charlotte dried her tears and began to worry, not for her lover's safety—though that was in her mind: 'if anything were to happen to our friend I should feel it excessively'—but for the safety of the letters she had written him, and the little gifts she had lovingly pressed upon him.

She spent the next two years trying, with the help of Mercer and ultimately Mercer's father, Lord Keith, to trace the whereabouts of everything that she had sent to her lover, and to ensure that it was burnt or returned. They had vowed mutually to burn all letters, and this vow was faithfully carried out by Charlotte: she could not be sure, however, that Hesse had done the same. As the months went by she grew more and more apprehensive: Hesse was lost in the smoke of war: she could not tell if he was still carrying her gifts and those tell-tale notes accompanying them—'much *too full* of *professions* and *nonsense* . . .' As time went on, she became haunted by the thought of that 'paquet' of letters—'those dreaded letters'. She scanned the casualties in the papers: what if he were killed and the letters found in his possession? And she describes herself 'still smarting for my own folly'.[6]

Mercer, after several attempts to reach Hesse, succeeded at last in running him to earth in France and at last receiving an answer.

'The greater part of the articles demanded from me, I left in England,' wrote Hesse . . . 'are in a small trunk—this trunk I left in charge of a TRUE *friend of mine* with the particular request that "should he hear of my death to send this trunk *unopened* to the bottom of the Thames". I can rely upon the execution of this promise.'[7]

Mercer wrote back briskly, not believing a word of this, and asking him to 'return, without loss of time, all the letters or presents you may now have with you'. At this, her father Lord Keith summoned Hesse to an interview when he was next in London. Hesse, who must by now have begun to regret that he had ever met Princess Charlotte, duly presented himself, and Lord Keith, with Scottish thoroughness, handed him a sheet of twenty-six questions regarding his relationship with Princess Charlotte, the part played in the affair by the Princess of Wales, and the whereabouts of letters and trinkets not contained in the packet presented to Mercer the day before.

Captain Hesse answered carefully and plausibly. Everything, he said, had been returned except Charlotte's letters, which he 'burned so soon as I received them', and a small blue ring which he wore round the feather in his hat when he rode into battle—and which was unfortunately lost.

And so the affair ended. 'The little Lieutenant does not occupy a thought of mine,' wrote Charlotte, now totally disillusioned. Even when she was in love with him, she had never been quite sure, she said later, whether Hesse was her lover or her mother's. And in the end, as will be seen, it was Caroline who bore him away. Meanwhile, having bestowed Charlotte's picture upon '*l'aimable sujet*', as she called Hesse, and clasped him to her enormous bosom in farewell, Caroline was able to give full attention to her own plans and pursue the battle for Charlotte's rights, which were of course her rights also. She enjoyed the role of innocent distressed heroine, the role in which the British people saw her and in which Brougham was ready to reintroduce her. Accordingly, she presented him with a rough draft of a letter which she had composed to the Prince, stating her grievances. Brougham tidied up the English and the spelling; then he decided to rewrite the whole thing. His version was long, and set forth in grandiloquent language all Caroline's grievances: her enforced separation from her daughter, the insulting treatment she had met with at Windsor, the ostracism she had received from the Queen and Princesses. In spite of her complete vindication by the Delicate Investigation six years before, she was treated now as if she were 'still more culpable', and was held up to the world 'as a mother who may not enjoy the society of her only child'.[8] She pleads that her honour is at stake: Sapio and other intimates are forgotten, or thrust aside as belonging to another part of her life: she is the virtuous, forlorn, forsaken wife and mother.

A eulogy of Princess Charlotte follows, leading into a vehement protest against the young Princess's secluded life. 'She who is destined to be sovereign of this great country' is being deprived of all the social advantages which lesser people take for granted.[9]

It was a masterly letter when Brougham had finished with it, though nobody could have believed it to have been written by Caroline. However, she pronounced it 'exquisitely perfect', signed it 'Caroline Louisa', and dispatched it to Carlton House.

It was not so easy, however, to persuade the Prince to read it. The very thought of any communication with his wife filled him with horror and disgust: he refused even to touch the letter, and ordered it to be returned unopened. But Caroline was undeterred. 'Three different times at least' the letter shuttled between Prince and Princess, till finally she sent it to Lord Liverpool, asking him to open it and read the contents aloud to the Prince. This, rather surprisingly, he did, and a week later the Prime Minister wrote to tell the Princess, adding that 'His Royal Highness was not pleased to signify any commands upon it'.

Brougham immediately released a paragraph to the Press, giving the story of the letter and its adventures; and the following day the *Morning Chronicle* published the letter in full. It was a triumph for Caroline, who became a national heroine: the print shops seized upon the story and sold copies at sixpence, and Caroline found herself being presented with loyal addresses from London boroughs, while the Kensington band played loyal tunes in the background.

But it achieved nothing for Charlotte, and only served to widen the gap between her father and herself.

For some time she had hoped that after her seventeenth birthday she might be considered old enough to be given an establishment of her own with ladies-in-waiting instead of governesses. At the end of 1812 Lady de Clifford opened the door to this by resigning. Ever since the Hesse affair there had been a coldness between herself and her charge: Lady de Clifford felt that she had lost the young Princess's confidence, and Charlotte suspected that the Dowager was making mischief with her detested aunt, Princess Elizabeth. 'I am far from comfortable,' she said, 'with the old Dow.'

Brougham supported Charlotte in her hope of an establishment, and told her that the question would be discussed in Parliament. Encouraged by this, Charlotte wrote to her father. The letter was carefully thought out, diplomatic, and over-anxious. Her greatest ambition was to win his respect, and better still, his affection; but she never knew from day to day how she stood. Her letters to Mercer contain sharply contrasted reports of his behaviour to her: on the whole he chose to treat her with cold indifference.

There were several reasons for this. The chief was that she was Caroline's daughter, and remained loyal to her mother in spite of his efforts to keep them apart. He was jealous of her because she was young and high-spirited and because she was his heir. He cannot have enjoyed, after opening

Parliament in November 1812, the cheers and joyful shouts with which Charlottes' carriage was greeted by the crowd, while he had been allowed to pass in stony silence.

At times he relented, and allowed himself to try and please her, to respond to her attempts to please him. But he was unpredictable, and it was in some trepidation that she put her request for a Lady Companion instead of a governess.

'I trust my dear father will pardon the freedom & candour with which I have addressed him upon so interesting a subject to me. I feel the difference of my age. I cannot help judging from the view of other young people of my own age, who cease to have governesses at 17.'[10]

The letter had a disastrous reception. The Regent flew into a rage and summoned Lord Eldon to accompany him instantly to Windsor. John Scott, first Earl of Eldon, was known to the royal family as Old Bags, because his father had been a coal merchant in Newcastle. He was a pompous lawyer of sixty-one, totally unsympathetic to Charlotte's point of view. For Charlotte the scene which followed was an intolerable and unreasonable ordeal. An inquisition in miniature, it was held in the presence of the Queen, Princess Mary and a tearful Lady de Clifford. The Regent opened the proceedings by demanding of his daughter why she refused to have a governess. Charlotte, tongue-tied, could only refer him to her letter. The Queen accused her of being obstinate, headstrong and perverse, and the Prince added that she was a fool. 'Besides,' he said, 'I know all that passed in Windsor Park.' This must have frightened Charlotte, but she remained silent, showing remarkable self-control. 'You can conceive, during the time it was going on, I could command my temper and everything,' she told Mercer; 'afterwards it was too much.'[11]

'If it were not for my clemency,' the Regent continued, 'I would have you shut up for life. Depend upon it, you shall never have an Establishment unless you marry.'

Lord Eldon now took over, and in a rough, hectoring voice told her that she had no right to make demands of this kind: did she not know that the law of England gave her father supreme power over her? She did, for Brougham had said so, but she remained silent, and the Prince turned impatiently to the Chancellor. What would *he* have done, as a father? he is said to have demanded, to which Old Bags replied in his Tyneside accent, 'If she were my daughter I would have her locked up.'

'Charlotte never spoke, or moved a muscle,' said her mother proudly. 'Nothing could be more determined or immovable than she was.' And Caroline alarmed Lady Charlotte Campbell by her triumphant declaration

—'We must *frighten* the man into doing something . . . I do not think gentle means will ever prevail.'[12]

But Caroline had not the imagination to grasp what Charlotte had had to suffer. All her hopes of gaining her father's affection and sympathy were dashed; her pride trampled by Eldon's rough treatment. When they had gone, she ran into the room of one of her aunts and burst into tears, exclaiming, 'What would the King say if he could know that his granddaughter had been compared to the daughter of a collier?'

'Thank God, my spirit is not broken,' she wrote in her next smuggled letter to Mercer, 'tho' my health suffers & my own spirits very much.' She had lost her sleep and 'apitite' and had a heavy cold. It was cold comfort to learn that the Prince had regretted his harshness and wished her '*to think it was all a moment of heat*'.[13] She realized now that it was of no avail trying to stand up to her father. In the long run, he held all the aces. Wiser than her mother, she forced herself to accept the situation.

Caroline was disappointed in what seemed to her Charlotte's weakness. But she eagerly awaited the twelve-page letters that Charlotte managed to smuggle to her, feeling that she, not her daughter, was the heroine of this new drama. She felt complete confidence in her own power to overcome the Regent, and she brushed aside all Brougham's warnings. After the publication of her letter, she prepared to compose another. She did not realize that the Prince was already planning his answer to the first.

To Charlotte's appeal for an establishment his reply was rapid. Lady de Clifford was hustled unceremoniously away after a brief cold note from the Prince acknowledging her resignation, and the Duchess of Leeds was appointed to be Charlotte's governess.

In the circumstances it was natural that Charlotte should detest everything about the Duchess. As the second wife of a duke, she put on airs: 'what can be expected of a *low woman* who has been *pushed up* & *never* found her *level*?'[14] The Duchess had been a Miss Anguish, her father Accountant General to the Court of Chancery; but Charlotte was determined to find fault. Even the riding school where the Duchess took her exercise on an old, quiet horse was second-rate. She fussed over her health, took shower baths and sucked calomel, but was almost always ill. The only hope was that she would be too ill to put up with Charlotte. But as if in anticipation of this, she was given an assistant. 'An excellent and valuable person is come,' said Charlotte, 'wh. is Miss Knight . . . Besides being clear-sighted & firm, she is accomplished & talented. She is a blessing . . .'[15] The blessing had been Lady Companion to the Queen, who did not wish to part with her. A quite considerable row broke out over her appointment, and—persuaded by the

Regent to accept—Miss Knight found herself ostracized for many months by Queen Charlotte, whose temper since the King's illness had become alarming.

Miss Knight accepted the situation and tried not to mind being cut: she was happy in being chosen for Princess Charlotte, whom she liked and admired.

A tall angular lady of fifty-six, Miss Knight—soon to be known as 'notte' or 'The Chevalier', from her surname—was proud of being the daughter of a Rear-Admiral. After his death, she and her mother had lived abroad from economy; Carnelia had been the devoted friend and supporter of Nelson and Lady Hamilton, whom she met in Naples and in whose relationship she saw, she declared, no impropriety. She was a romantic, had written verses, sentimental or patriotic, and a novel called *Marcus Flaminius*. It was her fellow novelist, Fanny Burney, who introduced her to the Queen.

With the arrival of Miss Knight, Charlotte's life became less difficult. It almost seemed as if her father were trying to please her. She was allowed to go back to London, and it was at Warwick House that she hoped to stay, at least for the winter months. To her delight, Miss Knight was to be known as her Lady Companion, and Cornelia herself went so far as to contradict the announcement from Windsor of her appointment as sub-governess by inserting a paragraph in the *Morning Chronicle* (4 February 1813): 'Miss Knight is one of the *ladies companions* to her Royal Highness and is the daughter of the late Sir Joseph Knight.'

She was a fighter, and in time would fight for Charlotte. At first she was puzzled to understand the relationship between the young Princess and her parents. Her introduction to the Regent was at a small dinner party to which she and Charlotte were invited, where the only other female present was Miss Goldsworthy, the Princesses' governess, very old, very deaf and inclined to fall asleep over her plate. The presence of three royal Dukes—York, Cumberland and Cambridge—somewhat mollified Miss Knight, who was inclined to resent the Regent's lack of attention to herself and her charge. He hardly spoke to Charlotte, she said, and showed her no affection.

After dinner he took Miss Knight aside: he wished, he said, to make clear to her the position between Charlotte and her mother. The Princess of Wales, he told her, had shown little regard for Charlotte as a child, and it was through her negligence that Charlotte had a mark of smallpox on her nose, for she had left the child's hands free whereas *he*, her father, had watched continually beside the cradle. Even Miss Knight could not accept this charming domestic scene quite seriously, but the Prince went on to shock her by recounting at length and in detail the disgust and resentment he felt for Caroline. 'What could I think of such a mixture of serious and frivolous complaint?'[16]

To Charlotte's delight she was invited to a ball at Carlton House. Her mother told her that she should refuse to go unless she, Caroline, were invited. Charlotte had not been presented yet, and it was for her mother to present her. But for once Charlotte's loyalty did not prevail: she wanted to go to the ball—her ball—and she went.

She looked beautiful, said the now devoted Miss Knight, 'in white and silver, and wearing white ostrich feathers in her hair'. Her aunt, Princess Mary, dancing with the Duc d'Angoulême,* opened the ball—'though it was given for me', said Charlotte, who was obliged to take the second place in the set, with her uncle Clarence as partner. Princess Mary 'was *always the cupple above me*, as jealous & ill-natured the whole night as she could be'. But 'I did not care', she added. In fact, she enjoyed herself, and danced every dance. And the chief source of happiness was to know herself in favour with the Prince, who found her partners and was '*just* opposite to what he had *been before*'.[17]

Two days after the ball she announced triumphantly, 'The Queen & the whole pack of *devils* leave town.' The Prince, still amiable, had agreed to her remaining at Warwick House, 'so I am fortunately rid of all I hate most, at least for a little while'.

To her delight, Charlotte was allowed to remain in London when her grandmother and aunts returned to Windsor. According to Miss Knight, plans were afoot for Charlotte to have more pleasure and entertainment. 'We were to . . . go to the Play and Opera, and to have a party at Warwick House.'

But only a few days later, Charlotte was writing to Mercer: 'What will you say when I tell you, added to what you *must see* in *the papers*, that I am *deprived* by a *positive* order of seeing the Pss at all?' 'This', she added, 'was made known to me by the P.R. *himself* in person and *alone*, when we had a scene most painful . . .'[18]

* Eldest son of le Comte d'Artois (Monsieur).

Chapter Fourteen

THE PRINCE, with his instinctive feeling for drama, called suddenly and unexpectedly at Warwick House and demanded to see his daughter. He would see her alone, he announced, and mounted the stairs to the drawing room, leaving Miss Knight to entertain the Prime Minister, who had come with him, down below.

The scene which now took place was 'most painful' said Charlotte. After violent protestations of affection for her, the Prince let fly with equally violent abuse of her mother. She listened to him in silence, waiting for the *coup de grâce*. At last it came: his reply, said the Regent, to the Princess's publication of this abominable letter was to send for all the documents connected with the Delicate Investigation of 1806, and also some further evidence which had since come to light, and to appoint a council to form a new assessment of the Princess's behaviour and morals. Till they had done so, the Princess would not be permitted to see her daughter.

Charlotte, who had been ten at the time of the Delicate Investigation and consequently knew very little about it, was intelligent enough to envisage the sort of evidence that would be dragged into the light against her mother. She was appalled by the thought of this fresh attempt to expose her follies, of which Charlotte was only too well aware. But, as always in scenes with her father, she remained speechless, fighting not to betray her feelings.

The Prime Minister and Miss Knight were summoned. 'I found the Regent and Princess Charlotte standing near the chimney,' said Miss Knight. 'She looked penetrated with grief . . . The Prince said he wished Lord Liverpool, as his confidential servant, and me, as Princess Charlotte's friend, to hear him repeat what he had been saying to her.'[1]

By the time the Prince had finished, Charlotte was in tears. If he had deliberately set out to break down her reserve, he could not have done so more successfully—or more cruelly. Just as she had been bitterly hurt by Lord Eldon's interference in her last scene with the Prince, so now she could not endure his lack of feeling in discussing family affairs 'of so delicate a nature' before outsiders. Miss Knight was sensitive enough to realize this and would have liked to intervene—but there was nothing she could do. When the Prince took his leave she followed him downstairs. 'He told me that he was surprised at Charlotte's behaviour; for that she had taken everything he had said to her, when they were alone, perfectly well.' Miss Knight, unafraid, spoke up for Charlotte. 'The Prince's own feelings would suggest to him that what her Royal Highness could bear from him, she could not support to hear mentioned before subjects and persons unconnected with the family.' The Prince took this 'remarkably well' and left, promising to call 'the next day, or the day after'. And as if conferring a great favour, he would himself, he said, let Charlotte know the result of the investigation.

This was poor comfort. Charlotte soon realized that the assembly of twenty-three Privy Councillors, obliged to read through every shred of sordid evidence, would take their time before reaching any conclusion. She refused to go out: she felt that it would be insulting to her mother to appear in public while the inquiry was going on. Her health suffered: indeed, she was far more affected by the strain than was the Princess of Wales, who wrote from Blackheath 'in good spirits' assuring her daughter that there was nothing to fear, as she 'stood upon such very good ground'. As usual, Caroline's natural optimism manifested itself. 'Some of the Opposition dined with her,' said Charlotte, 'wh. has put her into good spirits.'[2] She had complete confidence in Brougham.

The Prince, encouraged by his advisers, set out to win public favour by the same means that Caroline had used—by playing the part of devoted parent. 'He comes here for ever now,' said Charlotte, 'and always with highflown expressions or actions.' She was not taken in by this new attitude. 'He is *determined* to make the *most*, if he can, of this intermediate time, to make himself appear in the best possible light & to get me over.'[3]

She was thankful, at least, that she had been allowed to remain in London during this wretched period, and told Mercer, touchingly, 'Here I feel somehow *nearer*.'[4]

Although the inquiry was held in the strictest secrecy, gossip was busy and the newspapers filled in the time by publishing any material that they could obtain from the Prince's spies or from Caroline's Whig supporters. The more sensational parts of Spencer Perceval's *Book* which had appeared after the Delicate Investigation, in Caroline's defence, were dug up. Caroline was always a gift to the Press, and she did not disappoint them now. According to Lady Melbourne, it became 'the fashion amongst ladies to burn their newspapers that the servants may not read such improprieties'.[5] Even Charlotte found herself the object of malicious gossip. In a society which seethed with mischievous rumours about the royal family, the story circulated that Princess Charlotte had had a love affair with her cousin, Captain FitzClarence, and dared not show herself in public because she was pregnant. This rumour was brought to Warwick House by two lady well-wishers, the Misses Hervey, 'very intimate at Windsor Castle', who warned Charlotte that if she persisted in not going out, her reputation would be lost. Charlotte —relieved perhaps that the gossips had picked on the wrong man—promptly ordered her carriage, and from then on drove out for an hour or two every day.

During one of these drives in the park, she happened to meet her mother. They had not seen each other for weeks; Caroline stopped her carriage and they had a talk—a natural and harmless enough encounter between a mother and her daughter. But needless to say, it would not be so regarded if the Regent were to hear of it, and immediately on returning home, Charlotte hurried to write to him.

'I am this moment returned from my drive in the Park, & do not delay an instant informing you that I met the Princess, who stopped her carriage & spoke to me for five minutes as she came to town to see the Duchess of Brunswick. I trust this circumstance will not happen again, but as it was entirely unexpected by me, I wished to give you the earliest intelligence, as I make it a point *never* to have *any concealments* from *you*.'[6]

On 1 March 1813, Charlotte and Miss Knight had just returned from their morning drive when the Duchess of Leeds arrived at Warwick House, bearing the report of the investigation. It had just been handed to her by the Prince, with the request that it should be read out to Princess Charlotte in the presence of the Duchess and Miss Knight. However, the Duchess 'to do her justice did not ask to see or read it' but with unexpected delicacy put the sealed document straight into the Princess's hands.

Charlotte read it through to herself, twice. To her 'very great surprise' it proved to be 'nothing in the world but a sort of answer' to Caroline's published letter. The conclusion reached by the council was that Charlotte should be allowed to visit her mother 'subject to *restrictions and limitations* as usual'. 'After all this farce, it leaves you just where you were before,' said Charlotte.

But Caroline was not going to let matters rest there. She had triumphed, once again, and she was jubilant. Her character was redeemed, her popularity greater than ever. Letters of congratulation poured in: she had 'escaped a conspiracy against her life and honour', her supporters told her, and the Lord Mayor and Aldermen of the City of London begged permission to present a loyal address to her at Kensington Palace.

An enormous crowd assembled, 'flocking through all the walks of the garden in file and in crowds'. Mary Berry and her sister managed to get into the palace through a side gate, and 'found the Princess with her three ladies and Miss Hayman, all dressed and eating in haste, awaiting the arrival of the Lord Mayor'. She was to receive the City dignitaries in her dining-room, which opened on to the gardens, and the shutters were thrown open for all to see the group with Caroline in its centre. There were roars of applause, indeed so great and so noisy were the shouts and cheers that 'they were obliged to threaten the crowd outside to shut the windows if they would not be quiet'. Caroline then made a speech, expressing herself, said Miss Berry, 'with a good deal of feeling, and seeming to be moved when she spoke of her daughter, which had a very good effect'.[7]

Carried away by these signs of popularity, and abetted by her Whig supporters, Caroline pranced joyfully into battle. She wrote to the Speaker, the Chancellor, and the Lord President of the Council, demanding that the report of the inquiry should be read in the House of Commons. She asked 'to be proved and treated as she deserved, as innocent or as guilty'.[8] In due course, 'Mr Whitbread spoke in the House as her champion', said Miss Knight, and so eager were the English for some royal person to admire that all the filth so avidly spread by the Press in the last weeks was forgotten, and she emerged, a little rumpled perhaps, but in the eyes of the nation a heroine.

'The Princess of Wales looked better than I ever saw her,' wrote Miss Knight, after accompanying Charlotte to Blackheath. This visit was authorized by the Prince, a gracious act on his behalf, prompted by the death of Caroline's mother, the Duchess of Brunswick. News and rumours of the inquiry can hardly have failed to reach Hanover Square, but long before her death the old woman had washed her hands of Caroline's misdemeanours. 'Her excuse is that, poor thing, she is not right here,' she would say, striking her forehead.

The Duchess's illness and death had not been ignored by the royal family, who immediately went into deep mourning. Queen Charlotte expressed a fear that 'the poor Dutchess's Health was hastened by Her anxiety and by suppressing Her feelings . . .' And she noted with relief that though she had once disliked her sister-in-law, lately they had been the best of friends: 'I loved the Dutchess much since She came amongst us & feel a Satisfaction in having been able to show Her the little Attentions that were in my power to offer . . .'[9]

The Duchess was seventy-six. Since her arrival in England after Napoleon's seizure of Brunswick, she had lived on a pension provided by her brother, George III. In spite of Lady Charlotte Campbell's dismal account ('dirty, empty, devoid of comfort') her lodging in Hanover Square is usually described as being spacious and comfortable, and it is to be hoped that she kept warmer than in Brunswick. Lady Jerningham, invited to dine with her, enjoyed 'a very good dinner', and noted that there were 'a great many tall well-dressed attendants, some German and others English, all particularly civil'.

The Duchess's passion for ombre did not leave her when she fled from Brunswick, and Lady Jerningham was invited to 'look at her game'.[10] She had become in her old age deeply religious: indeed, religion and ombre seem to have shared her thoughts. 'In an interval of the game she turned to Lady Jerningham and softly announced, "I have great confidence in the mercy of Almighty God. I think he will save us, if we do not make it impossible. My opinion is that we do not confide sufficiently in his mercy." '

She was buried, as the King's sister, in the royal vault at Windsor. As extra space was being dug to make room for her coffin, it was discovered that the corner of a much older coffin had come to light. With the Dean's permission the undertaker descended into the lower vault, and found that they had opened up the lost resting-place of King Charles I, under the choir aisle where King Henry VIII and Queen Jane Seymour also lay.

In his excitement over this discovery, the Regent forgot his cares. Sir Henry Halford, physician and friend to all the royal family, was ordered to accompany HRH into the vault, and to superintend the opening of King Charles's coffin which had lain there, lost, for many decades. It was enclosed in another coffin, made of lead, which was inscribed by some faithful Royalist, *King Charles, 1649*.

Sir Henry Halford has left an account of this fascinating but grisly experiment. He seems to have opened the lead coffin 'with his knife', and the body of the Stuart king, closely wrapped in waxed cloths, came to light. When unwrapped the well-known face was found to be in a remarkably good state of preservation. 'The forehead and temples had lost little or nothing of their muscular substance: the cartilage of the nose was gone, but "the left eye, in the first moment of exposure, was open and full though it vanished almost immediately, and the pointed beard, so characteristic of the period of the reign of King Charles, was perfect . . ." '

The doctor gently disengaged the head from its wrappings, and found that it could, without difficulty, be 'taken up and held to view'. The Prince and the doctor examined the sad relic: it was perfectly possible to see how the head had been severed from the body 'by a heavy blow inflicted with a very sharp instrument . . .' The Prince, fascinated, asked that the severed vertebra should be removed from the neck and shown to the Queen and Princesses.

That evening, Princess Charlotte and Miss Knight dined at Carlton House. Miss Goldsworth was there again, to the annoyance of Miss Knight, who observed that both she and the Duke of Clarence fell asleep after the second course. They certainly should not have been bored, for the Prince, at his most sparkling, entertained the company with the details of his ancestor's exhumation, and went so far as to demonstrate, with Miss Knight as model, exactly how King Charles's head had been sliced off. Charlotte was in high favour; and her father presented her with what seemed a suitable present—the central sapphire from King Charles's crown, which—by a coincidence—had lately been sent to the Regent from Rome, on the death of Cardinal York.*

Loyal addresses to the Princess of Wales still continued to arrive from all over the country: there was no doubt of Caroline's vindication in the eyes of the British people. Naturally, she hoped—and felt justified in hoping—for more cordial treatment from the royal family; but she was still totally ignored by the Regent and the Queen. Her birthday, 17 May, was acknowledged by a visit from one royal Duke—Kent—and Princess Charlotte, who announced that she could only stay for the inside of an hour. ('The meeting', said Lady Charlotte, 'was as dry and formal as possible.')

Charlotte was, as usual, torn between her warring parents. She had applied to the Prince for permission to pay her mother a birthday visit, and had received an unexpectedly cordial reply.

'I cannot express to you how delighted I am with yr most kind & affectionate letter,' he wrote. 'I shall not object to your visiting your mother upon the occasion of her birthday, but I confide so much in your own discretion, sense of propriety, & what you must feel is the delicacy of both our situations at the present moment, that you will see how desirable it is to make this merely a morning visit, & not to extend it to the hour of the day when you might be subject to society . . . which I might not approve of.'

It was a clever letter, and left Charlotte no alternative but to tell her mother that she had been ordered to be at Blackheath at half-past one, and back at Warwick House at half-past two. This, we are told, did not please.

Caroline was disgusted by what she considered Charlotte's weakness, and complained of her lack of character. Lately, under Brougham's influence, she had pictured herself as Charlotte's friend, her devoted mother: together, she had believed, they would fight the Regent and win. 'We must frighten the man,' she cried. With Brougham's help, she had scored the first victory, only to find that Charlotte was no longer fighting on her side.

* Younger brother of 'Bonnie Prince Charlie'.

Lady Charlotte Campbell, always a little grudging in her praise of the young Princess—conceding that she had 'very pretty legs and feet' but criticizing her for showing them—noticed that Charlotte's manner to her mother had undergone a change. The Prince's ban on Mercer Elphinstone had been lifted, and Charlotte, at Warwick House, had been enjoying the happiness of her company and also the benefit of her advice. 'Miss Elphinstone', wrote Lady Charlotte, 'is not friendly to the Princess of Wales. Since her return to the Princess Charlotte, the latter is not half so kind to her mother.'

But it was not so simple as that. Three months at Windsor, amid the 'tracasseries, cabals and wheels within wheels' which went on there, had made Charlotte unnaturally cautious and on her guard. She was wise enough to know that she could not be on good terms with both her parents at once: if she desired to please the Prince she must, to all intents and purposes, abandon the Princess. This was a painful fact which had to be faced, and which she fought shy of facing, because she could not help feeling some fondness and pity for her mother. The half-true 'revelations' about Caroline's behaviour, dredged up from the Delicate Investigation and now published gleefully in the Tory press, horrified Charlotte. But she remained loyal to her mother. '*She was ill used* & is *still* more *now* than before.' Nevertheless Mercer's advice was that she should try and please her father, and Charlotte tried. What Brougham called 'the little flirting between the Prince and the Princess Charlotte' had begun.

That summer, with no fresh drama to occupy her, Caroline was restless and bored. Brougham implored her to remain quiet while he was away on circuit. Canning had made a careful speech in Parliament saying that the Princess was proved pure and innocent, and that he now hoped that all this business would end for ever. Whitbread, in 'the finest speech that ever was made', succeeded in reducing his hearers to tears over the Princess's wrongs. Unhappily, he blotted his copy-book later by suggesting in a delicately worded letter that the Princess should not expose quite so much of her bosom when she went to the opera. 'She absolutely wept,' said Lady Charlotte Campbell, 'tears of mortification and anger.'

But there was no doubt, the Princess's appearance was becoming increasingly bizarre, as was her whole way of life. In spite of her popularity there were many who disapproved of her. Even at her kind friends, the Angersteins', house where she invariably received a welcome, a certain Lady Buckinghamshire 'like a true vulgar' ran off the moment she saw the Princess enter the room.

The Sapio family—the Squallinis—were still in favour: an expensive luxury. We hear of the 'old Orang-Outang dining at her table, and Chanticleer was joyfully received at all times'. They were her intimates, and Caroline in her foolish generosity showered them with presents and paid their bills, including the rent of their Bayswater headquarters. She was now renting a second cottage next door where she could be 'alone'. Her ladies—Lady Townshend and Lady Charlotte Lindsay—outraged by these low-class goings-on were horrified when she talked of sleeping there. Her servants were on the point of giving notice; 'there is no saying how long their fidelity may hold out'.[11]

At last, Mr Whitbread was consulted: her ladies begged him to tell the Princess that the cottages were becoming a cause of scandal, and to advise her to let the musical evenings take place elsewhere.

'Perhaps he will not dare to give her this advice,' said Lady Charlotte. It was even more doubtful whether she would take it.

Caroline was becoming very odd. It might be thought that after narrowly escaping conviction in two inquiries into her morals she would try to give an appearance of respectability, but she was incorrigible. By way of amusement, she suddenly shed her corsets, and alarmed her ladies by appearing with an unfettered stomach. Playing at being pregnant was, as we have seen, one of her little manias. Now she announced that she must have another little boy, leaving her audience open-mouthed. Could she really mean what she appeared to mean? Willikin, she then said, was getting too old. 'I must have a child in the house. Poor dear Willikin, I am sorry he is growing big, but I am determined to have *another* little boy . . .' 'Poor dear foolish woman!' said solemn Lady Charlotte, 'that she should not see that, in taking another child under her protection, she will lay herself open to fresh accusations. I wish', she added, 'that she had some friend who would tell her the truth.'

But Caroline did not care to be told the truth. She preferred to live in her own world of fantasy, and she demanded flattery to build up her image. It was natural that a gypsy fortune-teller whom she met in Greenwich Park should delight her with the Romany blend of rubbish, romance and credibility. Caroline believed every word. 'Shall I tell you something very curious?' she demanded of Lady Charlotte. 'Why, they told me that I was a married woman, but that I should not be married long; and . . . that I should go abroad and there marry the man I loved, and be very rich and happy—they did, by God, tell me so—and how could they know that?'[12]

And she began, soon after this encounter, to indulge in a form of witchcraft. Every day after dinner she modelled a wax figure of her husband wearing a large pair of horns. She then 'took three pins out of her garment, and stuck them through and through, and put the figure to roast and melt at the fire'.[13] There is something both pitiful and sinister in this picture of Caroline, her face reddened by spite and heat from the fire, sitting back to watch the flames consuming her husband.

She had reason to be vindictive, for worries and disappointments beset her. At the end of 1813 she was obliged to move: Montague House was being sold to pay off some of her debts, and a large house in Bayswater, Connaught Place, was given to her. Its being in Bayswater may perhaps have pleased her, as being so near her Sapios; but the close friendship was beginning to show signs of wear. Chanticleer had deserted her. It is possible that she may have frightened him with her suggestions of pregnancy: all that is known is that he was no longer at her beck and call. 'Chanticleer did not come to dinner, which caused great rage and despair.'

His son's defection did not stop Old Orang-Outang, who was constantly dining at Connaught House. Caroline offered him a performance of her pregnancy act. 'The Princess went downstairs for some music, and when she came up was ready to fall with breathlessness. This lasted for some minutes . . . I saw her look significantly at Sapio and say "If you know *what it is.*" Then catching my eye, she added, "So soon after dinner, to *run up down staircase.*" I looked stedfastly at her Royal Highness,' said Lady Charlotte, 'but she never flinched beneath my gaze.'[14]

Caroline had been bewitched by the faithless Chanticleer and behaved now as if she were heartbroken. She became increasingly difficult to live with. She quarrelled with her servants, complained of being surrounded by spies, and nothing entertained her 'except talking of her grievances'. She did not like her new house, and announced that she wished to have a lodging in the country, where she might go unaccompanied by her household.

Lady Charlotte went with her to take leave of Montague House, of necessity a melancholy and nostalgic occasion. As they walked together through the wintry gardens Caroline must have remembered sunny days when the peacocks strutted over the smooth lawns, the neat borders of flowers, some of which she had herself planted, the honeysuckle bower with its branches trained to frame a view of the Thames. It had been a garden for dancing and love-making, for revelry and laughter; and now she must leave it forever. 'She had not money to keep a house at Blackheath and one in London also.' Lady Charlotte felt genuine pity for the Princess; but Caroline was not defeated. 'I will go on hoping for happier days,' she said. 'Do you think I *may*?' Her lady answered 'with heartfelt warmth, "I trust your Royal Highness will yet see many happy days." '[15]

Chapter Fifteen

In the summer of 1813 news came of Wellington's triumphs in Portugal and Spain, where he succeeded in driving a wedge between two of Napoleon's armies, under Soult and Marmont, and forcing them back over the Pyrenees. Slowly the tide of war turned, and by the end of the year Holland, Germany and Sweden were freed. Over the lands through which Caroline had passed on her journey to England eighteen years before Napoleon's armies fell back. Wellington was the hero of the hour. The Regent wrote to him, an outpouring of praise and gratitude, and sent him—what he himself had always coveted—a Field-Marshal's baton.

After the Battle of Vittoria the Prince gave a 'magnificent breakfast' in the gardens of Carlton House, and he decided also to hold a grand fête in Vauxhall Gardens to celebrate Wellington's victories. This was just what he enjoyed, to display to the public all his skill in planning a scene of extraordinary splendour and magnificence in honour of the glorious victory. He would, he announced, be there himself.

But Caroline wanted to celebrate the victory too. She gave out that she intended to join the revels, and Brougham wrote gleefully to his crony, Thomas Creevey: 'Mother P certainly goes to the Tea Garden tomorrow night to meet her husband.' He added that 'the consternation of Prinny is wonderful. I'll bet a little money he don't go himself.' He didn't: purple with rage, he declared that he would give anything in the world that he had never thought of 'this damn'd fête'. 'Poor wretch,' said Brougham, 'could not summon up courage even to go in the evening [after Caroline had gone home] so his benefit, as it was meant to be, turned out to be hers.'

Caroline had won this round; but her triumph was short-lived. She was finding her position increasingly difficult. The ostracism she received from Windsor had spread to the circle who used to visit her. Charlotte was sorry for her mother. 'The Princess, I find, feels *extremely* her situation, that is to say, the *very few* who will . . . come near her, & the numbers who now refuse, decline & keep out of the way. She has a great deal of pride & high spirit & feels *mortified* ... One moment she is in tears & another you see they are smothered in *indignant feelings*.'[1]

But Charlotte was powerless to help. After the brief alliance of which Caroline had hoped great things, mother and daughter found themselves forced apart. The Prince had his own plans for Charlotte. She was to marry, and the sooner the better.

He had no wish to force her into marriage with an unsuitable person, indeed he wished her to be happy; but she had shown herself too easily pleased. After the Hesse affair, she had been seen exchanging loving glances with the young Duke of Devonshire, and the print shops displayed a cartoon of her dancing with him: 'The Devonshire Minuet', it was called. The Regent was obliged to reprimand Miss Knight, who had accompanied Charlotte on a drive to Chiswick, where the Duke was giving a 'great breakfast' at his Palladian villa on the Thames. 'I had proposed to drive that way,' said the Chevalier, shouldering the blame, 'that Princess Charlotte might see the carriages.[2] Her life has so little variety in it,' she added, lamely; but the Prince was not interested. Stories continued to circulate about the Duke and the Princess. The Regent, Brougham told Creevey, 'was angry at her for flirting with the Duke of Devonshire and suspected she was talking politics'. He believed that 'she really had a great penchant for the Duke'. 'I have not given him the smallest encouragement in any way,' Charlotte told Mercer; but at one point they were meeting daily in the park where the Duke drove his curricle—though perhaps they were only discussing politics.

As things fell out, nothing came of it, and, despite being 'followed by all the mothers and misses in London', that charming but sadly deaf young Duke remained unmarried till his death at the age of sixty-eight.

There was also trouble over the Duke of Gloucester, Charlotte's cousin. Pop-eyed and chinless, he had a strong sense of his own importance and a strong appreciation of Charlotte's charms. He was ready, he told her, to 'come forward' if she needed him: in other words, he would very gladly offer himself as a candidate for her attractive and important hand.

But the Regent looked for something better than an English duke or a lesser member of the royal family. His first choice, for strategic reasons, was the Hereditary Prince of Orange, eldest son of the Dutch Stadtholder, who would now, with the retreat of the French from Holland, be reinstated as King of the Netherlands. An alliance was being planned by the British Government with the liberated Dutch; and a marriage between the English Princess and the Hereditary Prince would triumphantly seal this alliance.

The Prince decided to arrange a meeting between the young people as soon as the Prince of Orange could obtain leave of absence from Spain, where he was serving on Wellington's staff. Meanwhile, the plan was not to be mentioned to Charlotte.

But of course Charlotte was well aware of what was going on. She was not opposed to the idea of marriage; but a misguided marriage would be 'worse than death'. She was determined to find out all that she could before she met the Prince of Orange.

As it happened, her friend Georgiana Fitzroy had met him and described him as 'amiable, very agreeable and sensible'. He was said to adore Wellington, and he had excellent manners said Miss Fitzroy, but was not good-looking. A month later, after waltzing with him, she sent a less encouraging report. He was, she said 'excessively plain' and 'thin as a needle'. His hair was 'excessively fair' and he had 'fine teeth that stick excessively out in front'. This was not encouraging, but perhaps it was a comfort to learn that he waltzed well and was 'very gentlemanlike, very informed and pleasant'.[3]

Rather to Charlotte's relief, the autumn of 1813 passed and the Prince of Orange did not put in an appearance. On 8 December she wrote to Mercer, 'I have agreed without any demur or hesitation to see the young P when he comes.' She was encouraged by further accounts of him and felt that after all he could not be so bad: for one thing, 'he is lively & likes fun & amusement'.

On 13 December he arrived, and was met at Greenwich by the royal barge—a more flattering welcome than that accorded eighteen years before to Caroline of Brunswick. Two days after his arrival, having done the rounds at Windsor and Oatlands, the young man was to dine at Carlton House and meet his prospective bride. A small party was invited, which, said the Prince, 'would take the glare off it, if it was put into the papers'. He did not wish any conclusions to be drawn. The whole thing, he said, was arranged with regard for Charlotte's feelings; but she must promise to give him her 'fair and undisguised opinion' of the Hereditary Prince immediately after dinner. To this request, Charlotte agreed. But as soon as she was alone she realized how unreasonable and how unfair it was. The decision had seemed to lie in her hands; but to be forced to make up her mind in so short a time on a matter which affected her whole life was truly alarming.

Trembling with nerves, she dismissed her ladies several hours before dinner, and, when the time came, emerged from her room looking 'pale and agitated' and in a dress of purple satin trimmed with black lace which may possibly have suited her mood, but can hardly have done her justice. 'Her toilet,' said Miss Knight, 'was by no means recherché'; but Miss Knight was upset because she had not been invited, while the Duchess of Leeds had.

It was with the Duchess that Charlotte, trying desperately to master her nerves, made her entrance at Carlton House.

The young people met and were presented. They were both extremely shy, and Charlotte was at her worst, throwing her arms and legs about, laughing too much and stuttering. But the Prince of Orange, she observed, was 'lively and animated'; and seated at dinner with him on her right, Charlotte began to revive. As she had expected, he was plain, very plain, and far too thin, but he talked, when he did talk, intelligently and well.

After the long dinner, there was among the guests a certain amount of walking up and down, as was the custom. The Regent made a graceful exit, and after a short interval an equally graceful entrance, whereupon events began to move with speed. He swept Charlotte into the next room, and immediately demanded her decision. 'What do you say?' he cried, and when she hesitated seemed overcome with disappointment. 'Then it will not do,' he groaned. But Charlotte assured him that he was mistaken, and that she liked what she had seen—'an answer as fair and as little as I could give, upon two hours of acquaintance', she said afterwards. Her father ignored the careful wording, and clasped her in his arms exclaiming emotionally, 'you make me the happiest person in the world!'

Now the Prince of Orange was called in, and, said Charlotte, 'We really had such a terrible overcoming scene with the Prince that I was quite unstrung. His whole soul and heart seemed moved with real parental affection.'[4] Tears, real tears, welled up in the eyes of this practised performer as the Hereditary Prince of Orange politely gave his promise to marry Princess Charlotte and permitted the weeping Regent to join their hands and give them his blessing.

Of course, Charlotte had second thoughts. She felt that she had been tricked, that the Regent had set out during the past weeks to charm her in order to exercise his power over her. Politically the marriage would be valuable, and that was all he thought of.

These and other sour reflections assailed her after her return to Warwick House, even though she was able to write to Mercer that the meeting had passed off pleasantly. 'I feel rather afraid of him, I confess, & shy, but he is so very amiable & kind in his manners that I do hope it will go off.'[5]

But the next day the Prince of Orange told her what her father had not had the honesty to tell her—that when they were married she would have to divide her time between England and Holland. There was no question of the young Prince making Charlotte's country his own and, if he wanted to 'visit his frogs', going to Holland by himself. Charlotte, at this, burst into tears. It was impossible, she cried, she would never agree.

Meanwhile the Regent, who had brought the Prince of Orange to Warwick House, was sitting with Miss Knight 'by the fire in the adjoining room'. He hoped that the Chevalier would give Charlotte good advice, particularly—during the four or five months before the marriage—against *flirting*. Suddenly, they heard Charlotte 'break forth into a violent fit of sobs and hysterical tears'. 'The Prince started up,' wrote Miss Knight, 'and I followed him to the door of the other room, where we found the Prince of Orange looking half-frightened, and Princess Charlotte in great distress.'

'What! Is he taking his leave?' the Regent asked archly, but Charlotte, in floods of tears, could only stammer out 'Not yet'. She tried to run out of the room, but her father stopped her, saying that the Prince of Orange was due at a City Banquet given in his honour, and tactfully drew the young man away.

Charlotte dried her tears; and the next day was able to write to Mercer, 'I will fairly tell you that the *little* I have seen him I am *delighted*.'

She was doing her best to accept the situation, but her feelings fluctuated from day to day. 'I had no idea,' she said, 'of its being the Regent's plan to fiancé us straight away.' She had believed that he had brought them together to make friends, 'hoping that sometime hence we might like each other well enough to marry'. As it was, her father's kindness, his displays of affection, which had made her so happy before her meeting with the Prince of Orange, had been a fraud, a careful plan to win her consent to the marriage. As for the question of living abroad, she now knew that it was 'to have been kept from her till it was too late to retreat'.

One of Caroline's charges against the Regent in the letter which she and Brougham had published was that Princess Charlotte had not been confirmed. Perhaps to confute this charge, the Regent arranged to have the ceremony performed at Windsor on Christmas Day, 1813. Caroline, her mother, was neither invited nor told: the confirmation was attended by the Queen, the Prince, and Princesses Elizabeth and Augusta. 'It was,' said Charlotte, 'so awful a ceremony that I felt during it and afterwards exceedingly agitated'; and she added that all the royal ladies showed signs of 'agitation' on their faces after the service.

Charlotte had dreaded this visit to Windsor, the first since her betrothal, and had looked forward with apprehension to her first encounter with the Queen, who for some time had not been her friend.

Queen Charlotte was seventy and so swollen by dropsy that an unkind person commented that she appeared to be carrying all her fifteen children at once. She was courageous, and in spite of all that she had endured kept a sense of humour and exchanged little jokey letters with her eldest son. But her sufferings had embittered her: when she was thwarted she lapsed into cold, violent anger which her daughters dreaded.

The Regent feared breaking the news of Charlotte's engagement to the Queen, and had employed the Duke of York to prepare her, in the hopes of preventing a scene. It was a delicate situation: the Queen did not care for the Dutch alliance and would have preferred Prince Charles of Mecklenberg-Strelitz, who was German and her nephew. So it was with some trepidation that the Regent ushered his daughter into the Queen's presence, and waited during the conversation in case anything should go wrong.

'The Queen', said Charlotte, 'was *gracious* but *added good advice*, wh. I saw rather put the Prince out of patience.' No wonder, since the advice consisted of a series of warnings against following in her mother's footsteps, which, said Charlotte, 'was *excessively* unpleasant . . . to me'.[6] 'I see very evidently,' she added, 'the Queen in her heart hates the whole marriage & connection'; but since the Prince had arranged it, 'must now put the *best leg foremost*'.

Chapter Sixteen

THE YEAR 1814 was an eventful one for both Caroline and her daughter. It was ushered in, ominously, by a thick dark fog, followed by snow and frost. The Thames froze, and a fair was held on the ice. From Charlotte's windows at Warwick House she could watch the skaters on the lake in St James's Park, while Caroline in Bayswater looked out morosely over the snow-covered streets. Perhaps she thought nostalgically of her own youth, and the sledge-drives through Brunswick, the brilliantly coloured sledges in the shape of birds and beasts, and the cries of the drivers flourishing their long whips. Now the picture was in monotone, grey and black against the snow. Life, which had seemed to stretch ahead, continually changing, continually offering fresh delights, had little by little become purposeless, stale, and utterly dreary. For once, Caroline could see no way ahead.

She made no secret of her misery, and Charlotte soon heard of it. 'I . . . cannot conceive what it can be owing to,' she wrote to Mercer, 'as there are no new restrictions and she seems to be delighted with her new house.'[1]

The fact was that Caroline had no specific grievance, and at the moment had no new scheme, no mischief in which to indulge. She looked forward to Charlotte's birthday party on 7 January as an opportunity to enlist her hero daughter's sympathy. 'She wished me to dine and have some musick in the evening,' said Charlotte, 'which I wrote to the P about, & as I expected, has *been refused* . . . I propose going to her from 5 till about seven, & then dining quietly at home. I shall endeavor if I can to find out what particularly grieves her.'[2]

This shortened visit was no consolation to Caroline, who bitterly resented the refusal. The meeting between mother and daughter was formal and constrained, and Charlotte felt doubly hemmed in by the Prince's regulations, for he had forbidden her to make any mention of her engagement.

At this party Caroline, 'arrayed in crimson velvet up to the throat' was described by Lady Charlotte Campbell as 'looking very well'. According to this observer, Princess Charlotte took very little notice of her mother. 'I do not wonder,' she said, 'the Princess of Wales was hurt. She took me by the arm and led me to the fireplace, and I saw that she was ready to weep.' But later she gives a more lively description of Caroline—'pouring dissatisfaction into her daughter's ear'. Everyone, she said, had expected great national celebrations on Charlotte's coming of age (she was eighteen that day)—but 'no testimony of joy had been shown, and the day had passed away in mournful silence'. To this Princess Charlotte is said to have replied, 'Oh, but the war and the great expenses of the nation' made any celebration impossible at present. 'A very good excuse, truly,' said her mother, 'and you are child enough to believe it!' Charlotte felt genuine compassion for her mother's plight, and she saw a new advantage to be gained from her marriage: the Regent would no longer be able to govern her relationship with the Princess. She was convinced that the Prince of Orange would 'never interfere or prevent my going 'as often as I wished to go, & my mother to have me'.[3]

She had had a letter from the Prince of Orange—'really a manly feeling one'—and had sent him a ring, which, she heard to her amusement, he wore night and day. At the Regent's request, she had sent carefully composed letters to the Dutch royal ladies, the Prince's mother and grandmother. They seemed to be rather dull ladies who spent most of their time knitting for the troops, but from what she had heard, Holland was 'a very odd place . . . in which society & everything else is quite different from any other place'. 'We *must see*,' she told Mercer, '*what we can do* to make it more Londonish & Dandyish, &c.'[4]

Early in March, the Regent sent for Charlotte and Miss Knight. They found him with his leg propped up on a chair: gout had assailed him. He told Charlotte that he had received a letter from the King of the Netherlands formally asking for the Princess Charlotte's hand in marriage to his son.

His Grand Master of the Household, who bore the impressive name of Baron Van der Duyn Van Maasdam, was invited to be presented to Princess Charlotte in a private audience with the Prince Regent. '*Un jeune garcon mutin en cotillon*,' the Baron commented after seeing her, surprised by her mannish stride and handshake.

The betrothal had already been made known in Holland, which was a little irregular as it had not yet been announced in England; but the Dutch ministers were anxious that this sign of an alliance with England should be known immediately, in order to strengthen the Dutch King's hand. It seemed that there was great enthusiasm in Holland for the marriage, and also for England, who had armed and clothed the Dutch in the war.

Charlotte now felt that she was being rushed into marriage, and wrote to her fiancé, emphasizing her determination not to leave England. But on this point he could not reassure her: she would be expected, he said, to spend half of every year in Holland. He tried to cheer her by reminding her that she would always have her English ladies around her: but this was cold comfort. She felt that she should have been told this before she met the Prince of Orange; and she became convinced that her father wanted her out of the country. 'The Prince of Orange,' wrote Lady Charlotte Campbell, '. . . wishes his wife to go with him to his own Dutch land: and so does the Prince Regent, who does not like a rising sun in his own.'[5]

'When the marriage was proposed, I had not the slightest suspicion that my residence was not to be in England,' she protested to her father. She had heard from the Prince of Orange that their marriage contract had been sent for his inspection; and she ventured to hope that she too might see it, 'that I may have an opportunity of considering, before they are finally settled, the conditions of an engagement on which the whole happiness of my life must depend'.

It was a carefully worded letter, probably written with the aid of Miss Mercer, but inspired by strong feeling and a genuine longing to gain her father's confidence.

The answer came like a thunderclap. Miss Knight was summoned to Carlton House, as if to emphasize that Charlotte had no say.

Neither she nor the Hereditary Prince had any business to see the contract, which was 'a matter to be settled by fathers'. The Prince considered that the provisions made for her were magnanimous, but he did not wish to listen to any arguments, or indeed to see Charlotte until the whole thing was settled. With his remarkable gift for twisting the truth to suit the situation, he now announced that it was Charlotte herself who had been so anxious for the Orange marriage, and that he had not even known of the Hereditary Prince's arrival in this country till Sir Henry Halford had brought him word from Charlotte begging to be allowed to meet the young man.

Charlotte was amazed. She refused to retract one word. She was determined to make it appear that the blame for this attempt to banish her to Holland should rest with the Dutch and not with her father. And she indignantly disputed the Regent's version of her attitude to the young Prince. 'I am most astonished to find . . . you thought the marriage was first proposed by me . . . I can most solemnly declare I never sent any message of that sort relative to the Prince of Orange to you.' And she blamed Sir Henry Halford for making mischief.

The Prince, gouty and querulous, was tired of the whole thing, and wished that the Dutch alliance had never been thought of. Other more important events on the Continent were claiming his attention. So, for the moment, there was deadlock. Charlotte herself found it impossible not to be caught up in the excitement of the news from across the Channel. The restoration of the Dutch monarchy was only one of the signs that Europe, after years of oppression, was shaking off the Napoleonic fetters; and the hope of peace seemed near.

At the end of March the Tsar of Russia and the King of Prussia rode into Paris, and on 6 April Napoleon signed an Act of Abdication. Peace had come, and the Bourbon monarchy was to be restored in the person of the guillotined king's brother, Louis XVIII.

'France', cried Lady Charlotte, 'is holding forth repentant arms to her banished sovereign. The poissardes who dragged Louis XVI to the scaffold are presenting flowers to the Emperor of Russia, the restorer of their legitimate king.'[6]

Alexander, Tsar of Russia, was acclaimed on all sides as the conqueror of Napoleon; but the Prince Regent thought that he too had a claim to glory, and he suggested to his mother with becoming modesty, 'I trust, my dearest mother, that you will think that I have fulfilled and done my duty at least, and perhaps I may be vain enough to hope that you may feel a little proud of *your son*.'[7]

It is hard to see just why: he had never visited any of the liberated countries, had never even crossed the Channel; but he knew how to celebrate a victory, and this he was now determined to do. England, he believed, should take the lead in peace as in war, and he accordingly wrote and invited the allied sovereigns to London.

He also decided to honour King Louis XVIII, who with other members of the French royal family had been living in exile at Hartwell, in Buckinghamshire. So in April, on his way back to France, King Louis received a loyal welcome in London, where he stayed for three nights at Grillon's Hotel in Albermarle Street. Here the Regent invested him with the Order of the Garter, encountering some difficulty in fastening it round the King's vast leg; and on 23 April Louis set off for France, escorted to Dover by the Dukes of Kent and Sussex, while the Prince went ahead to make sure that there would be abundant cheers and displays of white cockades at Dover, and to escort the French party to the royal yacht. Unfortunately, once aboard King Louis made a dive for his cabin, and so missed the sight of the Regent (surely in a Field-Marshal's uniform) bowing and waving at the pier-head as the vessel drew out.

In Paris, the French King found to his annoyance that it was generally considered that Russia had won the war. The Russian Tsar evidently thought so too, and resented King Louis's recent declaration to the Prince Regent, 'It is to the counsels of your Royal Highness, to this glorious country, and to the steadfastness of its inhabitants, that I attribute . . . the re-establishment of my House upon the throne of my ancestors.'[8]

This was an inauspicious opening to the glorious peace; but it was hoped that the Prince Regent's plans to entertain the allies in London would smooth over the misunderstanding.

It was to be a magnificent celebration, and the Prince was in his element ordering and organizing the decorations and illuminations, the banquets and balls. Only the Austrian Emperor was too lazy to accept the invitation, but —as he generally did—he sent Prince Metternich to represent him. As well as the heads of state there would be numerous princes and grand-dukes, as well as field-marshals and generals and other officers who had distinguished themselves in the war.

This vast assembly of guests was due to arrive in June; but at the end of March the Tsar's sister, the Grand Duchess Catherine of Oldenburg, with her large suite of attendants and her four carriages, sailed into Sheerness in the frigate *Jason*.

She was a widow of twenty-six, of striking apperance. Rumour had it that the Regent, if he succeeded in divorcing his wife, might offer her his hand. But would he? The Grand Duchess was a woman who liked the centre of the stage. She was small, but with a commanding manner; she had a flat slavonic face, glittering almond eyes and black hair which stood out round her head in tight curls. According to Princess Lieven, the Russian Ambassador's wife, she was 'very seductive in glance and manners'. Princess Lieven disliked her intensely.

She was to stay at the Pulteney Hotel, Piccadilly, the whole 'furnished mansion', as she called it, being reserved for her by her royal host at a rent of 210 guineas a week. She was there for over three months, which was unfortunate since her visit, as far as the Regent was concerned, was a dead loss.

Soon after her arrival he gave a magnificent dinner in her honour and, as was usual at Carlton House, a small band provided carefully chosen music as an accompaniment to the meal. But the Grand Duchess could not abide music: it made her vomit, she said. The musicians must be stopped, at once. After a moment, in a loud angry voice, the Prince gave the order. The musicians broke off abruptly and trailed out in a ghastly silence, 'during which', said Princess Lieven, 'we no longer knew what to do'. The only person who remained calm was the Grand Duchess, who, having got her way, seated herself with dignity and assurance beside her host.

Conversation flagged. The Grand Duchess had come to England bent on making a conquest of the Prince; but now, it seemed, she only wanted to annoy him. At this dinner she was dressed in deep mourning, and she indicated that her thoughts were still with her dead husband. The Regent, with an attempt at gallantry, suggested that after two years it was time for such an attractive female to be thinking of other things. She gave him a haughty stare and refused to answer. Try as he might, he could not please her; 'his much boasted affability', she told her brother, 'is the most licentious, I may say, obscene strain I have ever listened to'. She was shocked, she added, by his 'brazen way of looking where eyes should not go'.

Princess Lieven, seated on the Prince's other side, observed with dismay how the conversation was languishing. Then it took a dangerous turn. The Grand Duchess mentioned Princess Charlotte. It seemed a pity, she said, that this interesting girl should be kept in the background. 'Why does she go nowhere with you?'

'My daughter is too young, Madam, to go into the world.'

'She is not too young for you to have fixed a husband for her.'

'When she is married, Madam, she will do as her husband pleases; for the present she does as I wish.'

The Grand Duchess's face betrayed no emotion, 'Your Highness is right. Between husband and wife there can be only one will.'

'The Regent', said Princess Lieven, 'turned sharply towards me and observed pretty loudly, "This is intolerable." '

From that evening, the Grand Duchess and the Regent hated each other wholeheartedly. She did everything she could to annoy him, treating his ministers and their wives with coldness, and being rude to Lady Hertford, his mistress. She drove about London in an open carriage, cheered wherever she went, her unusual appearance and the fact that she was the Tsar's sister creating awe and wonder, as if she were a being from another planet.

She then fired her most lethal weapon: she let it be known that she was going to visit the Princess of Wales. This proposal caused chaos at the Embassy, and Count Lieven threatened to resign his post as Russian Ambassador. The Grand Duchess was obliged to give in—at least till the arrival of the Tsar; but if she could not go to see the Princess of Wales, she would befriend her daughter, and she called at Warwick House.

Since the contretemps about the marriage settlement, Charlotte was in disgrace, and her father had given orders that she was not to be invited to any of the parties. This prompted the Grand Duchess's campaign. She thought Charlotte by far the most interesting member of the royal family, and wrote enthusiastically to the Tsar of her 'great intelligent eyes of pale blue', her plump 'appetizing' figure, and her 'manners so odd that they take your breath away'. 'She looks like a boy,' she added, 'or rather like a young rascal, dressed as a girl.' It seems likely that in this description of the young

Princess, point by point, she may have been recommending her to her brother for marriage to one of the Russian Grand Dukes. It was not long before the British ministers began to murmur anxiously about the headlong friendship between Charlotte and the Grand Duchess, and the Regent sent Sir Henry Halford to warn Miss Knight that it was not on any account to be encouraged.

A number of people were trying, for their own advantage, to influence Charlotte's decision on the Dutch marriage. Lord Liverpool, for the Government, was persuasive and eloquent in favour of it; Brougham, backed by his fellow Whigs, Grey and Whitbread, begged her to stick to her guns and refuse to leave the country; and this counsel was echoed by her Whig uncle, Sussex, a kind but unreliable adviser. He told her—possibly with some truth—that her uncle York wanted her out of the country because he, York, 'aimed at the Regency in the event of the Regent's death'. This sad event was evidently considered quite likely by those in the know, including the Regent himself; and, as we have seen, Caroline was basing her future happiness upon it. For the present she was playing a waiting game. She was against the Dutch marriage for reasons of her own. She knew that being mother to Charlotte was her most valuable asset, and when Prince William of Orange sent her a polite letter introducing himself as her future son-in-law she did not respond. If Charlotte were to marry him and go to Holland, she decided, she would have no reason to remain in England. She would go abroad too.

To this announcement, Brougham's nimble mind foresaw alarming consequences. Caroline, foot-loose and fancy-free in Europe, might well provide the Regent with grounds for divorce. Prinny would then be free to marry again, and—always providing he were capable of begetting a son—Princess Charlotte would lose the crown.

Charlotte, though she may not have foreseen this contingency, was well aware that her marriage was of importance to a number of people. She was also aware that she was in her father's black books; but she had no intention of coming to a deicision at least till the visit of the Allied Sovereigns was over. Her attitude to the Dutch Prince fluctuated. At one point she told her mother that she was determined not to marry 'young frog': 'I think him so ugly,' she said, 'that I am sometimes obliged to turn my head away in disgust when he is speaking to me.'[9] Two weeks later she said that 'everything was fixed for her marriage; that she did not love the Prince of Orange but that she must be married'.

The truth was that she had not made up her mind because she did not wish to. A number of interesting and personable princes would, she had learned, be arriving in the wake of the allied sovereigns; and she believed that she should be allowed to have a look round, so to speak, before committing herself any further.

Fortunately, with the arrival of the foreigners, her problems were swept aside as a wave of wild excitement broke over London. The victory over Napoleon, believed to be total, and his banishment to Elba, were events to be celebrated by every man, woman and child in the capital. Flags and streamers greeted the victors, and at night the streets were brilliantly illuminated. Doves of peace and patriotic sentiments adorned the houses of the rich, while the poor showed candles in their windows. In Piccadilly, Pulteney's Hotel displayed a banner bearing the words, 'Thanks be to God', while across the front of Devonshire House the young Duke spelled out the one eloquent word, 'Peace'.

The Regent might well have been delighted by London's response to his call for celebrations. Every night there were banquets, balls and gala performances at the theatres and opera houses. There were feastings in the City, and dinners, suppers and breakfasts arranged by society hostesses. London, for the next few weeks, was *en fête*.

But all Prinny's pleasure was spoiled by a series of calamities.

The Queen had agreed to hold two Drawing Rooms in honour of the visitors. When all the arrangements had been made, a sudden ghastly doubt arose: what was to be done about the Princess of Wales? Several of the visiting royalties were her relations, the two Wurtemberg princes were her nephews, the Prussian princes her cousins. Already the Russians were asking awkward questions. Was Caroline, or was she not, to be invited to meet them?

Naturally she expected to be, and was happy at the prospect.

'Mrs Thompson,' wrote Sir William Gell, one of her few faithful friends, 'Mrs Thompson* has quite recovered her spirits, laughs and is merry.'[10] She was wildly excited, her gloom vanished as she prepared to receive illustrious company at Connaught Place.

A letter arrived from the Queen.

'The Queen considers it to be her duty to lose no time in acquainting the Princess of Wales that she has received a communication from her son, the Prince Regent, in which he states that her Majesty's intention of holding two drawing-rooms . . . having been notified to the public, he must declare that he considers his own presence at her Court cannot be dispensed with, and that he desires it . . . to be his fixed and unalterable determination not to meet the Princess of Wales upon any occasion either in public or in private.

* This was one of the names by which discreet friends referred to the Princess of Wales.

'The Queen is thus placed under the painful necessity of intimating to the Princess of Wales the impossibility of her Majesty's receiving her Royal Highness at her drawing-rooms. Charlotte, R.'[11]

It was the worst possible moment for this to happen, and the Regent, in deciding to ban Caroline from the Queen's Drawing Rooms, had made a disastrous mistake. 'If the Princess were to wish for a thing, it should have been this,' said Brougham. 'The Prince must be really mad.'[12]

Far from being quelled by the Queen's snub, Caroline set to work with Brougham's aid, to plague her husband with a new series of letters. With the same precision as that with which she had stuck pins into his wax image, she now aimed her verbal darts. 'Occasions may arise', she reminded him, '. . . when I must appear in public, and your Royal Highness must be present also. Has your Royal Highness forgotten the approaching marriage of our daughter, and the possibility of our coronation?' 'I suppose he will shake a little at this,' commented Brougham drily, and added, 'He is in such a mess that I question if they don't retract and countermand the drawing-rooms.'[13]

It was particularly unfortunate that at this moment, with illustrious foreigners crowding into London, the newspapers should be filled with reports of a classic royal row. The Prince was already on the worst possible terms with the Grand Duchess Catherine, and did not relish the arrival of her brother the Tsar.

He had planned to meet and welcome the Emperor of Russia at Shooter's Hill, Woolwich, and conduct him to St James's Palace after a triumphal drive through the City. But the Tsar did not want to go to St James's Palace: he wanted to join his sister at Pulteney's Hotel, so after briefly greeting his host, he jumped into Count Lieven's carriage and drove through the waiting crowds without being recognized. The cross, flustered Regent, all his plans awry, hurried back to Carlton House, and sent a message to Pulteney's Hotel, saying that he would visit the Tsar there. But once again everything went wrong. The Emperor Alexander and his sister waited for two hours, when another message arrived from the Prince. 'His Royal Highness has been threatened with annoyance in the street if he shows himself; it is therefore impossible for him to come and see the Emperor.'

The Emperor who had, on the whole, behaved rather badly, now drove with Count Lieven to Carlton House, where he held a short conversation with his ruffled host. It was to be their only private interview. The Prince had evidently dropped all attempt at charm; and the Tsar, already prejudiced by his sister's account of him, now found his ally quite insufferable. 'A poor Prince,' he commented to Count Lieven as they drove away.

During the first weeks of the Tsar's visit, London swooned with hero-worship. 'The Emperor of Russia is my hero,' wrote Lady Charlotte Campbell, 'and everybody's hero.' Tall and blonde, he was an impressive figure, though in Lawrence's portrait at Windsor he has a feminine look which may account for his unreliable behaviour. Francis, Lady Shelley, after watching his arrival at Pulteney's Hotel, declared that he was 'very gentlemanlike looking'. But it was the simplicity of this god-like figure that enchanted the people: he actually walked with his sister in the park, returning for breakfast, followed at a respectful distance by a rapturous crowd. 'On ascending the steps of his hotel,' said *The Times*, 'His Imperial Majesty turned round to the people and most condescendingly took off his hat.'

On 3 June, the King of Prussia, the Tsar, Prince Metternich and a number of foreign personages went to the opera, escorted by the Prince Regent. It was a gala performance of Pacitta's opera, *Aristodemo*, followed by *A Scotch Divertissement* and a ballet. During the first interval a hymn of welcome was sung by the stars, Madame Grassini and Signor Tramezzani, followed by *God Save the King*. In the middle of the anthem, the Princess of Wales suddenly and unexpectedly arrived. There was a gasp from the audience as her party entered the box, which was exactly opposite that occupied by the Regent, the King of Prussia and the Tsar. A number of minor princes were crammed into the box next door. Confronted by all this magnificence Caroline remained standing till the anthem ended, at which the Regent covered his confusion by loudly applauding the singers. The Princess then sat down, amidst loud applause from the pit. One of her ladies begged her to rise and make a curtsy, 'but she sat immoveable' while the applause continued. 'I know my business better', she said, 'than to take the *morsel out of my husband's mouth*.'

The Regent had by this time recovered his self-possession, rose from his seat and performed his famous graceful bow, as if in acknowledgement of the applause. He thus, in his own way, obliterated his wife, but it could hardly be denied that the victory on this occasion was hers.

Caroline's heart was set upon meeting the Russians. 'My ears are very ugly,' she said, 'but I would give *them both* to persuade the Emperor to come to me . . .' Then Lady Charlotte Lindsay brought her a message: the Tsar and his sister intended to call upon her, that same day, or, if not, a week later.

Twice over, Caroline dressed in her best and sat down to wait. The Russian party never came.

Princess Charlotte was deeply sorry for her mother: she had been so certain that the Tsar meant to go and had told the Regent 'that he was determined to visit the Princess of Wales and to make his sister accompany him; that he would do so publicly, to show his respect for her Royal Highness'. But apparently, since receiving this message, the Regent had refused to speak to the Tsar. Presumably the Tsar had decided that it would be wiser to withdraw: Anglo-Russian relations were becoming dangerously strained.

'Prinny,' wrote Creevey, 'is in exactly the state one could wish . . . All agree that [he] will either die or go mad. He is worn out with fuss, fatigue and *rage*.'

All his plans were going wrong. And now his daughter was causing trouble.

Just before the allied sovereigns arrived, the Prince of Orange turned up in London incognito, hoping that face to face with Charlotte he might succeed in building up their rather shaky relationship. Charlotte greeted him coldly, but was mollified by his sincerity; he seemed genuinely fond of her. He decided to remain in London for the celebrations, though the town was so full that he was obliged to lodge with his tailor. But he managed to get himself invited to a number of balls and assemblies. Unfortunately, however, Charlotte by her father's command was not appearing in public, and it would have been wiser and kinder on his part to have stayed away.

At only one party, at Carlton House, did the couple meet.

In the midst of a glittering assemblage—royalties, statesmen, distinguished soldiers—Princess Charlotte made a superb entrance, dressed in silver lamé, with ostrich plumes on her head and diamonds round her neck. The Prince of Orange was entranced. 'You are in great beauty!' he cried. 'You know I must do you credit now,' replied Charlotte. But this happy encounter was forgotten as the evening advanced and 'young frog', swallowing more and more glasses of the Regent's excellent champagne, was treated to cold looks from his fiancée. Alas, this was not the only occasion on which he drank more than he could carry, and if Charlotte had ever begun to accept the marriage as a reality, she was now utterly disillusioned.

She was accustomed to see her father and her uncles 'cut', but she was not prepared to accept a drunken husband. Then on 10 June, the young Prince went to Ascot Races where, incited by Prince Paul of Wurtemberg, he drank himself into a stupor, and returned to London insensible on the top of a stage coach.

By this time, Charlotte was in no mood to make allowances, or try to forgive him. She no longer cared what he did, and only wanted to see the last of him, because she had fallen violently in love.

At the Carlton House Assembly, among the numerous foreign princes who waltzed and clicked their heels was one who, to Charlotte's dazzled eyes, appeared quite perfect. He was a distinguished soldier, and had been invited to London on account of his bravery at the Battle of Leipzig. His name was Prince Friedrich August von Preussen but as practically every prince in Europe was named Friedrich he was generally known as August. Princess Charlotte, to confuse matters, refers to him in her letters as 'F'.

After their first encounter, Charlotte and Prince August met clandestinely and often. He was an experienced philanderer and had no difficulty in winning her vulnerable heart. Deluded as she was, she believed their passion to be mutual and for ever. He was thirty-five, she eighteen but that was of no account. She hung upon his every word: they exchanged rings, and he swore that when he returned to Prussia he would write. And romantic, misguided, idiotic Miss Knight encouraged what she believed to be a *grande passion*, admitted the Prince to Warwick House, and—with almost the same reckless abandon of Caroline's management of the Hesse affair—left him alone with Charlotte.

She could hardly have encouraged a more hopeless romance. Prince August was a notorious philanderer. But no one gave Charlotte a word of warning, till one day Mercer Elphinstone arrived unexpectedly at Warwick House and was met by an agitated Miss Knight. Charlotte, she whispered, was in the drawing room with Prince August: they were alone. Mercer insisted that the tête-a-tête must be broken up immediately, and, as Miss Knight demurred, did so herself. Although a month later Mercer was lending a sympathetic ear to Charlotte's outpourings on the subject of 'F', she saw at once the danger of the situation. Miss Knight, she said, must be mad to encourage it.

On 16 June Charlotte sent for the Prince of Orange. She presented him with a new argument against the marriage. She must stay in England, she said, to be with her mother, whom she could never desert and who had received such abominable treatment from the Regent and the Queen during the victory celebrations. She added that if she married she would expect always to be allowed to invite the Princess of Wales to her house. This final challenge met with a shocked refusal, as it was meant to, whereupon, without demur, Charlotte broke off the engagement.

Thus it was that Caroline, who had taken no share in Charlotte's problems, and who was already making plans which would cut her off completely from her daughter, played a major part in Charlotte's decision. 'Never desert your mother!' the people cried to Charlotte, but though she did not yet know it, Caroline was already planning to desert her.

Chapter Seventeen

THE REGENT received the news of Charlotte's broken engagement with 'astonishment, grief and concern'. He refused to comment further.

Her mother, though flattered by Charlotte's loyalty to her, was not sufficiently involved to take her part. Mother and daughter had for so long been forced apart by the Regent that it is hardly surprising to find that on both sides there was a certain detachment. Caroline was not in Charlotte's confidence: perhaps her conduct of the Hesse affair had been a warning to Charlotte. Her mother was not told about 'F'; and so little did she know of her daughter's violent reaction against the Dutch marriage that we find her suggesting—with what Grey called 'utter want of all sense of delicacy and propriety'—that Charlotte might have a look at Prince Frederick of Orange, 'Slender Billy's' younger and brighter brother, who was now in England. Charlotte dealt with this typically Caroline suggestion briefly: it was 'quite out of the question'. 'I could never think of the brother of a man I had been engaged to, & then broke off with.' And she added that it was not her intention to marry for some time, 'as I really wish for quiet'.[1]

As we have seen, Caroline's objection to Charlotte's marriage was simply that she herself would lose by it. Charlotte, on the other hand, genuinely hoped that if she married she would be in a position to make her mother's life less wretched. She was truly sorry for her, and she respected the tie between them. So when her own affairs became intolerable, it was to Caroline that she turned.

There was a dreadful silence from Carlton House, but rumours were rife. The Duke of Sussex, Charlotte's fervent partisan, feared that she had not heard the last of the Dutch business.

The Bishop of Salisbury called at Warwick House and carefully let fall that unless Charlotte wrote a submissive letter to her father, promising to reconsider her decision and marry the Prince of Orange, 'arrangements would be made by no means agreeable to her inclinations'. This sinister threat was received with dismay by Miss Knight, who believed that one of the 'arrangements' would be her dismissal: the Duchess of Leeds had already been asked to resign. Indeed, it looked as if Warwick House and its entire household were about to be given up. Charlotte became ill with worry and when, finally, a summons came from Carlton House, she was too ill to obey. 'But I went,' said Miss Knight. It must have taken all her courage.

The Regent, she wrote, 'was very cold, very bitter, and very silent'. This frightening silence caused the wretched Cornelia to blurt out a long apology on behalf of Prince Leopold of Saxe-Coburg, who admired Princess Charlotte and had called at Warwick House, but the Princess 'was by no means partial to him, and only received him with civility'. This red herring did not deceive the Prince who was well versed in duplicity; and he laid his trump card on the table. Prince August of Prussia, he said, had visited Charlotte not once, but several times. Why? Why was this permitted?

Miss Knight boldly lied. We do not know exactly what she said, but in her journal she wrote, 'I justified Prince Augustus, as he well deserved.' She had no right to think this, and she certainly had no right to assure the Regent that she had always been present when the Prussian Prince called. But she was fighting, she believed, for Charlotte's happiness. The Regent, she recorded rather doubtfully, 'seemed satisfied'.

Then, through her Uncle Sussex, Charlotte heard rumours of the Prince's plans, which convinced her that if once she set foot in Carlton House she would be kept there. 'Whatever is done,' she told Mercer, 'is to be *sudden*.' She was sure now that Cornelia would be removed from her, and that in itself was agonizing, for 'no letters perhaps will reach'—no letters from Prince August, sent to Warwick House under cover to Miss Knight. 'I dread everything & I know not why I fancy horrors in everyone and thing round me.'

The next day, 13 July, the Regent arrived without warning at Warwick House and was closeted with Charlotte for an hour. Cornelia waited on tenterhooks. At last the door burst open, and Charlotte rushed out 'in an agony of grief'. She had but one instant, she gasped, to speak to Miss Knight, and she then broke the news. All was over, she said, Miss Knight was dismissed; the servants were to be turned off; her new ladies were already in the house. Charlotte was to go to Carlton House for five days, and then to Cranbourne Lodge in the middle of Windsor Forest, where she would see nobody but the Queen once a week. 'God Almighty give me patience!' she cried, urging Miss Knight to go immediately to the Regent, who was waiting. Charlotte rushed up to her bedroom, seized a bonnet, ran down the back stairs, past the startled sentry, and into the street, where she managed to hail a hackney cab. The driver, whose name was Higgins, did not recognize her, but no doubt was suitably surprised and obsequious when Charlotte, landed on her mother's doorstep in Bayswater, handed him three guineas.

Caroline was out. She had gone to Blackheath 'on business'; but a groom was sent off post-haste to bring her back. The delay gave Charlotte time to compose her thoughts and to decide what to do. She had escaped to the only place where her father could not and would not follow her; but she knew that he would find some means of recapturing her unless she could be protected by the law. She ordered dinner, and then decided to send for her uncle Sussex, who was kind, and for Brougham, who was her legal adviser. As it happened, both were dining out and had to be run to earth, which caused a further delay.

At about nine o'clock the Princess of Wales returned; she had been met on the road by the galloping groom, and had hurried back, sensing trouble. She now heard the whole story. Charlotte threw herself upon her mother's protection, and announced that she wished to live with her always. This declaration may have been prompted by hysteria, but there is no doubt that Caroline found it disconcerting. Already, in secret, she had begun to make plans for leaving the country, plans which did not include her daughter. Charlotte by this time had recovered from the first shock of her escape.

When Brougham arrived, she ran forward and seized both his hands, crying, 'I have run off!' She was radiant and brushed aside his questions, saying, 'Oh, it is too long to tell now.' She was in high spirits, 'seeming to enjoy herself like a bird let loose from its cage'.

As they sat at dinner, other uninvited guests were announced, the Regent's law officers. The two Princesses, far from being awed by the importance of these dignitaries, treated their arrival as a sort of game—and here we may detect the mind of Caroline. As each personage was announced, she or Charlotte decided what to do with him. Eldon, the Lord Chancellor ('Old Bags') was told to wait in his carriage, which gave Charlotte peculiar delight as it happened to be a hackney cab. John Leach, the Prince's fussy, affected legal adviser (dubbed on the spur of the moment, 'Little Bags', 'Ridicule', 'Reticule') was accorded, amidst hysterical laughter, the same humiliating treatment. Even Lord Ellenborough, the Lord Chief Justice, was made to wait outside. Brougham pleaded for him as 'my Chief', but in vain. The Princesses were enjoying themselves.

The Bishop of Salisbury, arriving much later with an ultimatum from the Prince, was put in the dining room downstairs, where the Duke of York, who arrived later still, representing the Regent, was obliged to join him. Only the Duke of Sussex, 'not having been sent by the Regent', was asked to step upstairs. He had come in answer to a second summons, sent by Brougham. Charlotte's note, said her uncle, was such an illegible scrawl that he had put it into his pocket unread.

Caroline and the Duke of Sussex fell into each other's arms, greeting each other affectionately in German. Brougham found this surprising, for they had not been on speaking terms since the Delicate Investigation nine years before, when the Duke had carried the charges made by Sir John and Lady Douglas to the Prince.

Brougham was presented as Charlotte's legal adviser. 'Pray, sir,' the Duke demanded in his blunt way, 'supposing the Prince Regent, acting in the name and on behalf of his Majesty, were to send a sufficient force to break down the doors of this house and carry away the Princess, would any resistance in such a case be lawful?'

'It would not.'

'Then, my dear,' said Sussex to Charlotte, 'you hear what the Law is. I can only advise you to return with as much speed and as little noise as possible.'[2]

But Charlotte had no intention of doing this. While her uncle settled down to a lively conversation in German with the Princess of Wales, Charlotte, serious now after her high spirits during dinner, took Brougham aside and tried to explain to him what had happened and why she had been driven to run away. Brougham noticed that she kept harking back to her terror of being forced into the Dutch marriage. He assured her that 'without consent freely given' it could never take place; but she remained unconvinced. 'They may wear me out by ill treatment, and may represent that I have changed my mind and consented.'

She realized that whatever came of the affair, it would be a matter of public concern, and she was determined to stick to her guns. She again announced her intention of living with her mother if the Regent would not agree to her terms—which were the reinstatement of Miss Knight and the Warwick House servants, and no restrictions upon Mercer's visits.

Brougham listened, betraying no sign of approval or disapproval. At last Charlotte demanded what he advised her to do. His answer came instantly. 'Return to Warwick or Carlton House, and on no account pass a night out of your own house.'[3]

Charlotte burst into tears. This was not the advice that she had hoped for from Brougham. She accused him of turning against her; but he assured her that returning home was absolutely necessary. In this view he was supported by all the others—by the Duke of Sussex and even, alas, by her mother. Charlotte was shattered: after the desperate unhappiness of her plight at Warwick House she had believed that here she would be among friends. She felt betrayed: they were forcing her to go back, to face imprisonment and isolation, surrounded by a female bodyguard chosen without reference to her feelings. Worst of all, she thought in this moment of despair, she would be cut off from Miss Knight and so from her only means of communication with Prince August. This was the most cruel deprivation of all, and hardened her determination not to give in.

(She believed that her action in running away, though it might have been rash and misguided, would be abundant proof in the eyes of Parliament and the public that she was unhappy and unjustly treated. Her rights, she now hoped, would be the subject of debate in Parliament. No one could persuade her to go back.)

The night wore on. The company at Connaught Place passed the time in desultory conversation, awaiting the Regent's answer to Charlotte's proposals. Some of the legal gentlemen, including Lords Eldon and Ellenborough, had driven away. These two were now at Carlton House awaiting the Regent, who was still playing cards at the Duke of York's.

In his account of the affair, Brougham rather surprisingly pays tribute to the behaviour of 'the old Princess'. 'She gave no selfish advice,' he said, 'but took her daughter's part entirely.' Indeed, Caroline seems, after the first hysteria over dinner, to have played an oddly silent part in the drama. Usually so vociferous, she evidently accepted Brougham's opinion and wished that her daughter would be quiet and go home.

As dawn broke, Brougham made a sudden, dramatic move. He walked with Charlotte to the window, which looked eastwards towards the City of Westminster. On the day which was now beginning, there was to be an election there; and as they stood together looking out, he told Charlotte, 'In a few hours all the streets and the Park, now empty, will be crowded with tens of thousands. I have only to . . . show you to the multitude, and tell them your grievances, and they will all rise on your behalf.' There would be violence and bloodshed, he said. 'Carlton House will be attacked . . . perhaps pulled down; the soldiers will be ordered out; and if your Royal Highness were to live a hundred years, it would never be forgotten that your running away from your father's house was the cause of the mischief.'[4]

Brougham's eloquence won the day. Charlotte gave in. She consented to see her uncle York, and to go with him to Carlton House. She had only one stipulation: she would go back in a royal carriage.

While the party waited for this to arrive, there was an altercation about Charlotte's maid, Mrs Louis, who had been sent from Warwick House with a bag containing Charlotte's night things. The Duke of York had no instructions about how Mrs Louis was to get back, and objected to her travelling in the royal carriage. Here, we learn that Caroline intervened. Of course Charlotte must have her maid with her when she arrives, she said, and the Duke wearily gave way.

This was almost the last time that mother and daughter met, and as the royal carriage drove off, Caroline must have felt that there was little hope of a closer alliance: their lives were to follow separate paths.

At Carlton House the carriage was kept waiting in the courtyard because nobody had been told how Princess Charlotte should be received, and her new ladies had to be hastily roused from their beds. Eventually, Lady Ilchester, Lady Rosslyn and Mrs Campbell were rounded up and, the bodyguard being formed, Princess Charlotte was permitted to enter her father's house. She was a prisoner.

'The thing is buzzed over town, of course,' Brougham told Grey. 'All', he added, 'are against the Prince.'

Two days after her capture, Charlotte, with the aid of her drawing-master Mr Starkie, succeeded in smuggling out two pencilled letters: one to her uncle Sussex and one to Mercer. She dipped the letters in milk, to preserve the pencil. 'I am a complete prisoner,' she wrote. 'Not a letter or thing could get to me, except by some merciful private hand.' 'Shall you venture,' she asked, 'upon asking leave to come and see me? Oh, I wish you would . . . Pray, do it.'[5]

She was never alone, she said, even at night, and the atmosphere of watching and suspicion was intolerable. In this frame of mind, she was inclined to detest all her new ladies, but had to admit that Lady Ilchester was the least awful. When they moved to Cranbourne Lodge things seemed less appalling; for one thing, the house did not seem like a prison, but was 'cheerful and very good, the view lovely . . . It is an *honourable retreat*,' said Charlotte. She was still watched and guarded, and could never be alone, but she was determined to accept the situation in the hopes of things improving. She saw faint gleams of light ahead. Her uncle Sussex was to ask questions in Parliament about her treatment; and her doctors were agreed that she needed sea air. Perhaps, after all, this imprisonment could not be for long.

In spite of inflicting this heavy punishment upon his daughter, the Regent was all charm when they met. 'I heartily begged his pardon for my rash act,' she said, and he told her that he had forgiven her. 'He cried a vast deal,' said Charlotte, 'did not know what to do for me, but would try not to make my life miserable,'—an extraordinary statement which cannot have given Charlotte much comfort.

Some ten days later, he arrived at Cranbourne Lodge, 'amiable but not effusive'. He had news for Charlotte, he said, and asked the ladies to leave the room. He then told Charlotte that the Princess of Wales had asked permission to leave the country.

Charlotte told him that 'sometime back' her mother had mentioned that she might go abroad, but that she had not said a word about it since. It was all settled, said her father. The Princess was to set sail from Worthing in about ten days' time; he told her that he was breaking the news himself, thinking it would be kinder. As yet, none of the royal family knew, and he was on his way to tell them.

The Prince was cheerful: it was the wisest act of Caroline's whole life, he said, and he wished her happy. If it made her more so travelling on the Continent, he could not but agree.

As always with her father, Charlotte fought to hide her feelings. This news came as a shattering blow, and in her present forlorn state the loss of this supporter—however raffish and unreliable—was almost more than she could bear. When the Regent took his leave, she gave way to her misery. She would do anything, she cried, to persuade her mother not to go.

'She decidedly deserts me,' she told Mercer. 'Could any letter I could write now be of the least avail, do you think . . .?'[6]

It was too late. She was allowed to pay a farewell visit to Connaught Place, guarded by her two she-dragons. She found her mother calm and even cheerful, and the short interview that they were allowed passed without emotion. Caroline had made up her mind to leave, and no one could shake her decision. She kissed her daughter good-bye as if they were meeting again in a few days. 'I feel so hurt at *that* being a *leave-taking*,' wrote Charlotte to Mercer. 'For God knows how long, or *what events* may occur before we meet again, or if *ever* she will return.'

Caroline had acted against all her advisers: now Brougham stepped in with a last-minute attempt to stop her. He wrote a letter filled with warnings —'a strong dose, but necessary', he called it.

'Depend upon it, Madam, there are many persons who now begin to see a chance of divorcing your Royal Highness from the Prince.' And he begged her to face the truth. 'As long as you remain in this country,' he said, 'I will answer for it that no plot can succeed against you.' With prophetic insight he went on, 'But if you are living abroad, and surrounded by . . . spies, who will always be planted about you . . . who can say what may happen? . . . In England, spies and false witnesses can do nothing; abroad, everything may be apprehended from them.'[7]

But Caroline refused to listen. Nothing and nobody could shake her. Flouting the arguments, the entreaties, the warnings of her friends, she proceeded with her plans. As we have seen, she had one fervent supporter in her determination—her husband. He wished to give her a good send-off (though he drew the line at bidding her farewell), and by his orders the Admiralty arranged for HMS *Jason* to be in readiness to receive the Princess and her suite at Worthing, and to set sail with the full moon on 9 August for Cuxhaven on the way to Brunswick.

England had kept her for nineteen years: now, with an annuity of £35,000, granted her by Parliament, England was returning her. The Prince considered that she had been handsomely treated.

On 9 August large crowds assembled on the Steyne at Worthing, awaiting the arrival of the Princess of Wales and her entourage. At half-past four her carriage drove up, amid cheers which she gracefully acknowledged. Although it was August, she was dressed in a dark, military-style overcoat with large gold claps. On her head she wore a velvet and satin hussar's hat, sporting a bright green plume. Her cheeks were red, but whether from rouge or emotion, it was not easy to say. Beside her sat a youth with light hair and pale protruding eyes, who seemed to absorb the Princess's attention: this was our old friend, William Austin, now thirteen years old, and rather more sedate than when he last appeared suspended by his braces over the dining-table.

The crowd surged to and fro, staring at the carriages and the wagons piled with baggage, among which they observed a large tin trunk, bearing in white letters the interesting words, *HRH the Princess of Wales*, *To be always with her*. What this box contained was a matter of speculation—one of the mysteries with which Caroline liked to surround herself.

There was a delay, an exchange of signals between sea and shore, while the Princess's acknowledgement of her welcome became a little strained. The *Jason*'s commander, Captain King, was unfortunately late in his preparations, and apologized for keeping the royal party waiting.

Caroline decided to drive along the shore and embark at Lancing, which would give the Captain time to finished his preparations. She and her ladies, and of course Willikin, were driven in a small pony-cart along the sands, to where the Captain's barge waited to take them to the frigate. Such crowds as were able to follow watched the Princess's departure in silence, realizing that shouts of joy might be misconstrued. From the barge, she waved and kissed her hand, and was seen to be in tears: indeed, according to the *Sussex Advertiser*, which must have had a reporter on board, 'she was considerably agitated on leaving the English shore, and was so much affected that, immediately she arrived on the quarter-deck of the *Jason*, overpowered by her emotions, she fainted into the arms of her attendants'.

5a Bartolomeo Pergami.
Lithograph by G. Engelmann

5b Countess Oldi.
Engraving after sketch
by A. Wivell

5c The Villa d'Este

6a William Austin

6b Lieutenant Flynn RN.
Engraving after sketch by A. Wivell

6c Alderman Wood.
Engraving by R. Page

6d Theodore Majocchi.
Engraving after sketch by A. Wivell

I do love these Pears!
but I hate the Windsor Pears
Pergami Pears — or — Choice Fruit !!

7a A caricature of Caroline eating 'Pergami Pears'. 'I do love these Pears! but I hate the Windsor Pears.'

SWEARING
MORE PROFITABLE THAN
FIGHTING!
ENGLISHMEN, ATTEND!
Look at the Price of the Evidence against your Queen!
Two Witnesses have been brought forward, who confess, that they receive from our pious Ministers One Thousand Eight Hundred Dollars a Month!
Englishmen, ruined Englishmen, look at this! Here are two Italian Sailors, the Master and Mate of a little beggarly vessel, who receive out of the fruits of your labour, more than the pay of Two Hundred and Fifty of OUR BRAVE SOLDIERS, or of OUR BRAVE SAILORS!!!
Englishmen, think of this! See how much more profitable it is to swear than to fight!!!
If you want to know all about the Queen's Judges, look at the "PEEP AT THE PEERS." There they are all.—Price Fourpence; No. 269, Strand.

7b Patriotic Poster

8a *Brandenburg House*

8b *The trial of Queen Caroline in the House of Lords.*
Engraving after a detail of the painting by George Hayter. Left to right in the front: Thomas Denman, Stephen Lushington, Henry Brougham, William Vizard (seated), The Queen, 2nd Earl Grey

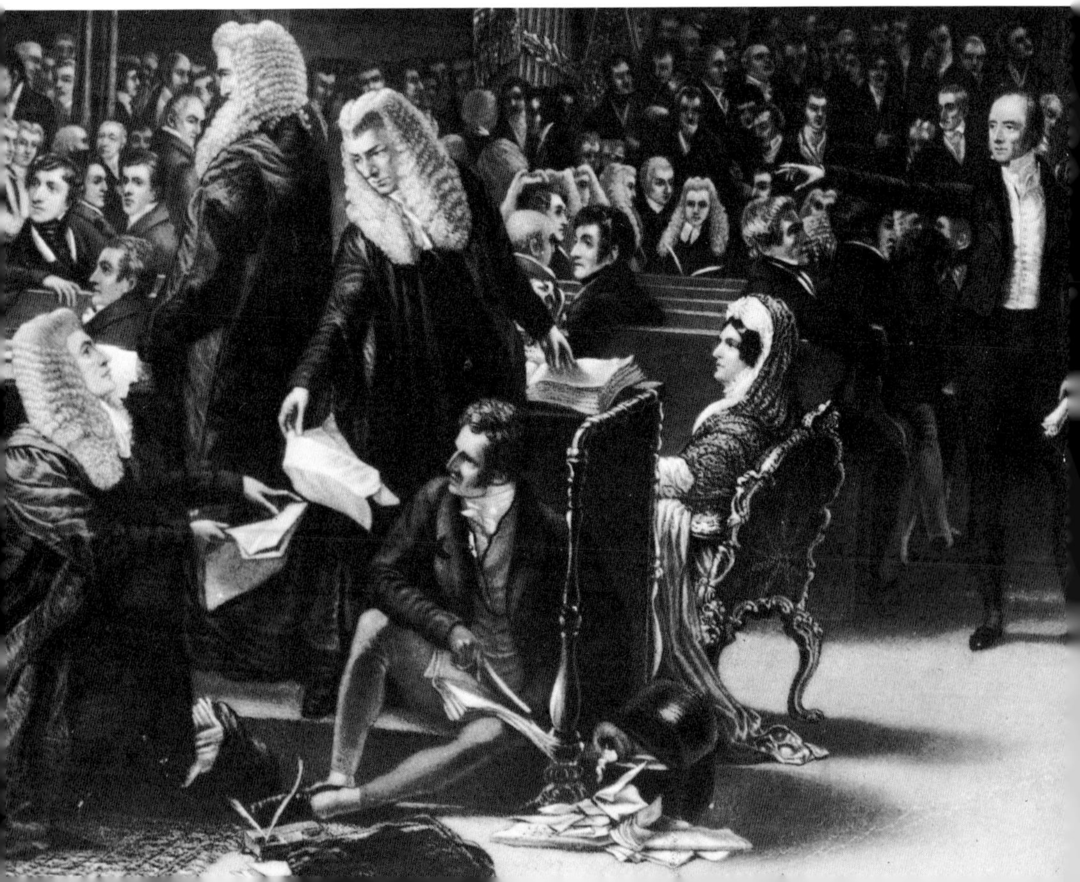

Chapter Eighteen

WHEN CAROLINE left England she managed to scrape together an entourage which gave the enterprise an air of respectability, if not—as it turned out—of stability. Her ladies-in-waiting were Lady Charlotte Lindsay, who was obliged to leave after a few weeks to join her ailing sister, Lady Glenbervie, at Spa, and Lady Elizabeth Forbes, who left after a few months. 'Our inclination nor temper did not well agree,' said Caroline, and awarded her a pension. Her chamberlains, as she called them, were Sir William Gell and Colonel St Leger; but the latter was obliged, through ill health, to return home almost at once. He was replaced by the Hon Richard Keppel Craven, devoted friend of Sir William Gell, but neither of these would commit himself for more than six months. Dr Henry Holland, a young man 'of pleasing countenance' was recommended by Gell for the post of travelling physician, and was still part of the household in the following summer; but her equerry, Princess Charlotte's once-loved Captain Hesse, was obliged to rejoin his regiment when Napoleon escaped from Elba in March 1815.

This dramatic event had its effect upon all who had taken advantage of the Peace of Paris and were idling about in different parts of the Continent. Many fled, panic-stricken, back to England; but Caroline was not afraid. The uncertain state of Europe and the thoroughly uncertain state of Caroline's plans were discouraging to the holiday humour in which she and her companions first set out; but she was determined to make a success of her new life; and perhaps she bore in mind the gipsy in Greenwich Park who had told that she would go abroad and there marry the man she loved, and be 'very rich and happy'.[1]

At the outset of her tour, she was encouraged by the warmth of her reception in Germany. In Brunswick her solemn brother, the Duke, received her with great kindness.* Her relations embraced her, tears were shed, and the town was illuminated.

She was travelling under the name of Countess of Wolfenbuttel; but as the tour progressed this was dropped, and she entered Switzerland under

* This was to be their last meeting: 'Brunswick's fated chieftain' died at Quatre Bras.

her own name. There was no need for disguise: once seen, Caroline was unforgettable; and in the enthusiasm of her desire to throw etiquette overboard, she declared that she was no longer Princess of Wales, but Caroline, a happy, merry soul.

Her attendants, remembering just how happy and merry she could be when in the mood, may have quailed, for her most innocent pranks could, in a foreign country, lead to trouble. Their fears were justified when the party arrived at Lausanne. She heard that a ball was in progress at a house opposite the Golden Lion where she was staying, and asked for an invitation. 'After dancing with everybody and anybody,' wrote a local gossip, 'she finished up by dancing a Savoyard dance called a "fricassée" with a *nobody*. The honour of England,' announced this pompous ass, 'the honour of England has been compromised.'[2]

On arrival at Berne, Caroline found that Marie-Louise, Napoleon's second wife, was in the town. The ex-Empress lost no time in inviting the Princess of Wales to dinner, and Caroline accepted enthusiastically.

'She appeared enveloped in yards of white muslin, trimmed with priceless lace. On her head she wore a long veil held in place by a magnificent diadem of diamonds. Around her neck was displayed a superb necklace of several rows of pearls.' It may be that she was not going to be outdone in magnificence by an ex-Empress; but the writer, Baron Meneval, believed that 'she travelled everywhere dressed in this bizarre manner'. He added, 'Although fantastically unbalanced, seemed to be an excellent woman, simple, frank, making everyone feel at their ease.'[3]

During the evening, which we are told was 'charming and gay', the Princess offered to sing. 'She sang only amongst friends,' she said. 'It was just as well,' commented the Baron, 'as her voice seemed to fall in and out of tune most easily.' Then Marie-Louise was persuaded to sing in duet with the Princess, but apparently, though she had taken singing lessons to please Napoleon, what voice she had was unequal to the occasion, and she was overcome by nerves. 'It was not an inspiring occasion,' said the Baron, 'but they were all very merry, and when the Princess of Wales bade us goodbye, we all retained a rather pleasing remembrance of the woman who half the world abused, and the other half praised.'

At this stage of her journey Caroline did not linger, and the cavalcade moved on through Switzerland and into Italy. Already the procession had a slightly ramshackle air, a heterogeneous collection of horse-drawn vehicles, followed up by an old London–Dover mail-coach which still bore on its panels the English ports of call, and which now lumbered over the Simplon Pass carrying servants and luggage.

Caroline was not concerned by appearances. 'I must confess that Independence, Curiosité, and also Economy are the real motive of my travelling,' she announced. And at first there would be no dallying. Keppel Craven wrote to his mother that he had 'gallop'd through Italy with the Princess of Wales, who just stops long enough to receive Royal Honours everywhere'.[4] Foreign rulers (uncertain, since Napoleon's defeat, of their future), felt that it was important to please the English Princess; but many persons were taken aback by her appearance, which became wilder as the tour went on. During her travels she took to a wig, and chose a black one which evidently did not agree with her natural colouring. Lady Bessborough describes her at a ball in Genoa . . . 'a short, very fat, elderly woman, with an extremely red face (owing, I suppose, to the heat) in a girl's white frock-looking dress but with shoulder, back and neck quite low (disgustingly so), down to the middle of her stomach; very black hair and eyebrows, which gave her a fierce look, and a wreath of light pink roses on her head . . . I was staring at her,' said Lady Bessborough, 'from the oddity of her appearance, when suddenly she nodded and smiled at me, and not recollecting her, I was convinced she was mad, till William* pushed me, saying, "Do you not see the Princess of Wales nodding to you?" It is so long since I have seen her near before, she is so much fatter and redder, that added to her black hair and eyebrows . . . I had not the least recollection of her . . .'[5]

Caroline was forty-six. Perhaps, from the unnaturally flushed face, and unbalanced behaviour, it would not be unreasonable to assume that she was suffering from the menopause. If this were so, it was rash of her to embark upon a series of journeys which would inevitably cause her hardship and discomfort. But she was not one to allow such considerations to interfere with her pleasures. She was Caroline, a happy, merry soul: she dressed her gentlemen in costumes *à la Henri Quatre*, and it evidently pleased her to display her own legs in pink satin boots by day, and her naked breasts by night.

The same impulse which as a young woman had made her let down her hair before the Prince of Wales, now, twisted into eccentricity, caused her to display herself, ridiculous and yet pitiful, to all the world. 'I could not bear', said Lady Bessborough, 'the sort of whispering and talking all around about the Principessa d'Inghilterra che era vestita da leggiera &c . . .'[6]

She had her own half-crazy courage, which sometimes involved her in serious scrapes. She also had moments of wild happinesss when she could believe herself the heroine of an exotic drama—as, for instance, when she used her royal prerogative to set free a number of slaves belonging to her

* Lord William Bentinck, Commander-in-Chief of land forces in Italy.

host, the Bey of Tunis. 'I am as happy as the day is long,' she cried, delighted with herself and everybody else.

But unhappily she was what we now call accident-prone. In the course of her journeys she was dogged by thunderstorms, epidemics, sudden risks of being drowned. Rivers overflowed before her; she was obliged to sleep on the road, lit and warmed by fifty flambeaux, because the Po had burst its banks. Next day, she continued her journey on foot, walking till her shoes wore away under her.

At sea, sleeping in a tent on deck, she was nearly swept overboard by a high wave; hurrying to disembark from another ship on her way to visit the Pope, she tripped over a coil of rope and fell headlong, giving herself a black eye. Undeterred, she went ashore and continued her journey, making a joke of the accident. 'What will His Holiness say when he sees my black eye? He will think I have been fighting!'

The Empress Marie-Louise invited her to dine at her castle in Parma, and Caroline, remembering their merry musical evening at Berne, accepted delightedly. But unfortunately, in the extremely formal Austrian court her propensity for disaster displayed itself once more. The story is told with relish by Sir William Gell in a letter to Miss Berry, and he describes how 'in full dress feathers . . . the two ladies sat before the fire in a very long tête-a-tête before dinner . . .'—and imitating Caroline—'You imagine it is not very entertaining; I assure you, very doll [dull], I yarn, and she de same; mein Gott, I balance on my chair mit my feet pon die fire. What you tink! I tomble all back mit di chair, and mit mein legs in die air; man see nothing more als my feet. I die from laugh, and what you think she do? She stir not, she laugh not; but wit the utmost gravity she say, "Mon Dieu, Madame, comme vous m'avez effrayé." I go into fits of laugh, and she repeat di same word . . . I . . . die to get away to my gens to tell die story. We all scream mit di ridiculousness for my situation.'[7]

Caroline was hurt and angry when, in February 1815, Sir William Gell tendered his resignation. Not only was he one of her oldest and most faithful friends, but also he was a learned classical scholar whose presence lent distinction to the Princess's entourage. Byron, on first acquaintance, dubbed him 'coxcomb Gell'; but after reading his *Topography of Greece and Ithaca* respectfully altered the sobriquet to 'Classic Gell'. With his constant companion, Keppel Craven, Gell had spent years exploring the treasures of ancient Greece, and wrote books which laid his knowledge before the world, opening the eyes of those who cared to travel in his steps.

Gell was an unexpected person to find at Caroline's table; but we must remember that when she began to choose her own guests she looked for talent and intellect rather than social position. She was fascinated by his enormous knowledge, and nicknamed him 'Anacharsis'.*

He was a wit—and, though he may have traded in Caroline stories elsewhere, he made her laugh and enjoyed her outrageousness. It seems likely that Gell inspired some of her journeys and taught her what to admire. Altogether it was a sad misfortune for the expedition when he was forced to leave. He may have found things too rowdy, but his proffered excuse was genuine: he was ill. He suffered from gout—or could it have been arthritis?—which gave him agonizing pain and sometimes completely crippled him. But 'I think I never knew a man of a more kind and gentle turn of mind' said Lady Charlotte Campbell.

The Princess was an enthusiastic amateur water-colourist, and evidently went sketching with Gell and Craven. Indeed, her admiration for their skill led her into dishonesty. Princess Charlotte at Windsor received a number of sketches from her mother, 'views of all the places she had stopped at'. Caroline had blandly claimed these drawings as her own unaided work, but her daughter was certain that this was untrue. 'They are Mr K. Craven's drawings and the names of the places are in his handwriting, though the Princess of Wales has wrote over some of the names in her own handwriting.'[8]

From a sketchbook of Caroline's which still survives (now in the safekeeping of the Mother Superior of an English convent) one may see what Princess Charlotte meant: there are several styles, and, amongst the meticulous architectural drawings, what must be Caroline's own dashing portraits of carefully posed peasants stand out unmistakably. Dressed in the brightest of colours and a little wobbly on their feet, they are brave reminders of the contemporary scene, and it is a pity that she did not send some of these to her daughter.

Rome was crammed with foreign royalties, and Caroline, who was bored by Court etiquette, decided to move on to Naples, where she arrived in November. King Joachim Murat, Napoleon's puppet ruler married to Napoleon's sister, met her with a great show of military pomp and much banging of drums.

Murat was the son of an innkeeper, and spectacular in appearance. Tall and god-like, with flowing black locks and clothes designed to make him look even more conspicuous, he believed Caroline's visit to be 'an acknowledgment of his title by the English Government'.[9] The year 1815 was one of feverish excitement: in Naples, balls and assemblies, masquerades and

* Anacharsis, a Scythian philosopher (592 BC) who, on account of his wisdom, temperance and expansive knowledge, has been called one of the World's Seven Wise Men.

operas, levées and military reviews followed in hectic sequence; and Caroline became caught up in the whirl. But the news, in March 1815, of Napoleon's escape and landing in France brought the gaieties to an abrupt end. Murat immediately began to raise an army in support of the Emperor.* 'It was in truth the dropping of a curtain upon a gorgeous drama,' said Dr Holland. 'The days of revelry closed with painful abruptness . . . and no-one saw what lay in the future.' 'At this crisis,' he added, 'we departed very hastily for Rome.'[10]

They departed so hastily that some of Caroline's luggage was left behind. 'There has been most dreadful blunders at Naples,' she told Gell, 'with all my goods and shattels, the three fin lamps which I had at Connaught House—the whole Box No. 63 has been lost and all my things which had been bought at Naples are gon I suppose to the Divel . . .'[11]

Rome was only to be a temporary resting-place, for the reorganizing of Caroline's sadly depleted entourage and for the replanning of her journeys. She was tired of wandering and wished to find a villa where she might settle for a few months. She had lost both her chamberlains, Gell and Craven; she had also lost both her ladies and her equerry, Captain Hesse. She sent to England for Lady Ann Hamilton, odd-looking but loyal; and for her faithful Lady Charlotte Campbell, who was ready to come if she might bring her six daughters and their governess. An even more peremptory summons reached a young naval lieutenant, Joseph Hownam, to join her immediately at Naples. If the Admiralty should refuse to let him go he was to throw up his commission. 'This', he wrote in his diary, 'would mean giving up my career.' Nevertheless, the order was received as sacred. He set off immediately.

Joseph was one of Caroline's orphans, not a foundling but the child of a page at Carlton House. When the Princess of Wales moved to Blackheath the Hownam family moved with her; but after three years the father died. Joseph had been devoted to him, and when, a few months later, his mother also died, the boy was heartbroken. The Princess sent for him, and told him to cheer up. 'I promise that from henceforward I will be as father and mother to you; you shall never want. Be a good boy.' He was put in the care of Mr Sicard, the Princess's major-domo, who treated him with great kindness till he was old enough to join the navy as a midshipman; and after successfully mastering the hazards and enduring the rough treatment of life at sea, he was eventually promoted to the rank of lieutenant.

When Caroline first began to talk of going abroad, she invited Hownam to

* On 2 May 1815, his forces were routed by the Austrians. After the final defeat of Napoleon, 'King Joachim' was captured, court-martialled, and executed.

dinner at Kensington. 'The conversation turning on the Mediterranean, Italy, Malta etc., she said to me with a sort of significant nod, that it was not improbable that in a few months she would see Malta, and even Jerusalem.'[12] Soon after this, Hownam learned that she wished him to join the party as her private secretary. Without hesitation he refused; he felt that he could not, so soon after promotion, leave his chosen profession. No more was said, and the Princess bade him a cold farewell. But now this order, which sounded like a *cri de cœur*, seemed to him one which must be obeyed at all costs.

By the time that he received the summons from Naples, the Princess had moved to Genoa where she established herself in a charming house, Palazzo Durazza. Here Joseph eventually turned up. 'My dear Hownam, here you are at last,' cried Caroline. 'I have sent for you to live and die with me.' This was a little alarming, but Caroline reassured him. 'You must not have any fears for the future, I take charge of that, therefore make yourself happy. Every comfort shall be at your wish.'[13]

From this time onward, Joseph worked devotedly for the Princess. Some instinct must have taught her to choose him as her protector, surrounded as she was already becoming with dubious or untrustworthy characters. In the shoddy, ephemeral atmosphere in which she lived, Hownam stood for sanity. He was a methodical and conscientious young man, and must have been a comfort to Caroline, dealing with all her correspondence and keeping her confused affairs as much in order as was possible.

At Genoa he found that he was to be 'surrounded with consideration, care and luxury'. He was to be paid £200 a year, the same salary as that received by Captain Hesse and Mr Keppel Craven. The Princess's household at this time was extremely modest. She was awaiting the arrival of Lady Charlotte Campbell; Lady Glenbervie, now recovered and living with her husband in Genoa, dined every day with her; and her male attendants were Dr Holland and Hownam.

Genoa was garrisoned by English troops and the town was full of English travellers. Caroline was well supplied with society. Hownam was suitably impressed when the Pope* came to call.

The visit His Holiness paid to the Princess was proof of the high respect he had for the English and the gratitude he felt for his re-establishment and his present protection from Napoleon. The old man in his carriage was given an escort of the 26th Dragoons, but had difficulty in reaching the Palazzo on foot owing to his age and infirmities. At last, at the entrance to the house,

* This was Pius VII (1740–1823). He had been captured by Napoleon and imprisoned in France.

the meeting took place. 'His objection to put his hat on in the presence of Her Royal Highness, and his regret that she should have come down to receive him, however little [wrote Protestant Hownam) we may think of his title to sanctity, could not but be touching when one reflected that so many thousands approached him on their knees and kissing his feet.'[14]

During her six weeks' stay at Genoa, the Princess occupied 'a most beautiful Palace, the situation the most enviable in the world, as it is close to the sea, with a most charming wood at the back . . .' She wrote to Gell (now forgiven) eulogizing upon the advantages of this idyllic place 'which is perfectly retired and free from all observations as it is out of Town. I ride in the woods every day upon a delightful donkey, which gives me a great deal of appetite . . . Beef and mutton', she adds, 'is equally good to that of John Bull's in England.'[15]

Enjoying sea and sun, beautiful surroundings and a healthy appetite, and at night dancing enthusiastically as Lady Bessborough described (see page 153) Caroline was happy. She did not know that already her enemies were at work. Hownam wrote innocently in his diary: 'A Baron de Ompteda who had been at Naples when the Princess was at that Court, was also at Genoa and frequently dined with Her Royal Highness in company with the Prussian Ambassador.'[16]

In the future, this name Ompteda would have a sinister meaning.

Chapter Nineteen

'I AM like Aladdin sitting in his beautiful Palace with his enchanted lamp about me, *namely* Lord and Lady Glenbervie which I found settled here at Genoa on my arrival.' So wrote Caroline to Sir William Gell. For the next few weeks she planned to remain in Genoa: with the friendly, amusing Glenbervies, joined by Lady Charlotte Campbell and Joseph Hownam, she would have a little court around her once more. As an officer in the Royal Navy, Hownam was accepted in Genoese society, invited to balls and parties; when the Princess went driving he sat in her carriage; if he wished to ride, her stable, she told him, was at his command.

It seemed that he had fallen on his feet: he could hardly believe his luck. Even his fears for the loss of his career were allayed. Far from being dismissed from the navy for desertion, he was treated with the greatest civility by Lord Exmouth, Commander-in-Chief of the Fleet, who happened to be on duty in the Mediterranean and accepted an invitation from the Princess to dine. Hownam was dizzy with excitement and gratitude to his patroness: the Admiral's manner was as kind as it was unexpected. 'His affability and his engaging me to drink with him was more than I anticipated; he even asked permission that I should sit beside him at table.'[1]

Hownam had never been so honoured, or felt so self-confident. But, alas, this blissful state of affairs did not last. One day he went as usual to the stables and asked for his horse to be saddled. Charles, the Princess's coachman, told him that he had received orders that Hownam could not ride that horse any more. Hownam was puzzled and indignant. 'I asked for another and another but something was the matter with every one of them.' 'I was at a loss to imagine who could take so much upon himself as to give such an order; and was told that it was, in Charles's language, "the long 'un".'

He had little difficulty in understanding who was meant. 'The long 'un' was Bartolomeo Pergami, the Princess's courier. She had engaged him when she was in Milan, at the recommendation of Count Gizziliere, Chamberlain to the Austrian Emperor. Pergami gave her to understand that he was doing her a favour in accepting the post that she offered, but he would expect to be promoted when the opportunity arrived. He later announced that he was of noble birth, but that his family had fallen on bad days. He had been in the army, and was, he claimed, aide-de-camp to General Pino. These boastings did not endear him to his fellow servants, but Caroline paid little attention to his credentials: she was dazzled by the splendour of his looks. He was god-like—'a man about six feet high,' wrote Lady Charlotte Campbell, 'a magnificent head of black hair, pale complexion, mustachios which reach from *here to London*'. And Count Ompteda noted, 'He is a sort of Apollo, of a superb and commanding appearance . . . his physical beauty attracts all eyes. This man,' he added, for the Regent's information, 'this man . . . has entered the Princess's service.'[2]

This was 'the long 'un'. Hownam lost no time in seeking him out and demanding what he meant by issuing such impertinent orders. But Pergami was disarming. In the gentlest manner he explained that he had been given superintendence of the stables, 'and that, as the Princess would want such and such a horse, he had desired as above'. He could not have been more polite, or more insistent that he was simply obeying orders. But Hownam gathered that when asking favours in future he would be wise to apply to Signor Pergami. This was not a happy discovery.

'It was far from my nature to stoop to my *equals* for any favours.' Instinctively he mistrusted the flamboyant Italian, and believed, perhaps wrongly, that he was a rogue bent upon charming the Princess to give him whatever he desired. For the moment, Hownam was obliged to accept the situation and pretend to ignore it; but at any moment it would explode into open war. Already he noticed a coldness in the Princess's manner which showed plainly which way the wind blew.

Pergami's position was firmly established. Little by little he was promoted from servant status and treated as one of the Princess's entourage. Then he played his trump card. While the Princess was still at Genoa, his mother Signora Livia Pergami, arrived, bringing Pergami's child, Vittorina, aged about one and a half. Caroline was enchanted: this beautiful Italian baby was her delight; she could not be parted from her, and had a cot set up for her in her own bedroom. If Pergami had ever doubted the success of his plans, his doubts were now at an end. He reigned supreme.

But his family shared in his good fortune. His mother was put in charge of the Princess's linen. His brother, Luigi, had already been introduced as a courier—not entirely happily, as it turned out, for sent ahead to make arrangements on an expedition, he forgot to order a meal and the Princess was kept waiting. But this did not lose him his job. Another brother, Voloti, was made comptroller of disbursements—presumably a position of trust, but we do not hear of him again. Shortly afterwards, two sisters arrived and were presented hopefully to the Princess. In fact, the only member of Pergami's family who did not appear was his wife.

The party left Genoa for Milan, and Lady Charlotte Campbell was regretfully obliged to resign—her excuse, 'family affairs' and the impossibility of following the Princess on the many voyages that she intended to make.[3] Caroline was left without a lady-in-waiting. She tried in Milan to find one; but enquiries among the English colony there proved fruitless: scandalous reports about her behaviour had preceded her and no one was prepared to take the social risk of joining her now notorious party. Pergami, ever resourceful, mentioned tactfully that his sister Angelina, unhappily married to the Austrian Count Oldi, might be prevailed upon to consider such a post. Caroline wrote delightedly to Gell: 'A fine Italian lady has been chosen for me. She is a married woman, her husband has been in the Austrian *Armee*, a very good old family from Vienna . . .'[4]

One morning in May, Joseph Hownam was surprised to find himself having breakfast tête-à-tête 'with an Italian lady who had arrived the night before. As she neither spoke English, nor I sufficient Italian, our conversation was not very edifying. She was about thirty years of age, a fine woman and pretty.'[5] (Hownam was susceptible to female beauty.) But his first impression soon changed. She was coarse-looking, provincial, and dull. In fact, she was the Countess Oldi, Pergami's sister, and she remained with Caroline to the end.

Caroline liked her, and treated her as an equal. After the vicissitudes of an unhappy marriage, the Countess settled down to enjoy the advantages of her position and pleased her royal mistress by her placid behaviour and interest in the domestic arts. She had learned to cook, and they cooked happily together. On journeys she was uncomplaining, and, as Caroline put it, remained 'always merry and pleased'. When things went wrong she had no wish to resign: she had nowhere else to go.

With the exception of Joseph Hownam and Dr Holland (who was shortly to leave) Caroline's suite was entirely Italian. 'We all now speak much Italian,' she told Gell, 'which is quite delightful.'[6] But it was not so delightful to find herself ostracized by the English in Milan; and it was not long before she realized the reason. Here, in the north of Italy, under Austrian rule, the Prince Regent was able to keep in closer touch with his wife's movements; and Milan was chosen to be the headquarters of a Commission, which, it was whispered, was being set up on the Regent's orders to spy upon the Princess wherever she went, and to send reports to England. The Prince believed that his father's death could not now be far off (in point of fact, he had five years more to live) and determined that he, as King, must at all costs be freed from this intolerable burden, freed to remarry if he wished, to beget an heir—if he could. Through the Hanoverian envoy, Count Münster, the services of Ompteda were engaged; his instructions, 'to inform the English government all about the condition of Italian politics' and 'to obtain exact knowledge about the conduct of the Princess of Wales'. There were other agents, both English and Italian: among them the Austrian, Gizziliere, who actually found her the delectable Pergami to be her courier. Did he, perhaps, guess what might come of this introduction?

An elaborate system evolved, to follow the Princess wherever she went and watch for any move that might lead to her conviction. Divorce—grounds for divorce—were all that the Prince demanded. Somehow Caroline must be caught 'in the fact', as the housemaid at Montague House had put it, and then all would be simple.

The arrival of Pergami was exactly what the Commission wanted; but unfortunately he behaved, at this stage, with perfect discretion: he treated the Princess with respectful kindness, accepted her princely favours with modest dignity and was exemplary in fulfilling his duties. Caroline was quieter—less restless—than was her wont. The death of her brother the Duke of Brunswick at Quatre Bras was in a measure responsible: she describes herself (July 1815) as 'very miserable' on account of the death of her beloved brother. According to Hownam, the news 'depressed her Royal Highness so much as in a great measure to interfere with her plans for more trips'. She consoled herself by house-hunting, found a large and beautiful villa on Lake Como known as Villa Garovo, and bought it for £7,500, to be paid by instalments, with a further £2,500 for alterations and additions. A theatre was to be built, stables, and a wing: Caroline was carried away by her enthusiasm. There was no road to the villa: she would make one. 'I have already begun to make a beautiful road for carriages and horseback,' she told Gell. It was to be called '*La Strada Carolina*': 'I am very populaire here,' she added modestly. The road, she said, would only cost £2,000.[7] She found an Italian artist named Montielli and engaged him to design murals in her house, which she renamed Villa d'Este in honour of her (and her husband's) ancestors at Ferrara.

While the work went on, Caroline was living at Como in a rented villa, where with her much reduced retinue she remained for several months. Apart from expeditions into the countryside the party lived quietly. The smouldering resentment which Hownam felt for Pergami erupted from time to time. He had to remind himself that, 'as a gentleman in the suite of the Princess of my country and as an officer in his country's and her service', he must accept the duties—and drawbacks—of his position. Nevertheless, as an Englishman he resented Pergami's growing influence: he began to loathe his 'insolent stare' and easy assumption of a position to which he had no right. The Princess now called him her chamberlain. When they went on expeditions he no longer road on horseback ahead of her, but sat 'in a very handsome carriage' which he ordered to pass Hownam's and take its place directly behind the Princess. This sort of thing culminated in an extraordinary scene when, at the end of a long day, the party stopped at an inn. Here the Princess, 'feigning a sort of democratic oblivion of rank', invited the innkeeper to join the party at table, and, on his doing so, turned to Pergami and asked him also to sit down. This was, for Hownam, the last straw. 'I cannot describe my feelings,' he wrote in his diary. 'I suppose I turned all the colours of the rainbow and it affected me so much that the tears trickled down into my plate.' Poor loyal, emotional man, he felt that the Princess of Wales, his kind patroness whom he genuinely revered, had betrayed him.

Caroline realized in the 'morose silence' that followed, that she had gone too far. She tried by every means to make up for it, plying Hownam with food and drink, and 'with tears in her eyes' (tears were infectious) begging him to join her in a glass of wine. 'I drank', said Hownam, 'to her future happiness, but I forsaw that she was about to blast it for ever.'

As for Pergami, he accepted, gracefully, whatever he was offered. He desired position and power, and in return he was ready to arrange the Princess's life and to give her what she had always longed for—kindness. Accounts of him suggest that he appeared to be unassuming—'a plain, straightforward *remarkably good sort of man*', wrote one English visitor. Pergami was evidently something of an actor. But it must be remembered that he was Italian and not given to restraint: at an insult, real or imagined, he drew his pistol, shaking with rage, and only Hownam could, with difficulty, calm him. Hownam had to accept the situation—or leave. He chose to stay.

Caroline grew tired of waiting for her villa on Lake Como to be ready, and decided to proceed on the tour of the Mediterranean which she had long planned. She was being plagued by mysterious characters who turned up from time to time, applying for work or trying to bribe her servants for small pieces of information. Strangers bearing reputable introductions came to call. At intervals, Count Ompteda appeared, smiling, genial, professedly the Princess's friend and admirer. Caroline, always ready to receive visitors, began to be suspicious: there was an uneasy feeling that people were lurking in the grounds, though nobody was actually seen. Pergami grabbed his pistol and gave orders for house and grounds to be patrolled.

At last, through Lord Exmouth, Caroline received the welcome news that the battleship HMS *Leviathan* (Captain Briggs) had been ordered to carry the Princess and her party on the first stage of their journey. Caroline was overjoyed. She was bound for Sicily, she told Gell, and later would visit Tunis. 'Jerusalem is my great ambition to see,' she added. But for the moment the world was her oyster.

At Genoa, the Princess went on board HMS *Leviathan* 'under the salute of two lines of battleships', reported Hownam, conjuring up a picture which evokes for a moment her true status. The lovely line of ships 'dressed over all', the Royal Standard raised as the Princess boarded *Leviathan*, are part of a different world from the odd assortment of travellers which made up the Princess's retinue. Onlookers can only have felt astonishment or pity at the sight of the little crowd which trailed behind the Princess of Wales. A friend of Pergami, Count Schiavini of Crema, had joined the party ('my Gentleman', said Caroline, 'a very passable, good man'): he was dressed, according to Hownam, like a barber's assistant, and was 'disgustingly ugly. I never, in my whole life, saw such an assassin's countenance.'[8] Pergami was now, of course, a member of the Princess's suite, the rest consisting of William Austin aged fourteen, the Countess Oldi, the child Vittorina and Hownam. They were followed by seventeen servants of various denominations and nationalities. 'How, alas,' cried Hownam, 'shall I paint in respectful terms and colours the ensemble of our motley group, when the court of a Princess of England, wife of its sovereign, is composed of such uncouth, I would say, such ignoble members.'[9]

He passionately blamed Pergami for the demoralization of Caroline and her Court, for surrounding her with second-rate Italians, and even more for her sudden, violent dislike of England. It was Pergami's influence, he believed, that caused her to betray 'an absolute hatred of the country and its rigid observance of decorum'.

This may not have been altogether just. The English in Milan had cut her, and she had been hurt that Madame de Staël, living close to her at Como, had never called. To Gell she confided her disillusionment, 'having made such dreadful experiences of Friends and Friendship'. But it was her own bitterness that caused her to disown her country-by-marriage, and ostentatiously, while enjoying the hospitality of the British Navy, to declare herself an admirer of Napoleon. The first port of call on *Leviathan*'s voyage was Elba. Here, she slept for two nights in the house once occupied by her hero, and left clutching a book from his library and his favourite billiard cue.

At Sicily, the *Leviathan* was under orders to leave the party for a time, and finding Palermo a grave disappointment—'nothing remarkable but its filth and its churches', said Hownam—the Princess decided to travel about the island by road. For the most part, she went by *littega*—a sort of sedan chair drawn by two mules.

Sicily was poverty-stricken, and in some places the travellers suffered from poor food and dirty uncomfortable lodging. At Syracuse, the Princess drove out into the country, where a house had been prepared for her at the Governor's orders. When they arrived, they could hardly believe their eyes. 'Bare walls, and a miserable house in ruins offered but a poor night's lodging, but it was too late to retract.' The rest was nightmare. The house, they discovered, was infested by rats, and the Princess's room no better than the rest. 'Rats, thirty or forty of them in a troop,' ran over Hownam as he lay in bed. The rats, like the peasants, were starving. The next day the party was thankful to learn that two miles away a Mr Buffadiace was building a house, and he offered it to the Princess. Unfortunately the doors and windows were not yet put in, but this should be seen to. 'A troop of workmen,' said Hownam, 'were immediately set to work.' The Princess and her party moved in that night. It can hardly have offered much comfort, but Caroline seems to have displayed amazing good-humour and fortitude in conditions better suited to a gipsy than a princess.

From Syracuse the travellers proceeded to Catania, and here they received a reassuring welcome. 'I never witnessed anywhere a more hearty and unanimous reception to the Princess,' said Hownam. It was the feast of Catania's patron saint, St Agatha, and the town was enjoying a carnival. Caroline was greeted with cheers and screams of enthusiasm, with much ringing of bells and waving of handkerchiefs. Indeed, so carried away were the people that shouts of *Viva Santa Agatha* were mingled with *Viva la Principessa*! Caroline, in an elegant carriage drawn by six bay horses, was driven to the Palazzo Patterno Castelfranco, where she was to stay—'commodious, well situated and rich', said Hownam. Catania was full of gaiety and the travellers enjoyed parties and balls. There was a masked ball: we do not know how Caroline was dressed, but Hownam created havoc by appearing as a skeleton: he had bought the costume at Messina. It was so life-like, or death-like, that the Sicilian ladies fled shrieking, and Hownam was asked to leave; 'the Master of Ceremonies spoke threateningly as to the consequences if I remained,' he said, 'so, to avoid trouble, I immediately withdrew'.

Caroline was with difficulty persuaded not to climb Mount Etna, which was in a dangerous state.

During the stay at Catania, enjoying with Pergami the warmth and sea air, Caroline decided to have her portrait painted. As we have already seen, she liked to appear *en Vénus*, and this was how she now posed. Pergami, of course, was to be painted too, but chose, like Byron, to dress in exotic national costume. 'A Young Turk' the picture was called. 'The two portraits', wrote Clerici, 'were afterwards removed to Milan where they for a long time decorated the Villa Barona; and perhaps they are even yet preserved somewhere.'[10]

It was now that Caroline found the solution to the problem of Pergami's rank. At Augusta, some ten miles south of Catania, a small estate was for sale, carrying with it the title of Baron. Without hesitation she bought it, and presented it, lock, stock and barony, to her beloved. Now, his status was unqestionable: from henceforth, after a few legal preliminaries, Bartolomeo Pergami was to be addressed as Baron.

Chapter Twenty

CAROLINE was angry when she learned that HMS *Leviathan* was no longer at her service and that she was being fobbed off with a frigate, HMS *Clorinda*. Already, at Naples, she had crossed swords with the commander of this vessel, who refused to have Pergami at his table. Now she decided that since the Royal Navy would not give her *Leviathan*—'I find myself remarkable comfortable on board the *Leviathan*'—she would hire a ship of her own. She consulted Hownam, who was flattered. 'The Princess', he said, 'now did me the honour in the most affectionate manner to place confidence in my guidance.'

At this juncture, a rather mysterious Lieutenant Flynn, RN, suddenly appeared. He was plausible, and claimed to have won decorations, Sicilian and British, in the recent war. Hownam accepted him as 'a gentleman and brother officer', and immediately presented him to the Princess. 'His agreeable, open, and candid manners pleased much.' Apparently, with the ending of the war he had decided to remain in Sicily, 'whether from private reasons or otherwise I do not know', said Hownam, displaying, it must be admitted, astonishing trustfulness. A handsome naval officer was a welcome addition to Caroline's entourage; the British Navy was accepted as a guarantee of his respectability, and it was not long before he was asking if he might join the party. The Princess was delighted, and so was Hownam, who was 'much pleased at having a companion a little after my own heart, for since leaving Italy, the household was composed only of Italians, and such a set as I could not in conscience make intimates of'.[1]

Hownam and Flynn set off together on horseback, their destination Messina, where they were to find the vessel recommended to the Princess. She was a polacca, a three-masted Mediterranean merchant ship, about 280 tons—'new, well fashioned and to all appearances would sail well'. These English sailors were critical of anything foreign, but the ship passed muster and the transaction was completed. Hownam set out alone to report to the Princess, leaving Flynn, who spoke fluent Italian, to superintend the refitting and restocking of the polacca, and to sail her, after two weeks' quarantine, back to Catania. 'The Princess was kind enough to approve and commend all I had done.'

On Monday 1 April 1816, the party sailed from the port of Augusta bound for Tunis. No sooner had they set sail than a thick fog enveloped them, obliging Flynn, who was in command, to lay the ship to. She rolled uncomfortably in the ground swell—oh, for HMS *Leviathan*!—and everyone was seasick; or, as Hownam put it, 'the bubble of the sea' made the ship 'rather uncomfortable to women and landsmen'. Soon he began to regret having undertaken the conduct of this voyage; and evidently the Princess, egged on by Pergami, blamed him for what he could not help, the behaviour of the elements.

Next morning when the fog lifted, cheerfulness returned. Cape Bon was sighted, and 'a good breeze led us under topsails and foresails safe into the Bay of Tunis'. Here Mr Oglander, the British Consul, came aboard, having sent to inform the Bey, Mamoodh Bashaw, of the Princess's arrival. She landed, said Hownam, 'under the long and heavy salutes of the cannon of the Goletta, Turks being fond of pomp and salutes'.[2]

The Bey did not make his appearance immediately, but sent three of his ministers, magnificent Arabs, to offer congratulations to the Princess upon her arrival, and to invite Her Royal Highness to stay in one of his palaces. Caroline, who professed to hate Court ceremony, now found herself the centre of an elaborate Oriental welcome which went on for days. The Bey was evidently determined to impress the English Princess with his wealth and power before he received her in person. Flags of all nations flew, and a long procession of carriages was formed, and round it tremendous state reception took place: horsemen careered wildly, flourishing sabres, 'changing their weapons at full gallop from gun to sabre, from sabre to pistol and dagger . . .'[3]

'Arriving at the palace,' said Hownam, 'we were saluted with guns and musketry and the howling of veiled Arab women who stood at the gate.' The noise was shattering but the scene was one of wild beauty, with horses and riders clothed in a rich variety of colours.

At the door of the palace the Princess was received by the two sons of the Bey, and escorted into his presence. He was a stately man of sixty-five, with a long white beard. He kept his seat when Caroline approached, but laid his hand on his heart, and bowed his head in greeting; then indicated to her to be seated. Beside him on his divan lay his snuff-box, his pistols and dagger, all thickly studded with diamonds; his love of glitter was comparable with the Prince Regent's.

Caroline was a great success with the Bey, who liked plump ladies. In due course the English Princess asked if she might visit his wife. This was a bold request and might well have been misconstrued, for the Bey had three wives and a number of other ladies in his seraglio. But, taking the key of the women's apartments from under him, and putting the dagger and pistols in his girdle, he got up, and offering his arm to the Princess entered the apartment by a strong door, through which only he and his two sons passed. 'His giving his arm to the Princess,' Hownam noticed, 'was a thing strange and uncommon, as we read in the faces of his courtiers.'[4]

'Her Royal Highness's description of the interior of the seraglio leaves me no reason to regret not being of the party,' said Hownam. The favourite wife of the Bey was 'so exceedingly fat as not to have been out of her room for several months'. Indeed, all the ladies were enormous. A certain berry, mixed with rice, was their regular diet, and successfully built up the attractive layers of fat. All the ladies, the Princess reported, were 'more or less embonpoint': she must have felt sylph-like beside them. They evidently regarded her with suspicion, and there was some whispering when, attempting European manners, the Bey once again offered Caroline his arm.

From now, daily entertainments were arranged for the party, and there were expeditions to Carthage and other ancient places which Caroline wanted to visit. In a letter to Sir William Gell, she boasts of her happiness.

'I am at Tunis living in the real [royal] Palace of the Bey . . . and I can assure you I am as happy as the day is long . . . I have been three times in the seraglio and received most kindly. I have seen the *Dancing of the Country*, and three very fine dinner the Bey's sons—very fin young men—have given to me. In short I could write a volume to you about all what I have seen here —I am living in a perfectly enchantment the dear Arrebeanin and Turcs are quite darlings their kindness I shall never forgette—I have received the most superb presents . . .' Among them were two lion cubs and three Arab horses—and a Roman bath covered in mosaic; she had also been collecting 'all sorts of curiosities' to take home'—'medailles and fin *Mosaiques* and a small statue which was found at Carthage . . . never have been taken much notice of'.

Caroline's archaeological research was given a free rein, and she was forced to tell her dear Anacharsis of some of her findings which she hoped would be keepings. 'As England has ever behaved so ill to me not to give me a Other ship to continue my voyage I shall certainly send them no antiquities not even my o[w]nself, good sound antiquite.' (She thought this funny.) And having cocked a snook at the British Admiralty, 'I have at last a most charming ship of my own . . . Sicilian polacca . . . Captain Flinn who has commanded for four years the flotilling in Itaila [Italy] is now upon half pay and he commands my ship besides L-ten Hownam who I have myself placed in the Navy and has been my protégé since sixteen years.'[5] She then outlined her future journeys, which were to culminate in a pilgrimage to Jerusalem. After that she had not decided what she would do; 'but I have not the most distance plan of returning to England'. 'My daughter', she adds casually, 'going to be married to the Duke of Coburg the *first of May.*' Caroline had not been invited to the wedding, and covered her feelings by making a joke. 'I shall not return till I shall meet a new race which will be my *grand children.* I can assure you,' she adds, 'I can assure you that the soi-disant Barberiann are much more real kind and obligeant to me than all the Civil people of Europe, for which reason I shall certainly remain with them as long as I can . . . I am quite a Philosopher I go my own way and I do not trouble myself about what their foolish tongues may say about me or not. I am in perfectly good Health and Spirit and I have all the Hearts of the People at Tunis.'[6]

This delightful state of things was interrupted by the sudden arrival at Tunis of the British Navy under the command of Lord Exmouth, threatening bombardment unless the Bey immediately handed over all slaves. It was an embarrassing predicament. Caroline had already been asked to intercede on behalf of five Italians captured as slaves in the war, and had obtained their release from the Bey. But the present situation was serious: many Tunisians were refusing to part with their slaves, and the British Navy was under orders to shoot. Caroline, accepting the Bey's lavish hospitality, was in an embarrassing and dangerous situation. 'I think', said Hownam solemnly, 'I saved Tunis from an attack by the Fleet.' As a naval officer and the Bey's guest, he was in a position to act as go-between. Negotiations were entered into in which Caroline figured as a heroine: 'The Minister of the Bey came to the Princess . . . to force they would not yield, but would surrender the slaves to Her Royal Highness, and in fact do everything that was required.'

This proposal could hardly have been taken seriously, but it paved the way to a peaceful settlement, and eventually to the abolition of slavery in Tunis. Meanwhile, Caroline proceeded with her plan for the day, which was to have dinner ('served in the greatest splendour and on the finest French china') with the Bey's elder son, Sidi Hassan. 'The magnificence of the banquet exceeds all imagination,' wrote Hownam (a good trencherman)—'and notwithstanding the present political circumstances, nothing was altered in the . . . gaiety of the host or of his numerous court.'[7]

During her stay in Tunis the Princess met Count Borgia, a fellow archaeologist, whom she had known in Naples. 'He was a general in the Neapolitan army,' said Hownam, 'a most agreeable and gifted man with great culture . . . a most amusing and instructive cicerone.' 'He has travelled all over the interrieur of Tunis,' said Caroline, 'and he writs his diary which he has in parts read to me, and I can affirm he is perfectly right and correct in all his remarks about the different antiquities . . .'[8]

Her interest was not just in the loot: she was genuinely eager to learn, indefatigable in her search for ancient places. Illiterate and uneducated, on this tour she displayed a talent—with no guide-book to help her—for studying the past, and an appreciation of beauty, which are unexpected. On setting out she had announced that she was going to write a history of her life and adventures. Had she done so, she might now be esteemed as an intrepid traveller—another Hester Stanhope—and the smears on her character would have faded into insignificance.

But she was preoccupied by other matters. We do not hear much about Pergami at this time, but he was undoubtedly there, close to the Princess and attending to her wants. It seems unlikely that he was deeply interested in archaeology, but undoubtedly he was deeply interested in pleasing Caroline. His success was beyond question; she adored him, she was 'happy as the day is long', and the informal, gipsy life suited her. By now she had discarded her carriage on inland journeys, and rode astride, in Hessian boots and with a sabre strapped to her side.

She planned to reach Jerusalem on 1 June 1817, but for one reason and another she was behind schedule. After a journey as fraught with perils as those of St Paul—chased by pirates, in danger of shipwreck by sudden storms, threatened by the plague, which was rampant—at last she anchored at Jaffa. Here the party was refused permission to land, as through some misunderstanding the Princess's permit was only made out for herself and five pilgrims. The journey to Jerusalem could not take place unless this janissary captain changed his mind, which was unlikely.

'I advised the Princess to up anchor,' said Hownam, 'which we did, and ran again for St Jean d'Acre where we arrived the next day, leaving our surly friend, who probably only awaited a present, to chew the cud by himself. I went on shore, accompanied by Pergami . . .'[9] The Pasha 'threw bright prospects on the voyage to come, and was indignant at the behaviour of the soldier in command at Jaffa'.

The celebrated defence of Acre against Napoleon by Sir Sydney Smith (Caroline's Sir Sydney) was not forgotten, and this Pasha was enthusiastically pro-English. He greeted the Princess with delight. The soldier who had refused permission for her party to land was reported and subsequently beheaded. Punishments in these parts, Hownam noted, were fierce and ruthless. 'The Pacha's prime minister is a Jew who wants an eye, an ear and a nose, it being a punishment of the former Pacha, and the quantities of persons one sees in the streets without noses leaves room for a thousand surmises.'[10]

That evening the party set out . . . 'A sort of litter, called a Tatchtarwen' and pulled by two mules, was provided for Caroline, but she preferred to ride, and asked that a donkey should be found for her on which she would ride into Jerusalem. This whim has been taken as an example of her dottiness; but it seems that she was taking the pilgrimage seriously. Brought up without religion, Caroline now described herself to Gell as 'a good Christhinne'. From time to time in Italy, she sat hand in hand with Pergami in Catholic churches, and evidently it was with complete sincerity that she applied herself to studying the historic evidence of Christianity.

The heat was intense, and Caroline decided to travel by night and rest during the day. The pilgrims were followed for some miles by a crowd of mixed nationalities. At three in the morning they arrived at Nazareth.

'We got most excellent bread here,' said Hownam: the most important citizen of this poverty-stricken town was the baker, 'who every day makes from two to three hundred loaves . . . to look at Nazareth, you would suppose that quantity was not consumed in a week.' Here they spent the day visiting the miracles and holy places, and in the evening proceeded on their journey. The kind and friendly Pasha of Acre had sent camels bearing tents for their protection against the hot sun. One, for the Princess, was 'very large, and double, having a corridor all round. The tent was green and might have been twenty or thirty feet in diameter. A large couch was prepared in the middle but she always lay on her travelling bed.' Eleven camels, Hownam noted with respect, carried this equipage.

At nine o'clock on the evening of 11 June the pilgrims entered the holy city.

'It would be impossible', wrote Hownam, 'to paint the scene. Men, women, children, Jews, Turks, Arabs, Armenians, Greeks, Catholics and infidels, all—came out and received us'—'*Ben venute!*' they cried, as the Princess with her train of pilgrims moved in slow procession by the light of flaring torches, and 'many fingers extended towards the Royal Pilgrim with "that's her" '. Hownam admitted that at this moment his feelings 'mixed up of fatigue and religion were almost solemn and certainly laughable'.[11]

This might describe the whole pilgrimage—solemn in intention, evocative and even emotional, but at intervals toppling from sublime to ridiculous. Hownam, the Protestant, was inclined to criticize the preparations made for their reception at the Catholic monastery. 'I was tolerably lodged in a cell with William Austin', but 'we were almost suffocated in the night by Friar

John not trimming the lamp properly.'[12] All the same, he enjoyed being sprinkled in the Church of the Holy Sepulchre with rose water and incense 'on our approach to anything sacred'. 'The padre', he said, 'did not economize at all: it is infinitely agreeable.'

On they went, to Mount Zion by torchlight, and the next day ('the Princess still on the same ass') to Bethlehem, 'a wretched habitation indeed', with a wretchedly poor population, who lived by the sale to tourists of cheap gew-gaws—beads and ornaments of mother-of-pearl. The spot where Christ was born was marked, said Hownam, by a round gold plate let into the floor of the Temple built on the site. 'In this temple were so many saints and apostles that I forget one half of them.'[13] The monks were anxious that the party should miss nothing, and they were encouraged to visit every shrine and every holy place, leading them finally to the Via Crucis, where they retrod the ground trod by Christ to Calvary—'the different places where He fell, where He was insulted . . . the house of Pilate . . . the room in which our Saviour was judged and rejected'.[14]

It is not surprising, at the end of the day, to learn that Caroline was 'rather fatigued'. The next day they went through the desert to Jordan. 'We wanted to go to the mouth of the river where it falls into the Dead Sea but everyone agreed that it was too far to venture.' The heat was intense, but the Princess wished to take home some Jordan water and would not rest till she had achieved this 'object of her voyage'. The party, which numbered about 200 began to flag: they had had enough. The Arabs were afraid of being attacked under cover of darkness by rival tribes. They spread a general uneasiness, and 'anxiety was strongly marked on the countenance of our Turkish escort while we remained on the banks of the river'.

Caroline was obliged, reluctantly, to give in. She was deeply disappointed: she had planned to pursue the journey into Egypt. Now, to oblige her followers she agreed to play safe and return to Jerusalem. Here, on their arrival, an important ceremony took place—the Dubbing of the Knights of the High Order of Jerusalem.

Three members of the Princess's suite were nominated to receive this honour: William Austin, Bartholomew Pergami, and Michele Schiavini, who boldly but not altogether truthfully took the oaths of being nobly born and of being persons of property which they would on occasion sacrifice for the defence of the Holy Catholic Apostolic religion; and upon these oaths they were booted and spurred and had buckled round their waists the so-called 'Epée of Godfrey de Bouillon'.

Hownam was clearly uneasy about the validity of this Order; but he does not even mention another ceremony in which he himself took part, and which is described by Graziano Paolo Clerici. In this the Princess established the Order of St Caroline, nominating Pergami its Grand Master and the other men of her party Knights—all this in the deepest solemnity and with regard to traditional ceremony. The order consisted of a red cross bearing the familiar motto *Honi soit qui mal y pense*, and was to be called by the name of St Caroline of Jerusalem. It was to be worn by 'all the faithful knights who have had the honour of accompanying her [the Princess] on her pilgrimage to the Holy Land'. The Grand Master was to wear the cross round his neck, the other Knights on a ribbon through their top button-hole. 'The ribbon shall be lilac and silver.'

And so, sporting this Order of which they were the only members, St Caroline's pilgrimage left the Holy Land. Their ship awaited them at Jaffa, and they set sail for home. But it soon became apparent that the long sea-journey would not be as easy as they had hoped. They were delayed by sheltering from storms, changing course to escape pirates, and worst of all by the laws of quarantine which were in full force at every port on their route. They were unprepared for such interminable delays and it became clear that their supply of fresh water was not going to last. Water had to be rationed. The animals aboard began to suffer from being cooped up in the hold without exercise. They were carrying a number of horses, including a beautiful Arab chestnut mare, a present from the Governor of Jerusalem; and there were two donkeys—'the jackass which had carried the Princess through Palestine', and a very small one which Hownam had bought (surprisingly) for 'little Victorina', Pergami's child, who must by now have been two years old. Then there were the two lion cubs presented to Caroline by the Bey of Tunis, and which she planned to give away as soon as she reached Italy (she was not fond of cats). All these animals grew restive, smelly and noisy as the hopes of being allowed to land became remote. It was an intolerable delay, and the whole party was overcome by 'ennui and a desire for fresh provisions and safety'.

The health officer at Syracuse was totally unhelpful. Neither the Princess's rank nor her physician's declaration that the whole company was in perfect health could shake the decision of the Governor, who was adamant. The ship cruised from Syracuse to Messina, where it was equally impossible to land; and it became clear that the whole coast of Sicily was closed. An American squadron anchored at Messina tried to while away the time with music, and asked the Princess to name a tune for their bands to play.

'In an unguarded moment,' said Hownam, 'she asked for *Rule Britannia*.' This unfortunate mistake was passed off good-naturedly, the Americans evidently accepting that Britons never, never would be slaves and liked their own tunes best.

Caroline was desperately tired. Life at sea had lost its charms, and she longed to have the dry land under her feet. With Pergami's help, she thought of a scheme. Hownam, afraid of some wild idea which might involve her in disaster, was on tenterhooks. 'Now, Hownam, I have a plan, you shall see, you shall see, a very good plan,' she told him. 'I hope, madam, you will do nothing rash.'

'The poor lady' he wrote, 'was so completely fatigued that she told me frankly she would die if she did not get ashore.'[15] Crossing the Bay of Naples, they sailed up the coast to Terracina. Here, 'about fifteen miles off the land', they anchored, and the ship's boat was hoisted out. Hownam realized that Pergami was about to take a brave but desperately dangerous step which might involve the Princess in disaster. 'Pergami, Camara and Majocchi [the Princess's couriers] went into the boat and pulled for the shore' (presumably sailors did the pulling), 'and towards dark the boat returned, reporting that they had run a great risk but that our party had landed unseen . . . and had started for Rome.'

Now the plan was revealed to Hownam. An appeal, signed by Caroline, was being presented to the Pope through the powerful Cardinal, Consalvi.

'Hownam, you'll see, Consalvi is such an excellent good man, and the Pope, I am sure, he will be too happy.'

On the contrary, Consalvi, on reading the dispatch presented by Pergami, was extremely angry. He regretted much that such a step should have been taken, for not only did it involve the Princess in a dishonest plan, breaking the law of Italy, but he was well aware of the amount of bribery that must have carried Signor Pergami and his companions from Terracina to Rome. Pergami had used all his skill and effrontery—and now even this last difficult ditch was crossed. 'As the thing was without remedy,' said Consalvi, 'the Vatican must make the best of it.' The Princess was given a grant of permission to land 'with all the politeness and delicacy of the court of Rome'. Carriages were immediately hired and apartments secured at the hotel in the Place d'Espagne, and Pergami returned to the Princess flourishing a polite letter from His Eminence the Cardinal.

It was while waiting for Pergami's return that the Princess so disastrously fell flat on her face. Late at night, while she rested on a couch, a boat was heard approaching. She jumped up excitedly, but 'before I could get to her', wrote Hownam, 'her foot had caught in a rope and she fell, giving herself a black eye.' She made nothing of it. 'Where's the boat?' she cried. 'My God, have they succeeded? I'm sure they have.' But it was not the boat they expected, only a fisherman. Three hours later shouts awakened them. 'It was our party. "Eh bien, all is arranged and you have permission to land . . ." ' 'I congratulated them with all my heart,' said Hownam, 'and feasted on the joy of the good Princess, who repeated frequently, "I should have died if I had stayed much longer." '

As soon as they arrived in Rome, Caroline, her face covered in a veil, presented herself before Cardinal Consalvi. He told her that she had committed a great fault, and that he did not know what he should say to her. But he invited her to dinner.[16] 'The Princess, sitting down to this meal,' said Hownam, 'after so long existing upon anything but luxury, was a real pleasure to witness.'[17]

She was happy. Pergami had triumphed and the Pope was still her friend. This was confirmed when, a day or two later, she visited him at the Palace of Monte Cavallo. 'On going up the stairs', said Hownam, 'we heard a terrible noise on the first landing, and Her Royal Highness asked what that could be' . . . Consalvi told her that His Holiness had heard that she had an aversion to cats, and that he, having a great many, for fear she should see one had had them all shut up in one room—which seems a fitting note on which to bring Caroline's travels to an end.

Chapter Twenty-one

'MY PALACE', Caroline told Sir William Gell, 'is most superbe.' The Villa d'Este was certainly larger and far more ornate than when she had bought it a year before. The architect had taken advantage of her absence to concoct a number of fanciful additions as well as the necessary alterations, and to run up bills on all sides, which, with the news of the Princess's return, began to pour in. Hownam was busy at his desk, sorting out the alarming mass of debts and trying to calm his mistress. Dispatches, she said, would have to be sent immediately to London and some arrangement would have to be made with the bankers. She had never had to worry about her debts before: if she exceeded her allowance she had been given credit. Now Messrs Coutts would have to sort things out. In any case, all this expense was nothing to do with her, she had not ordered all these things.

'The Princess,' said Hownam, . . . 'uttered to me bitter complaints of the licence the architect Batti had taken in furnishing the palace and making additions she had never ordered.'[1]

Hownam found that there were other debts as well as those for the house and road. It was decided that a letter must be sent to Brougham, who looked after the Princess's interests. Certainly her affairs were in a muddle, and her Italian bankers, Messrs Marietti, were unhelpful: her jewels, worth a considerable sum, were in their hands where she had left them before going away. Now Marietti refused to give them up until she paid back what she owed them. In Turkey she had had dealings with a firm called Scarramonger, from whom she had bought 'carpets, painted glass, etc., etc.' for a sum 'not to exceed £500'. Now a bill arrived from Messrs Scarramonger amounting to £1,200. 'This the Princess absolutely refuses to pay.' Altogether, the poor woman was in a fix. Her quarterly allowance from England, £8,000, was totally inadequate to meet the extra expenses in which she had involved herself: she was naturally generous, and had little or no idea of managing her money. Soon after arriving at the Villa d'Este she bought a villa for Pergami—Villa Barone: it was to be a present for his little daughter, Vittorina, and before long it was inhabited by numerous members of the Pergami family, including Pergami's wife, who seldom showed herself.

The Baron himself, not satisfied with this present, was clamouring like a spoilt child for yet another title: 'a titelle for a certain Baron', said Caroline. That of the Order of Malta, which he had received at Catania during their tour had not been validated, and Caroline begged the Austrian chamberlain, Count Gizziliere, to write to his Emperor and have this put right. Pergami would then acquire the rank of Comte, with leave to wear the decoration, as well as that of the Order of St Sepulchre which he had received at Jerusalem. It was, she wrote to Gizziliere, 'a matter of etiquette that any *subject* most ask leave of the Sovering to wear any forring order'.

Life at the Villa d'Este during the winter of 1816 was peaceful: 'we were pleased to be in what we might call a home', said Hownam. Casting aside her cares, Caroline appeared once more as 'the happy, merry soul' she had resolved to be when she left England. She kept open house, and her guests were allowed the run of the house and grounds. 'A hundred small amusements', said Hownam, 'passed away the time.' The Princess loved acting and dressing up, and 'sometimes a play was rehearsed in the theatre'. In the stables there were fifty horses, there were 'boats of all sizes', and the guests were free to fish or shoot if they wished. In the evenings they played billiards or card games or '*des petits jeux*' such as blind man's buff—and there was music. 'A Mr and Mrs Sapio', said Hownam, 'had come from England.' The Squallinis! Lady Charlotte Campbell would have groaned. They came 'not quite as guests of the Princess': it was their son, the once idolized Chanticleer, who had received an invitation, and arrived bringing his father, mother, and grandmother, his wife, and one child unnamed. The Princess gave them a house to live in at the end of the lake. There were now concerts at which Chanticleer gave vent to what Hownam—not so critical perhaps as Lady Charlotte—called his wonderful talent for singing.

Caroline passed the winter in this way, but it was not in her nature to remain quiet for long. 'I shall be in Rome the Holy Week,' she told Gell, 'which is the first week in April. I trust I shall not be a April Fool to the Respectable Pope.' She also planned a visit to the ex-Empress Marie-Louise, Napoleon's widow, at Parma. (This was the occasion when, sitting over the fire before dinner, she fell flat on her back with her legs in the air.) She knew that the Milan Commission was watching all her movements, and evidently she was determined to show that she was not ostracized by foreign royalties. She visited the King and Queen of Sardinia, but chose to stay at an inn rather than the Royal Palace. 'I do believe', said Hownam, 'that independent of the Princess's dislike to the etiquette of a court, and her intention to remain en famille with her own people, economy had a strong weight in her determination.'

She paid visits to some of her relations in Germany, driving in appalling weather to Munich where she was royally received by the King of Bavaria and the Hereditary Prince but again insisted upon staying at an inn. Her visit was 'one continued round of visits, dinners, concerts, balls, plays and soirees'.[2] In Hownam's account, the royal names are poured out: he obviously enjoyed his Princess's importance (and possibly felt that Pergami was temporarily put in his place). At Nuremberg Caroline was to meet her aunt, the Margravine of Bayreuth. Her castle had just been burnt down, and she had suggested meeting her niece in Nuremberg, where she stood in the window of an inn, watching Caroline's carriage approaching. 'Now, if that figure should happen to be my aunt,' Caroline said to Hownam. 'It were impossible, Madam: it is the signboard of the hotel.' 'But I had to apologize to the Princess afterwards when she, in fits of laughter, reminded me of my mistake.' This ancient lady must have presented an extraordinary appearance: 'Her face of eighty well marked years had the rouge plastered on like a mountebank,' said Hownam: she wore a black wig, with ringlets, among which her own white hair appeared in wisps, and her dress, in a bygone fashion, was that of a girl of sixteen. She was attended by two very elderly ladies and a chamberlain, and invited the party to take tea with her—a melancholy ceremony which evidently took place daily at this hour. 'A side glance from the Princess spoke all she felt,' wrote Hownam, 'and ten o'clock relieved us from the Dead March operation to the gaiety of our own little circle.'

After investigating the lakes and toyshops for which Nuremberg was celebrated, the Princess decided to go to Vienna. She sent a courier ahead, claiming her right as Princess of Wales to stay at the British Embassy. Unfortunately she was not on the best of terms with the British Minister, Lord Charles Stewart, who returned an answer that he could not receive her Royal Highness as he was about to leave Vienna. But the Princess, undeterred, gave orders to proceed immediately: she wished to confront Lord Charles who, she knew from the police, had visited the Villa d'Este several times during her absence and had offered bribes to local peasants and others to give information. 'The police at Milan', she told Gell, 'is very exact to give any proper information if any more spy are about the Villa d'Este.' In the meanwhile she would deal with Lord Charles herself. She wished to let him know that she was aware of his activities.

Her idea, wrote Hownam, was 'to confront him face to face . . . placing a couple of loaded pistols on the table, and calling upon him if he was a man to accept one and at least give her as a woman, an equal chance against her enemies'.[3] 'She wanted *my* pistols,' said Hownam, horrified at the whole project. Politely, he told her that nothing would induce him to be a party to such a scheme: but undeterred she said she would find others, and so she did . . . 'I easily recognized the owner,' said Hownam dramatically. 'It was Pergami.'

It was perhaps fortunate that by the time the party reached Vienna, Lord Charles had gone. Prince Metternich, suave, icily polite, represented the Austrian Emperor, who excused himself from giving the Princess a state reception owing to the preparation for his daughter's marriage, but offered not very enthusiastically to see her *en famille*. Caroline was not interested in this invitation: she decided to leave Vienna at once. After some aimless wanderings she returned to the Villa d'Este, where she learned that the new Governor at Como had been ordered by Metternich and Lord Charles Stewart to put a watch on the Villa d'Este, 'which', she said, 'has given me the plan to go to my island which upon the Lac Majore: Isola Muderi . . .'[4]

Life at Villa d'Este was becoming intolerable. To add to her worries, Caroline learned from the police that they suspected her *maître d'hotel*, John Heronymous, of spying and accepting bribes. This German was a trusted retainer—'I have never yet found Hieronymous a *traitor* in any way'—and she had just sent him to London with dispatches to Canning, and with orders to find out how much she was entitled to receive from the late Duke of Brunswick's will.

The sooner her debts could be paid the better. In the spring she would be visiting Rome, and to have a settled establishment there was her firm intention. At Como the atmosphere of spying, intrigue and bribery was overpowering, and she did not know whom to trust. It was discovered that English agents had been offering bribes to all her servants during her long absence abroad; and one of these, her outrider, Maurice Crede, a German, protested his innocence but was dismissed.

As it turned out, Ompteda did not get the keys; and Hieronymous was not involved in this or any other plot. 'I must now informe you', Caroline wrote to Anacharsis, 'that our mutual friend Hieronymous is not Guilty but a most innocent man possible.'

She went on to explain that Maurice Crede had been in the service of King Joachim, 'a former acquaintance of Baron Ompteda', and this man, Frederich Ompteda,* was the villain. 'Last years he visit sometimes me in the contry. I even offered to take him in my suite in my journey [but] he

* This Hanoverian Baron, accredited to the Papal Court, had been chosen to work for the Milan Commission by Count Munster, British chargé d'affaires. 'The Baron will locate himself as close as possible to the Princess, with the object of accumulating such evidence of her doings as can be brought up against her in Court . . .'[5]

refused on account of Ill Health.'[6] During her absence, Ompteda had tried to get statements from all the servants, and '*these all refused* to speak *ill of me* and even refused the money which [he] offered to them very riskelly'. Maurice Crede did accept money, and promised in return 'to have fals keys to my rooms and to interduice Mr Ompteda in the Night time'. All this he confessed in the presence of the Prefect of Como, begging with tears to be taken back into the Princess's household. He was forgiven, after signing a written statement that he had been bribed by Ompteda.[7] But unfortunately it was discovered that one of Caroline's maids, Annette Preising, was in the family way, and 'I found it necessary to send her back to Germany,' said Caroline, 'on account of this Maurice Crede.'

Hownam now decided that something must be done by him to protect the Princess from the perfidious Ompteda. He sent him a challenge: 'You will perhaps be surprised when you learn the object of this letter. It is not likely to be agreeable to you to know that your conduct has been unmasked, and that very soon the infamous and degrading manner in which you have responded to the infinite courtesies of the Princess will be made known to the world.' He went on to challenge the Count to a duel the following morning at eight o'clock.

Ompteda did not care for this at all, and wrote a slimy letter in which he appeared to accept the challenge but suggested a delay while arrangements were discussed and seconds appointed. While this was going on, Saurau the Governor of Milan was at the Villa d'Este, and learned from the Princess about the duel. He decided that Ompteda must be banished from Milan: the Count, immensely relieved, immediately wrote to Hownam explaining that he had given his word of honour not to fight, and that he was obliged to leave the country.

'Count Saurau', wrote Caroline, '. . . himself send him from Milan and even from all the states of the Empereur [of Austria]; I trust that the Pope in case he should come to *Rome* send him off *also*.'[8]

She had written to Mr Canning about it, she said, and went on to assure her dear Anacharsis that she was 'very happy never despondent. I have a charming Theatre at my Hause and very offen we play French proverbe and Italian operas. Count Saurau and all such good proper people have been present and where [were] much amused . . . We are all very merry indeed.'

But the days of the Villa d'Este were numbered. It was too near Milan, too easily accessible to the Milan Commission; in spite of her professed enjoyment there, the Princess began to hate the place.

Accordingly, after one or two business trips to her bankers in Milan and to Munich, where she succeeded in selling her 'fine Antiquite' (or loot from the Mediterranean tour) to the Regent of Bavaria, she and her entourage left Como for Rome.

As they drove away, Hownam bade adieu to 'this paradise of habitations'. 'A conviction crossed my mind that we should never see it again.' He began to regret the things he had left behind—'A quantity of Turkish pipes, three or four bags of the best tobacco Constantinople could afford, four quart bottles of the water I had taken myself from the River Jordan, and various ornaments which, though of no intrinsic value, I feel the loss of.'[9]

At Ancona on the Adriatic coast, Caroline had accepted Lucien Bonaparte's offer of a 'delightful palace' . . . 'near the sea and most charming air and situation'. She spent some weeks there, but a 'country villa' had been found for her near Rome, and—issuing broadcast invitations to Gell and others to visit her there—she hurried across Italy. She was light-hearted: she believed that her finances were improving. It is true the Prince Regent had prevented her receiving the capital from her brother's bequest, leaving her only the interest, but she was optimistic. 'Your two quarters are to be paid immediately,' she told Gell who had had to wait a long time for his promised pension. 'I have left Mr Marietti, my former banker,' she wrote, 'but a most honest one I have found at Milan and things will go now in a good Regular manner.' It was dishonest bankers, she firmly believed, rather than lack of money, that caused financial troubles. And wherever she went on her journeys she continued to sprinkle largesse. Whatever Pergami asked for, she gave him. He knew better than she did whether or not she could afford it.

After a month, Caroline had had enough of Rome. She thought of going back to Ancona, but Lucien Bonaparte's charming villa was occupied; and it was at Pesaro, some forty-five miles north, that she finally decided to establish herself. 'I am so happy so Tranquille and so Respected here,' she wrote, 'that I cannot wish neither for a better situation nor Company . . . Consalvi and the Pope have done everything to make me think this Place quiet a Paradis . . . I shall probably remain here all my life till my death . . .'[10]

What a tragedy it was that she did not.

But were things quite so idyllic? Caroline had left the Villa d'Este in a hurry, and evidently no one in her suite—except Pergami—was fully aware of what was happening. She was leaving for good because she could not pay her creditors, and as soon as she had gone the Villa was put up for sale. She owed large sums of money: the bankers, Messrs Marietti, were hanging on to her jewels, and her account with Messrs Thomas Coutts could not be touched without authority from the trustees appointed by the Regent.

There had been an unpleasant and rather worrying business when a person unknown presented to her banker in Venice a letter of credit for £2,500 signed T. Coutts. This signature, wrote James Brougham,* 'was as like T. C.'s as it was like the Great Mogul's'. Brougham took a serious view. The transaction, signing a false document on behalf of the Princess of Wales, 'would assuredly be in Chancery—and in Parliament in all its force if steps be not taken'. He advises extreme caution: 'I am alarmed lest a word be said to offend him [Coutts]: if he gives up the account all the veil that yet lays over the transaction would be withdrawn and then . . . only figure the destruction that must overtake that poor *lunatick* (I call her nothing more) if she rushes on in this way!'

Hownam became embroiled; and wrote an ill-judged letter defending the Princess and making light of the transaction, which infuriated Brougham. He told Gell: 'I admire him very much for his warmth and devotion towards the Princess (whom of course he don't know as she is) but for Godsake keep him from getting her into scrapes—she really is on the brink of one'.[11]

She certainly was. As well as the letter of credit, there had been three bills of credit in foreign countries, amounting to another £2,500. The Venice affair, wrote Brougham, 'was in a word—*forgery*—the three bills—only *swindling* . . . I saw the Venetian banker's letter detailing the whole. Our friend,' he added, 'went off early next day from Venice.' Our friend? There can be little doubt as to his identity.

Caroline wrote to Gell that she could not understand 'the muddle about Venice'. She must have had more grasp of her money entanglements than Hownam had given her credit for; for she eventually produced a document which stated (in French) that since a payment on 8 June 1815 a bank in Venice had not made another payment to the Princess or to any one of her suite.

The affair, which became known as the Venice Forgery, dragged on, and it was two years before Caroline was able to tell Anacharsis that the Villa d'Este was sold 'to the Marquis Antalte who is one of the first great family in the Roman Estate'. 'All Pecuniary affairs have been settled,' she announced cheerfully—adding 'that in the cours of three years these detes will be paid by me.' The bankers Marietti were bringing a lawsuit, she said, 'against Brougham and even Mr Coutts in the Court of Chancery'—but 'by having myself and my lawyer arranged this affair all lawsuit falls upon the ground'. She was delighted with herself, and with 'the Baron' (Pergami) who had 'very generously' offered to guarantee payment of all her debts 'which are

* James Brougham to Chevalier Tomassio, now Caroline's Chamberlain . . . 'a very delightful man in every Respect'.

14,000 louis d'or, and to pay these himself in case of *my death*'. These were brave words.

Meanwhile, the sea and sunshine at Pesaro were improving her health and spirits. She went riding and 'took the sea bathing almost every morning'.

Another cause of rejoicing was that after a break of nearly three years she was in touch once more with her daughter.

When Caroline had gone abroad, Princess Charlotte was forbidden to write to her. Only after the death of the Duke of Brunswick at Quatre Bras was she allowed to send a few formal lines of condolence. Mother and daughter were thus entirely separated; but of course Caroline knew from the newspapers and from friends of Charlotte's marriage to Prince Leopold of Saxe-Coburg. After this event, the Regent was no longer able to prevent Charlotte from writing, and letters began to be exchanged.

'I have received a very agreeable letter from my Daughter and from my Son-in-law,' she told Gell, 'surely these are true in their sentiments towards me which I can not doubt.' She saw practical as well as sentimental advantages in the reunion, encouraging herself with the thought that one day her daughter would be Queen. 'I have certainly a great deal of happiness in store for me if a certain *Tyrant* should ever *die* but I hear he has not such plan—that he is much better health than for many years . . .'[12]

On 29 October 1817 she wrote—'I receive very often letters from my Daughter they [these] both are very kind and attached to me they have sent their picture to me and a great many Prints of their Resemblance.' The couple were living at Claremont in Surrey, and were awaiting the birth of their first child. 'I shall now soon be a Grand Mother and I trust to Haven that then all cabals about me will be at an *End*. I am then a well established old lady and no more scandals can be created about poor me: besaids the great world I have quiet given up, and England I shall probably no more see.'[13] But she begs her daughter 'for the futuer' to give Sir William Gell 'the Situation of Minister at Naples, Which', she told Gell, 'she as promised to do if ever she was *Queen* . . .'

Anacharsis never received his appointment, for on 5 November 1817, after giving birth to a stillborn son, Princess Charlotte died.

The news did not reach Charlotte's mother for nearly three weeks, and then in a private letter delivered by a King's Messenger on his way to Naples and Rome. She received no official intimation, and the only person who thought of telling her was Prince Leopold. Too stricken to write himself, he ordered his private secretary to send a few lines to the Princess of Wales. In the small hours of 30 November Hownam was summoned to receive a letter addressed to the Princess. The messenger told him that it was to announce the death of Princess Charlotte.

Hownam did not know how to break this news: he feared that 'not knowing that she had even been ill, she would conclude immediately that it was a messenger of good tidings rather than the harbinger of death'. He delayed waking the Princess till nearly her usual time of rising. Then he knocked on her door. 'I said I wished to speak to her if she would permit me. In a few minutes she came out.'

' "Well, Hownam, what is the matter that you wake me?"

'I said, "I have something, madam, to communicate to you."

' "What is it?"

' "A King's messenger arrived this morning."

' "Ah, Princess Charlotte is delivered."

'I remained silent.

' "She is ill!"

' "I am afraid she is, Madam."

' "Dangerously so?"

' "From what I can learn from the messenger I think—" ' A pause.

' "Has he letters?"

' "Yes, Madam."

'Turning very pale, she said, "My God, Hownam, what is the matter?"

'She paused a little, then tears came into her eyes and she said, "Well, my dear Hownam, I am prepared for the worst, give me the letter". I put it into her hands . . . She seized it, and seeing the black seal, "My God, she is dead, poor Charlotte!" She opened and read it, and, giving me the letter, "It is just so, Hownam, poor dear Charlotte," and cried a great deal. I endeavoured all I could to encourage her. "Well," she said, "she will never know all the torments her poor mother has suffered or will suffer, it is probably better. This is not only my last hope gone, but what has England lost?" '[14]

What indeed? 'It really was as if every household throughout England had lost a favourite child,' said Brougham.[15]

The woeful news spread over the country like a pall. Such high hopes had been placed upon Princess Charlotte—the future Queen—and her heir. Shops, theatres, the Royal Exchange, the docks, were closed and buildings were draped in black. Linen-drapers sold out of black cloth, and even tramps and beggars showed their respect by tying scraps of black round their arms. In Pesaro Caroline went into deepest mourning. She wished her household to do the same, but 'there were persons', said Hownam, 'who would have persuaded the Princess that mourning not being the custom in

Italy, she might dispense with putting the household in black'.[16] This piece of sympathy proceeded from Pergami, who, said Hownam, professed to be trying to save the Princess an unnecessary expense, while at the same time 'grabbing all the money he could by any means filch'.[17]

'The poor lady was about to consent,' said Hownam, 'but after a moment's reflection repulsed the idea and ordered black.'

Chapter Twenty-two

HOWNAM hated Pergami. He made no attempt to hide his awareness of the Baron's dishonesty and was disgusted by his endless attempts to take advantage of the Princess's fondness. From time to time the antagonism exploded into rage; and it must have been after one of these angry scenes that Caroline decided to send Hownam to England with letters to deliver to Henry Brougham. There was evidently open war, in which Caroline sided with Pergami, for in Hownam's own words he left Pesaro 'for reasons which in honour and justice to myself I could not submit to'.

Nevertheless the Princess bade him an affectionate farewell and offered him a carriage, which he refused, and a suite of rooms at Kensington Palace which still belonged to her, and which he accepted.

The day after his arrival he called on Mr Brougham. 'What, Hownam, you here!' cried the great advocate. 'Then all is lost!' He went on to say that the Regent had often been heard to declare that while Hownam was with the Princess she would do nothing wrong, and that Hownam 'kept up the little respectability that remained'. During 'a couple of hours' conversation', Hownam must have made it clear that his position in the Princess's household was far from easy, and that he knew she was being swindled by the Pergami family. He believed that she was often prevented from spending money by Pergami's refusal to give it to her, and that the Princess's accounts were entirely in his hands.

Before going back to Italy, Joseph planned to pay a visit to his cousins who lived in France. Caroline, evidently anxious that he should not hurry back, had encouraged this. And so it was that when Brougham sent his younger brother James to visit the Princess at Pesaro and report upon what he found there, Joseph Hownam was away. James Brougham, like his brother, was a lawyer, but he was neither as asute nor as sharp at summing up a situation or a character. He was completely deceived by Pergami. 'I think him', he wrote 'a plain, straightforward *remarkably good sort of man*—assumes nothing, he has a great deal to do and is very active—quite a different man from what I expected.'[1] Pergami presented seemingly flawless financial statements which James Brougham accepted. 'If the Baron feathers his own nest, he takes care that no one else shall.'

The Princess was now established in her cottage, as she called it, which Pergami had bought with her money and which she named Villa Vittoria after Pergami's daughter. It is rather surprising to find that in this 'cottage' no less than eighty persons were employed—sixty-three indoor servants and seventeen in the stables. The Princess's establishment, on the other hand, was comparatively small, and consisted of 'le Baron' (Pergami); two Italian colonels who acted as chamberlains (very good sort of men, wrote the optimistic James); Pergami's brother Luigi, who was first equerry; 'a singer and his wife' (Chanticleer presumably); Pergami's sister, the Countess Oldi; Pergami's mother; and William Austin, now aged eighteen. There was also Vittorina, now a precocious child of five who addressed the Princess as Mama. Caroline, said Brougham, was as fond of this child as if she were her own.

Out to sea a ship lay at anchor, with a captain and eight men aboard, which cost the Princess 200 crowns a month; while at the Villa there was a regular guard of fourteen soldiers, which was allowed her by the Pope, to keep sentinel day and night.

This extravagance was made necessary by the Princess's fears. 'Great part is imaginary,' said Brougham, 'but still if she *has the fear* it matters little whether there are grounds or not.' From what we know of her it is hard to believe that the fears were Caroline's own: from what James Brougham says, it is more likely that they were invented and encouraged by Pergami, mindful of his own safety and solicitous on that account for Caroline's. 'She thinks', said Brougham, 'there are people hired to kill or poison her, and the kitchen is watched accordingly—two servants parade the hall all night, besides the guards on ye outside.' Pistols and blunderbusses, he added, were placed about the house, and dogs were on guard.

In spite of this melodramatic atmosphere, the Princess, he said, seemed very happy. She and the Baron were 'to all appearances man and wife, never was anything so obvious'. His picture was in every room. '*His room* [i.e. his sittingroom] is close to hers, and his *bedroom* the only one in that part of the house ... Perhaps there might be difficulty in proving the fact to find her guilty of high treason [which carried the death penalty] yet I should think that all the circumstances being stated wd. completely ruin her in ye opinion of the people of England. That once done, the Prince might get a divorce, or at any rate prevent her being Queen ...'

'I have had several very serious discussions with her,' Brougham said, 'on the subject of giving up England, and of all claims to be Queen.' This was evidently what she wished to do. With the death of Princess Charlotte the whole shape of future events was altered. There was no direct heir to the throne, and Caroline could no longer think of herself as mother and grandmother of future sovereigns. She could no longer make jokes about visiting England on the birth of her fifteenth grandchild, no longer promise tempting appointments to her friends when her daughter became Queen. She could see no future for herself in England, and she preferred to stay where she was, where she had made a home for herself and her motley crew of attendants, if only she might be allowed to live in peace. This mood of pious resignation was communicated to Sir William Gell.

'I only trust that the few years I have still to live to passe tranquille in a quiet removed place. I have given up for ever the great world and nothing can or shall bring me back to it.'[2]

'The Milan Inquisition', said James Brougham, 'has annoyed her most terribly. They have got hold of a maid, a Swiss, [Louisa Demont] who was with her . . . for some time . . . The Princess says that she [Demont] is a great *W*[*hore*] and her character being known, no one will believe her.' But Caroline was evidently uneasy about the evidence that this woman might give.[3] Demont had sharp eyes and a mind quick to jump to conclusions; moreover, her position as woman of the bedchamber had brought her into close contact with her mistress.

As well as Demont, a number of servants had been offered money by the Milan agents; but no evidence of any value, Caroline thought, could have been dragged from them. As for the gentry, 'all the good people and gentlemans have all declined to answer any questions and even the English which are at Milan . . . crie out oh shame! oh shame!'[4]

Nevertheless, month by month the scraps of evidence against the Princess grew in numbers if not in reliability. Then another event took place which made a dénoument inevitable. On 29 January 1820, the demented dream which for the last eight years had been the life of King George III came to an end. The Prince Regent, at fifty-seven, was proclaimed King George IV.

A divorce was now considered essential: the new King hoped to marry and beget an heir. But two days after his accession he became seriously ill from pleurisy and pneumonia and it was thought that he would die. 'What think you of the accounts of the King?' wrote Creevey to Brougham. 'He is, I apprehend rapidly approaching to his death.'[5] But just as the Duke of York was growing accustomed to the glorious vision of himself as King Frederick I, his elder brother rallied, made a miraculous recovery, and began to make plans for a coronation which would surpass in magnificence any other coronation in British history.

Caroline was on her way to Rome when news was brought of the death of

George III. As Brougham put it, she suddenly found herself Queen; moreover, she suddenly found that she had numerous supporters who expected her to return at once to England. Other, wiser friends implored her to stay in Italy, at least till arrangements as to her future position and income were made. Brougham had already suggested the terms on which she might consent to remain where she was; but Caroline had strong views as to her rights, and did not trust the Government. She would be prepared, she said, to ask 'for a Trial at Westminster Hall as I would have nothing to do with a *corrupted Parliament*'.[6] But now, determined to escape from the misery of continual espionage and to establish her claims for just treatment, she needed legal advice. Several Italian lawyers were already working for her, but at this point it was Brougham that she wished to see.

They were curiously wary of each other. He would not spare the time to go to Italy: the Baron assured her that she could not afford the expense of going to Paris. But finally, she went to St Omer on the road to Calais, where Brougham joined her at the Hôtel de l'Ancienne Porte. 'I found her', said he, 'surrounded by Italians and resolved to come to England.'

Brougham was accompanied by Lord Hutchinson, an elderly peer who was one of the King's cronies and was now entrusted with documents containing a proposition from His Majesty for Caroline's future. She refused point-blank to see him, but asked to see the King's proposals. Unfortunately Lord Hutchinson, upset perhaps by a very rough crossing, had lost the papers. He could not recollect, he told Brougham, exactly what the King had written. Caroline insisted upon being given, in writing, the terms of this proposition and was prepared, she said, to wait three hours for his answer. It was then 2 pm. At four o'clock, Brougham received Lord Hutchinson's effort of memory, written out for him by James Brougham as he had the gout and wrote 'with pain and difficulty'.

The Queen would receive £50,000 a year for life, provided that she agreed to renounce the title of Queen of England. She would also agree never again to live in England or to visit England. He forgot the bit about her name being removed from the prayer-book, but it made no difference: she dismissed the offer out of hand.

'Mr Brougham is commanded by the Queen to acknowledge receipt of Lord Hutchinson's letter and to inform his Lordship that it is quite impossible for her Majesty to listen to such a proposition.'

At this, Hutchinson wrote immediately that he was prepared to negotiate and would send a courier to England for further instructions, but before Brougham received this letter, Caroline had left St Omer and was on her way to Calais.

'Mr Brougham implores your Majesty to refrain from rushing into certain trouble; . . . or at least to delay taking this step until Lord Hutchinson shall have received fresh instructions . . .' Couriers sped post-haste along the road to Calais, bearing urgent letters of advice. 'I entreat your Majesty once more to reflect calmly and patiently upon the step about to be taken . . .' 'If your Majesty shall determine to go to England, . . . I earnestly implore your Majesty to proceed in the most private and even secret manner possible . . .'

But Brougham's advice was ignored. Like a commander-in-chief preparing for battle, Caroline of Brunswick had laid her plans and was fully equipped, she believed, to meet her powerful enemies on their own ground.

Caroline had hoped to arrive in London accompanied by an entourage of respectable and impeccably British supporters. 'Brougham has written to Lady Charlotte Lindsay to meet me and I think really Mr Craven should not lose any time to meet me at Calais,' she told Gell.[7] But at Calais her suite still consisted of only two persons. One was Lady Anne Hamilton, tall and angular, her 'Joan of Arc' of Blackheath days, for whom she had once tried to find a husband because 'she is so full of old maid's whims and prudery, it is quite tiresome to be under her surveillance'. But now Lady Anne's quirks were forgotten and Caroline was grateful for her loyalty.

The other, less reliable but even more ardent, supporter was Sir Matthew Wood, a City alderman and extreme radical who had urged the Queen to come to England in the hope of getting himself into the limelight and advancing his political career. He arranged for her reception at Dover, which was tumultuous, himself gave an interview to *The Times* about her plans and had arranged to escort her to London, where he offered her board and lodging at his house in South Audley Street. For the Queen of England, this invitation from the son of a Devonshire cloth-maker, himself a chemist and hop-merchant in the City, was unsuitable, not to say impertinent; but to Caroline it was an offer to be accepted without hesitation.

'The Queen's chief performer in this drama was that enlightened mountebank Alderman Wood,' wrote Lord Hutchinson, still angrily defending himself. 'I suspect that dull as he is the Alderman had . . . raised suspicions in her mind, not only against [Brougham] but against me.'

Queen Caroline crossed the Channel in the public ferry and landed at Dover on 6 June, to be greeted—presumably through some official oversight—by a royal salute of twenty-one guns from the Castle. The following day she drove to London, and her progress is described by Greville, the diarist, who rode out to meet the procession at Greenwich. 'The road,' he said, 'was thronged with an immense multitude the whole way . . . she was everywhere received with the greatest enthusiasm. It was a modest little procession of three carriages: William Austin and the Alderman's son were in one, and servants were crushed into another. The Queen 'travelled in a rather shabby open landau, Alderman Wood sitting by her side, and Lady Anne Hamilton opposite. Everybody was disgusted at the vulgarity of Wood sitting in the place of honour, while the Duke of Hamilton's sister was sitting backwards in the carriage.' He caused further disgust, according to Greville, when the procession reached London, by standing up and giving three cheers when the Queen's coach passed Carlton House.

'It is impossible', said Greville, 'to conceive the sensation created by this event; but all ask "What will be done next? How is it to end?" '[8]

Princess Lieven gives a description of the arrival at Alderman Wood's house, where Caroline came out on to the balcony in response to the cries of hysterical crowds who 'streamed through the streets all night with torches, making passers-by shout "Long live the Queen"! "Long live Queen Caroline and her son, King Austin!" '

For two days the crowds ran riot. The Duke of Wellington, returning from a Cabinet meeting, had the windows of his carriage broken, and Lord Exmouth was obliged to arm himself with sword and pistol and drive the mob from his house. Stones were thrown at the windows of Lady Hertford's mansion—but here the crowd was a little out of date, for this lady had been superseded in the King's affection by Lady Conyngham.

The King prudently retired to Windsor, where he found his family united in their determination to ignore Queen Caroline's return. But before leaving London he recommended that both Houses of Parliament should give their 'immediate and serious' attention to the contents of a certain green bag. These were the findings of the Milan Commission, a formidable mass of evidence collected and concocted over the past five years.

A secret committee headed by the Archbishop of Canterbury was appointed to study the evidence, and, a week later, issued its report. There was little doubt now: the Queen, by all accounts, had behaved scandalously during her sojourn abroad, and a 'solemn enquiry' must be instituted. This would be no Delicate Investigation: it would take place in the House of Lords, a public examination of witnesses to prove the Queen's 'licentious and adulterous Intercourse' with Bartolomeo Pergami, and to determine the passing of a Bill of Pains and Penalties, which was designed to remove the Queen's name from the liturgy and her person from the country.

It was a harsh move, but this was no ordinary trial, it was the culmination of twenty-five years' war between two bitter enemies.

The reactions of the King's subjects were varied. Caroline's ardent supporters were not limited to the lower classes; she had passionate sympathizers among the aristocracy; and it is interesting to find that in the whirligig of time one of the most enthusiastic of these was Lady Jersey. This, however, was not the once lovely Frances (now a widow and pestering the King for a pension), but her daughter-in-law Sarah, Creevey's 'gold and silver dickey bird' who 'sang till twelve at night without interruption. She changes her feathers for dinner, and her plumage both morning and evening, [and] is the happiest and most beautiful I know.'[9] And now this exquisite and influential creature was declaring herself 'absolutely in a raging fever, quite frenzied', in Caroline's defence.[10]

Caroline's supporters, who daily grew in numbers, protested that she was being cruelly and unjustly used, and George Canning, who had been her devoted friend in days gone by, decided that sooner than support the Government against her, he would resign. In Parliament he spoke of her 'in terms of warm admiration' and described her 'fascinating manners, formed to delight society'—a tribute which infuriated the King. Canning, accordingly, resigned, but King George refused to accept his resignation, and told the Duke of Wellington that he had almost made Canning confess to his former '*extreme intimacy*' with the Queen.[11]

Another old friend of Caroline's, Sir Walter Scott, was not so kindly disposed. 'By all accounts, her conduct has been most abandoned and beastly,' he said. But Byron brushed aside the charges of immorality, and thought that Caroline would win. 'You must not trust Italian witnesses,' he wrote from Ravenna; 'nobody believes them in their own courts; why should you?'

Caroline continued to insist that her name be kept in the prayer-book: she was determined to be prayed for, and her lawyers supported her. She should be prayed for, said Denman, 'among the desolate and the oppressed'. A deputation, led by William Wilberforce, walked from the House of Commons through hooting, hissing crowds to present an address begging her to give way, but she received them in stony silence. 'The Deputation found the Queen standing in her drawing room, dressed in a robe of black richly embroidered, and having on her head a bandeau of laurel leaves studded with emeralds, surmounted with a superb plume of feathers. . . . The Queen spoke not a word to them, and made Brougham read her answer . . . The Deputation returned among renewed hootings of the mob, and reported the Queen's answer to the House.'[12]

It was deadlock: the King refused to give in. 'You might as easily move Carlton House,' said Castlereagh.

The wrangle over this had been going on for five months, and had become of paramount importance to the King. We hear of him sending for all the prayer-books in Carlton House, 'of new and old date' and spending the evening poring over them. Clergy throughout the country were in a dilemma. 'In some Churches', said Croker, 'I understand the clergy prayed for "our most gracious Queen", in others, and I believe in general, they prayed for "all the Royal Family". It struck me', he said, 'that if she is to be prayed for, it will be, in fact, a final settlement of all the questions in her favour. If she is fit to be introduced to the Almighty, she is fit to be received by men, and if we are to *pray* for her in Church we may surely bow to her at Court.'[13]

The first reading of the Bill of Pains and Spikalties, as Caroline called it, was introduced immediately after the secret committee had made their report. The second reading was, in fact, the opening of the Queen's trial, and took place in the House of Lords on 17 August. It had been held up, pending the arrival in England of the Italian witnesses. Some of these had already been lodged for some time in London, at the Government's expense (according to Caroline, Mlle Demont & Co had been there for six months, being paid £30 a week each),[14] while others, arriving at Dover, were received by angry crowds expressing their loyalty to Queen Caroline. Stones and mud were thrown and the military had to be called in to protect the Italians and bundle them into a Channel boat. In London they were lodged in temporary buildings near the House of Lords, erected for the cooking of the coronation banquet. The wretched, bewildered Italians, unable to speak a word of English, were virtually prisoners, guarded by cavalry parading the streets and by a man-of-war anchored in the Thames.

When these arrangements had been made, the Peers were summoned by Lord Eldon. The Queen's trial, as it came to be known, was about to begin.

Caroline drove to Westminster accompanied by Lady Anne and Lord Archibald Hamilton, and her reinstated chamberlains, Sir William Gell and the Hon. Keppel Craven. Enthusiastic cheering crowds lined the streets, which was reassuring, but Caroline showed no pleasure and stepped from her carriage with a resolute, even stern, expression. In spite of some opposition from members of the Government, she was accorded the ceremony due to her rank: Sir Thomas Tyrwhit, in full fig as Black Rod, received her and conducted her to her place in the Chamber. Perhaps it was fortunate that, owing to the death of the Duchess of York, the Court was in mourning: Caroline could not indulge her freakish taste in dress, but presented a sober and highly respectable appearance in a large black bonnet trimmed with ostrich plumes, and wearing a dress of black figured gauze with white bishop's sleeves and frilled lace at the neck. Before entering the Chamber she exchanged her bonnet for 'a handsome white veil' which almost hid her face.

'I cannot resist the curiosity of seeing a Queen tried,' wrote Creevey to his step-daughter Miss Ord, and got himself a place 'within two yards of the chair which was placed for her'. From this point of vantage he watched with fascination as, escorted by Sir Thomas Tyrrhwit, she made her entrance.

Her appearance was a disappointment. He had been taught to believe, he said, that she was as much improved in looks as in dignity; but 'with much pain' he observed that 'the nearest resemblance I can recollect to this much injured Princess is a toy . . . called Fanny Royds.'*

Poor Caroline, she was not fitted by nature to play a heroic role. As the doors were opened for her she hurried in like some bourgeois housewife out shopping, 'made a *duck* at the Throne, another to the Peers, and a concluding jump into the chair which was placed for her'. Creevey was disappointed that her veil was so thick: he could not see her face and had to be satisfied by observing the 'few straggling ringlets on her neck, which I flatter myself from their apperance were not her Majesty's own property'.[15]

The Queen was not obliged to be present at every session: she had been provided with a room where she might retire and rest, and from which Brougham might summon her when her presence was necessary. Thus, while some 250 of the nobility were occupied in deciding whether or no their Queen had betrayed them, the Queen herself, the only person who knew the true story, was generally to be found playing backgammon in her retiring room with Alderman Wood.

The Lord Chancellor had duly summoned each peer to attend the trial, in which the King was represented by the Attorney-General (Sir Robert Gifford), the Solicitor-General (Sir John Copley), and a selection of Law Officers. The King's brothers were expected to be present, but Sussex managed to get himself excused on the ground of consanguinity to both parties, to the fury of the Duke of York. 'I have much stronger ground for asking leave of absence than the Duke of Sussex, and yet I should be ashamed not to be present to do my duty.' (In the course of this unpleasant duty he was obliged to listen to Brougham firing 'a body blow' at himself over the Mrs Clarke affair.)[16]

The Queen's Attorney-General was Henry Brougham and her Solicitor-General Thomas Denman, who later became a judge and a peer. It was soon evident that, as Creevey put it, 'the Law Officers of the Crown are damnably overweighted by Brougham and Denman. Denman,' he said, 'is speaking as well as possible, tho' I am all against him introducing jokes, which he has been doing somewhat too much.' But jokes, in this as in every occasion attended by Caroline, continued to creep in.

* This was a Dutch toy with a round bottom weighted with lead, so that it always jumped erect in whatever position it was laid.

On the second day of the trial, Creevey thought that the Lords rose to receive the Queen with a better grace than on the day before. He noticed that her procession had been smartened up. 'She has a most superb and beautiful coach with six horses—the coachman driving in a cap, like the old King's coachman; and a good coach of her own behind for Craven and Gell.'[17]

Caroline's entourage had increased. Mr Craven, who had disappointed her by failing to turn up at Calais, now proved himself a true friend. When it was known that the Government had no intention of offering her a royal residence, he persuaded his mother, the Margravine of Ansbach, to offer her Brandenburg House which looked down over the Thames at Fulham. Here she might find a refuge from the persistent and noisy crowds which milled round her carriage in the London streets, and a home where she could retire at the end of the day for rest and quiet. That, at least, was what she hoped. But unfortunately, as soon as the London public knew that they could reach her by water she was inundated by noisy river parties who made an outing of it. Boatloads jostled one another, eagerly waiting for a glimpse of the royal lady. Deputations arrived to present loyal messages, and altogether Brandenberg House became London's greatest attraction.

During the trial the Queen was suffering intermittently from pains in the bowels, and she decided to stay for the time being at a house in St James's Square, which was near to the House of Lords—and next-door to Lord Castlereagh, who hastily gave orders for all his windows to be shuttered. Perhaps he was wise, for great crowds assembled in the square each morning, waiting for a glimpse of the Queen on her way to the House. 'Not only the mob', wrote Lord Lyttelton, '. . . but people of all ranks, and the middle-classes almost to a man, and I believe the Troops too, side with the Queen . . .'[18]

The first two days of the trial were taken up with long speeches attacking or defending the principle of the Bill. One of the high spots was Brougham's broadside against the Duke of York: this young man Brougham had a deadly power; he could be venomous, the peers observed with relish. Then on 19 August, formalities over and methods of procedure being at last agreed, the Attorney-General opened his case against the Queen. '*Now*,' said Creevey, 'her danger begins.'

Chapter Twenty-three

As soon as the trial began it became evident that the Queen was fortunate in the two men who defended her. Brougham disliked her as heartily as she distrusted him, but his brilliance as an orator, his quick mind and cruel wit dealt with each piece of evidence like a tennis player returning a series of all-but unplayable serves. Denman, her Solicitor-General, with his handsome looks and pleasing voice, and a sense of humour less cynical than Brougham's, was a persuasive and gentlemanly speaker whose sincerity was beyond question.

The Italian witnesses were now called one by one to give evidence. They were for the most part uneducated, and not one could speak English. The size and impressive appearance of the crowded House, the whole panoply of British justice, must have been alarming. Moreover, they were being asked questions about events which were said to have taken place five years ago. Before appearing at the trial, the witnesses had undergone, as we have seen, rough treatment at the hands of the British public: as a result of this, they had been herded together for safety, and hurried off to Holland, and finally to improvised quarters in Cotton Garden, which was close to the House of Lords.

During this time they had had ample opportunities to talk to one another —and to recount the high spots of the evidence which they had been called upon to give. No doubt the stories about the Queen and Pergami grew more dramatic, more shocking, with the telling; and by the time the witnesses reached the House of Lords all may have become bewildered by the mass of impressions which, true or false, they found themselves pledged to recount. There were language problems: the finer shades of Italian speech were not always satisfactorily translated for their lordships. There were two interpreters, one for the Prosecution, and one, at his demand, for Brougham; and there were altercations.

The first witness to be called was Theodore Majocchi, who had been employed by the Princess as a postillion at Pergami's introduction. As this decent, respectable-looking man took his place, there was a dramatic moment. The Queen stared at him in horror, then gave a piercing cry, 'Theodore! No, no!' and was led out of court, looking, said one Lord, 'more like a fury than a woman'. This cry has been interpreted in several ways. The word used by the Queen was thought by some to be 'Traditore!' which seems more likely. The strong emotion with which it was charged suggests that it was not only Majocchi who was a traitor, but all the witnesses who had received kindness at her hands and who were at this moment waiting to betray her.

Majocchi confirmed that he had been engaged at Naples where the Princess was staying, and that he had been told to wait on Pergami, who was laid up after being kicked by a horse. He was questioned about the sleeping arrangements in this house, and said that he slept in a cabinet or ante-room between the Princess's room and that of Pergami. He twice saw the Princess come through on her way to Pergami's bedroom, where she stayed for ten or fifteen minutes the first time, and the second time fifteen or eighteen minutes. Each time he could hear, he said, 'whispering conversation'.

Brougham, cross-examining, pressed Majocchi to admit that there might have been another way to Pergami's room.

'I have only seen one that I remember.'

'Will you swear that there was no other way in which a person wishing to go from the Princess's room to Pergami's room could go, except by passing through the cabinet?'

'There was, I think, another passage going to the room of Pergami.'

Brougham had, for the moment, no more to ask.

The Prosecution proceeded with questions about the Princess's sleeping arrangements during the whole of her tour. It transpired that she had always chosen the rooms for herself and Pergami. Their two bedrooms were most conveniently arranged when their host was the Bey of Tunis, whose slaves no doubt were accustomed to making arrangements of this sort. On board the polacca, the heat during the day was intense and the Princess made use of the green tent given her by the Pasha of Acre, and had it pitched on deck. There were two tents, one within the other, and here, in the inner tent, the Princess had a sofa and a travelling bed. She slept, said Majocchi, every night in this tent.

'Did anybody sleep under the same tent?'

'Bartolomeo Pergami.'

'Were the sides of the tent drawn in, so as to shut them entirely in?'

'When they went to sleep, the whole was enclosed, shut up.'

He was then asked to describe what happened when the Princess took a bath. The bath-tub was in her cabin. Majocchi filled the tub, Pergami tested the temperature of the water. He then escorted the Princess down the companion-way and into the cabin, and shut the door. They remained alone in the cabin.

So far, Majocchi had given his evidence calmly and clearly: he had been well rehearsed, and the Attorney-General was encouraging. But when Brougham took over, he began to lose confidence. Either unable or unwilling to admit more than he had already said, he fell back on the evasive 'I don't remember'—'*Non mi ricordo.*'

This phrase, easily understood and easily pronounced by the British, became as it were the theme song of the whole solemn proceedings, reducing it to the level of the sort of entertainment in which Cockneys delighted, a comic song.

Theodore Majocchi is my name,
And everyone's aware,
From Italy I came,
Against the Queen to swear,
I was sent to Colonel Browne's,
When I was abroad O,
Who gave me many crowns,
To say *Non mi ricordo.* (and so on, for many verses)

Colonel Browne was one of the leading members of the Milan Commission. In his evidence Majocchi admitted that he had travelled from Vienna (where he was employed by the British Ambassador, Lord Stewart) in answer to a summons from Colonel Browne. He travelled with his father, who was 'a carter, a carrier, carrying merchandise with horses'.

'How does he happen to come to Vienna, your respectable father?'

'My father came to Vienna to take me . . . he told me that at Milan there was a Colonel Browne who wanted to speak to me.'

Brougham asked him, 'Do you go everywhere whenever anybody comes to say to you, "Colonel Browne wishes to speak to you?" '

'When my father told me so, I went to Colonel Browne directly.'

'If your father were to go and ask you to speak to Colonel Black would you go there also?'

The Solicitor-General objected to this question.

Brougham then asked how Majocchi and his father had travelled and whether they had lived 'pretty comfortably' on the road.

'We wanted for nothing.' (Obviously Brougham was out to prove that Majocchi was in the pay of the Milan Commission.) Well aware already of the value of the witness's evasive '*non mi ricordo*', he began to fire a number of questions calculated to confuse the witness and bring this answer. First he ascertained, gently enough, that Majocchi, his father and his wife, were living comfortably in a London lodging. Majocchi did not know if he was to pay for his keep. Had he received money for his journeys to Milan and Vienna? He could not remember. 'I remember to have received no money when I arrived at Milan. *Ricordo di no* ...'

Lord Rosebery interrupted to say that it was essential that they should know what the witness meant by '*ricordo di no*'. Apparently, after some consulation with the interpreters, it was decided that Majocchi meant, 'I recollect—not': he recollected that he was not paid. Pressed by the Solicitor-General, he added, 'When I say "*non mi ricordo*" I mean that I have not in my head to have received the money, for if I had received the money I would say yes: but I do not remember it now, but I do not recollect the contrary.'

Brougham now changed the subject.

'Do you recollect a German baron visiting the Princess of Wales at Naples?'

'*Non mi ricordo.*'

'Did any German baron visit the Princess of Wales during her residence at the villa on Lake Como?'

'There was a baron whom I think to be Russian.'

'Was the name of that person Ompteda ...?'

'Precisely I cannot recollect the name by which he was called ...'

'Was there not a room in the house of her Royal Highness at the Villa, which was called the baron's room?'

'*Questo non mi ricordo.*'

Questions were then thrown open to the House.

Lord Ellenborough asked, 'How was her Royal Highness dressed when she passed through the cabinet to Pergami's room at Naples?'

'*Non mi ricordo.*'

Lord Grey asked, 'Did you see her Royal Highness distinctly on that occasion?'

'Yes.'

'But you do not know how she was dressed?'

'I do no remember what dress she had.'

Keen interest was shown by the peers in the story of the bath on the polacca. Lord Duncan asked if Majocchi could be sure that none of the Princess's female attendants were with her in the bathroom. 'Yes, I can answer to having seen nobody go into the bathroom of her Royal Highness.'

Majocchi was stationed at the door to the bathroom when Pergami went upstairs to tell the Princess that her bath was ready. 'When they came down Pergami told me—"Be at the door, for if there be any need of water you shall give it me." '

Lord Grey then asked, 'Did you remain in the outer room during the whole time that the Princess and Pergami were in the inner room?'

'At the door with the two pails of water.'

'Did you see the Princess and Pergami quit the bathroom to go on deck?'

'No, but I have seen Pergami come out of the room to go on deck, to call the maid to come down and dress her Royal Highness, and I have heard, with my own ears, when he said "Mademoiselle Demont, come down to dress her Royal Highness." '

'How long had Pergami and the Princess been in the room before Pergami went to call the maid?'

'About half an hour.'

'Was Pergami on retiring from the bathroom, dressed in the same way as when he handed the Princess in?'

'He was.'

Brougham (with the Lord-Chancellor's permission) now questioned Majocchi about the efforts that he had made to get back into the Princess's service, through an upper servant called Camara. This man told him, 'and I remember it as well as if it was now—"Theodore Majocchi, do not enter into any service [with anybody else] because her Royal Highness wishes to have you back, and I shall pay you." ' Majocchi had evidently by this time recovered his nerve and spoke up boldly. 'This conversation must be put down, such as it is, and I beg to be allowed to speak . . . Camara told me, "Theodore, give me back the certificate of your good service . . . and I will tell to her Royal Highness that you have not taken a further engagement . . . and she will pay you for the whole time you have been out of service—all the time you have been out of service, and all the damages and losses you have suffered," and I told Camara, "Camara, give me back my paper (because I had already given him my paper) because rather than go to serve her Royal Highness, on account of the persons that are about her, I will go and eat grass." '

Majocchi, trembling with emotion, was directed to leave the court.

The next witnesses were the mate and master of the polacca, followed by Francisco Birollo who had been cook on board the polacca, and at Villa d'Este. He had left the Princess's service, he said, because there was too much hard work. He was asked to describe Mahomet's indecent dance, or trick. 'Describe what Mahomet did in the presence of the Princess.'

'He did so, [making a dancing motion] saying "Dami, dimi, dami, dimi." '

'Did he do anything with his trousers in the course of these gesticulations?'

'He made a kind of roll to represent something—I do not know how to call it decently . . . he took it in his hand, and made gesticulations . . .'[1] This dance aroused much interest and curiosity among the Lords, and several witnesses were later asked to describe it.

The first female witness was a German named Barbara Kress, who before her marriage had been employed at the Post Inn at Karlsruhe. When the Princess and her suite were staying there, she had carried up some water to one of the bedrooms and was disconcerted to find Pergami in bed, and the Princess sitting on the bed. She could not tell whether or no Pergami was clothed, but when she entered the room the Princess jumped up in alarm. 'I withdrew, I was frightened.'[2]

This witness, questioned by the Attorney-General, admitted that she had not wished to come to the trial: 'I am a married woman, and I have other business to attend to.' She had not been paid to come, she alleged, but a gentleman in Frankfurt had given her a ducat as compensation for time lost. She said that one of her duties was to make the bed in Pergami's room, and that once she had found a cloak in his bed—'it was of silk, the colour grey'. She had seen the Princess wearing a similar cloak. 'It was of the same colour . . . it was likewise silk.' In his cross-examination, Brougham ascertained that this woman was of humble background, and that she had been approached by several illustrious persons—the Baden Foreign Secretary, the ambassador from Wurtemberg, and by the Hanoverian ambassador, who examined her about the evidence she had to give. She was told that she might be obliged to go to England. After the Princess had left the hotel (she told Brougham) Herr von Grimm, the Wurtemberg ambassador, came back and went into the room that had been Pergami's 'to look at what was there'.

It was gradually revealed, in the testimonies of the witnesses, that the Princess and Pergami were constantly seen together, often in compromising attitudes. In fact, they were seldom apart: they travelled in the same coach, they slept in adjoining rooms. But it was strange that no witness had seen the couple in bed together, though no doubt many inquisitive eyes had peered through keyholes. It was always Pergami who was seen in bed, the Princess standing or sitting and bending over him. She was heard to call him '*mon ange*', '*mon cœur*': he called her '*Principessa*'.

The Princess's chambermaid, Louisa Demont, was Swiss, and of better class than Frau Kress. While awaiting the trial she had been living stylishly in Frith Street, Soho, on the money paid her by the Milan Commission. She called herself the Countess Colombiera.

Unlike the previous witnesses, Demont could read and write, and gave her evidence with assurance. She was demure in manner, but repeated, when pressed, a bawdy story told her by Pergami; the peers were 'much dissatisfied' with this as evidence, and the Lord Chancellor had it struck out as irrelevant.

Demont had been with the Princess throughout her travels, and was ready to supply detailed information about beds and night adventures. She described a masquerade in Naples to which she had gone with the Princess and Pergami, disguised in dominoes and hideous masks. The Princess's appearance, she said, was so shocking that they were obliged to leave in a hurry to escape the menacing crowds.

The Solicitor-General referred to an occasion when Caroline was in her bedroom dressing herself. 'Did you ever see her Royal Highness in pantaloons?' Demont said that she had, and that Pergami was also present. 'He turned her round, looking at her, and said, "How pretty you are, I like you much better so." '

'At the time when you describe her Royal Highness as being in pantaloons what was the state of her neck and breast?'

'Uncovered. She was at her toilet.'

We do not know how much of the evidence was heard by the Queen. She must by now have become hardened to hearing her character blackened, and that stout, upright figure with its attitude of proud defiance in the centre of Hayter's painting may well have been seated there during Demont's evidence, betraying no emotion but boredom.

Louisa was followed by Giuseppe Sacchi, who during the past year had been employed by the Princess as courier and equerry. He, like Demont, was of superior class, and his evidence against the Princess was more deadly. 'Much dirt and some damage,' Creevey commented at the end of the day. Sacchi was evidently, from Louisa Demont's account, something of a Don Juan. He described a conversation which he had had with the Princess after a ball given at Pergami's farm, Villa Barone. This ball had already been mentioned as being of a disreputable nature: the Baron's guests were a mixed lot, and his villa was regularly frequented by young women from Como in search of pleasure or profit.

'One day', Sacchi told the House, 'when I was in the courtyard, and her Royal Highness and Pergami were there, she said that she wished to make a present to some of these girls. "How can we dress these young virgins, Mr Sacchi?" Then she asked me, "Do you believe they are such?" I answered that as far as I was concerned I believed them to be modest girls, and I had nothing to say against them. Her Royal Highness said to me, "I know you,

you rogue, that you have gone to bed with three of them, and how many times you have had intercourse with them." I being surprised at this compliment, endeavoured to persuade her Royal Highness that she was deceived; and Pergami, who was present, began to laugh and to cry aloud, "It is true, it is true, it is true." '

Sacchi was smartly dressed, and had always been, he thanked God, 'in easy circumstances'. It transpired that he had been well bribed, well rehearsed as to how to give his evidence, and promised further payment when the trial was over. Questioned by Brougham, he admitted that he had been in England for some time, and that he had been living with the Rev. Philip Godfrey at Aston, near Stevenage. It is to be hoped that the Rev. Philip did not read the newspaper reports of Sacchi's evidence. Everything was reported verbatim.

Sacchi let fly his most damaging piece of evidence.

In July, he said, in very hot weather, the Princess decided to go to Senigallia for sea-bathing. As was her custom, she travelled by night. As soon as dawn broke, Sacchi went to the Princess's carriage to draw the curtains. He found the Princess and Pergami asleep, 'having their respective hands one upon the other'. 'Her Royal Highness held her hand upon the private part of Mr Pergami, and Pergami held his own hand upon that of her Royal Highness.' Apparently, this discovery was made not once, but several times. 'Once', asserted Sacchi, 'I saw that Pergami had his breeches loosed from the braces, and that he had the front part of his breeches, the flap, half-unbuttoned.'[3]

This was the nearest to *flagrante delicto* that any witness could produce. (In his speech for the defence, Brougham blew it to smithereens.)

Meanwhile, the weather in London was also very hot and the crowded chamber intolerably stuffy. Tempers were frayed, and there were angry altercations between the lawyers over matters of procedure. On 9 September, the twenty-first day of the trial, the Lords decided to adjourn for three weeks.

The Queen, according to Creevey, was all for going on without a break. But Brougham needed time to assemble his witnesses and prepare his defence. He believed that she was ready to 'fling her Counsel overboard' sooner than adjourn. 'In this situation of peril for the idiot,' wrote Creevey, 'Brougham thinks of asking only till Monday fortnight to be ready.'[4] He was given a week longer. It was decided that the proceedings should reopen on 3 October.

'The Queen is delighted,' said Creevey; 'she clapped her hands with delight when [Brougham] communicated it to her . . .'[5] But the peers were not so pleased. 'You can form no conception of the rage of the Lords at Brougham fixing this time: it interferes with everything—pheasant shooting, Newmarket, &c., &c. . . .'

Caroline, well aware of the public interest in her trial, determined to make good use of the interval. She drove about in an open carriage, appeared on the balcony of Brandenburg House overlooking the river, and sailed down the Thames in a state barge, cheered all the way by crowds thronging the banks. At Blackfriars, it was reckoned that over 200,000 people collected to see her. A few days later, on 13 September, Creevey, dozing in his club, heard a noise of hurra-ing and shouting in the street; 'so I ran out to see. It was, I may say, the "*Navy of England*".' It was what we now call a demo. 'I have seen nothing like this before,' said Creevey . . . 'There were thousands of seamen, all well dressed, all sober—the best looking, the finest men you could imagine. Every man had a new white silk or satin cockade in his hat. They had a hundred colours, at least, or pieces of silk, with sentiments on them, such as "Protection to the Innocent" &c.' Creevey considered that this procession would decide the Queen's fate. 'When the seamen take a part, the soldiers can't fail to be shaken.'[6]

It was astonishing that the evidence which seemed to prove her beyond doubt an immoral woman, unbalanced and totally shameless, had not the slightest effect upon the bulk of the British public, who insisted on treating her as a heroine. 'As to the Queen's affair,' wrote Croker, 'I can only tell you that all the disgusting details proved against her seem to make no change in the minds and numbers of her partisans.'

The print shops did a roaring trade in caricatures of the Queen and Pergami, whose portrait, published in Paris, crossed the Channel to be reproduced in countless comical situations. Never was there such a trade in patriotic posters.

> ENGLISHMEN, ATTEND! [shouted one of these in large black letters] 'Look at the price of the evidence against your Queen! Two Wittnesses have been brought forward who confess, that they receive from our *pious* Ministers *One Thousand Eight Hundred Dollars a Month*!
>
> Englishmen, ruined Englishmen, look at this! Here are *two Italian Sailors*, the Master and Mate of a little Beggarly vessel, who receive out of the fruits of your labour, more than the pay of *Two Hundred and Fifty* of OUR BRAVE SOLDIERS or of OUR BRAVE SAILORS!!!
>
> Englishmen, think of this! See how much more profitable it is to *swear* than to *fight*!!!!

This vehement broad-sheet added, for good measure: 'If you want to know all about the Queen's Judges, look at the "PEEP AT THE PEERS". There they are all—*Price Fourpence*; No. 269, Strand.'

The King was at Brighton, where he intended to remain till the trial and its attendant uproar had ended. He was well aware that the passing of the Bill of Pains and Penalties through the Lords, even without the divorce clause, would be in the public view a major victory for the King in the long-drawn-out war between himself and his wife. But there was little doubt as to who held the popular favour. Even at Brighton the manager of the Theatre Royal told Lord Darlington that he dared not permit the singing of *God Save the King* for fear of causing riots. And Wellington, who had been the idol of the whole country, was hissed and booed in the streets on his way to the House of Lords because, as he said, 'I am a King's man!'

When the Lords adjourned, there seemed little doubt that the damaging evidence had had its effect: the King's men were confident that from what had been said proofs of the Queen's guilt were incontrovertible. The Attorney-General, who had carried a second batch of witnesses from Italy, decided that their evidence could be dispensed with, and sat back to listen to what the Defence could possibly have to offer. But he reckoned without Brougham.

Chapter Twenty-four

WHEN THE House reassembled, Brougham opened the proceedings with a speech which, it was said, had been rewritten seven times. It was extremely hot in the Chamber, and Creevey found himself obliged to go out and walk about on Westminster Bridge. On his return, he wrote, 'He has been at it again for two hours . . . criticism in detail about the evidence—damned dull and damned hot.' But after listening to Brougham's demolition of some of the evidence, he was forced to admit that he had been spellbound. Brougham did not finish till half-past twelve the following day, a feat of endurance, and 'the most magnificent display of oratory that has been heard for years', Greville wrote.[1] Creevey was compelled to admit that the speech was 'perfection in all ways', adding, 'If he can prove what he has stated in his speech, I for one believe she is innocent, and the whole case a conspiracy.'[2]

Brougham began by criticizing in detail the evidence which had been given by the prosecution witnesses. With a fine blend of ridicule and moral indignation, he set about demolishing all that had been stated against the Queen's honour. The Milan Tribunal, he said, was 'a storehouse of false swearing'. And to show how easy it was to distort the evidence of unreliable and dishonest witnesses, particularly when the events described had taken place in a foreign country, he gave examples of Louisa Demont's allegations, showing how justly she had won from the British public the nickname of *La Chienne*.

Brougham happened to know Italy, having travelled widely there as a young man, and he showed off this knowledge to prove that the Prosecution, in their questioning of Demont, were woefully handicapped by ignorance of Italian customs. The Solicitor-General, he said, had criticized the Queen for going to a masked ball in Naples, disguised and in a closed carriage. His learned friend had clearly never been to Italy or he would not have made the criticism. 'What a pity that her Majesty did not, to suit the view of his learned friends, go to the masquerade in a state coach, with coachmen in splendid liveries . . . with all the pomp and show of state ceremony.' It was a wonder, he said, that his learned friend did not go on and say, 'Why did she go in a domino and disguised cap to a masquerade?' During Her Majesty's residence at Naples another . . . masquerade was held at a theatre. To this entertainment also she chose to go in a very extraordinary manner. She was accompanied, not by Lady Charlotte Lindsay or Lady Elizabeth Forbes, or even by any of the gentlemen of her suite, but by the courier Pergami and a *femme de chambre* of the name of Demont. The dresses chosen by Her Majesty for herself and her companions were, we learn from this witness, of a description so indecent as to attract the attention of the whole company and to call forth marks of general disapprobation. According to the evidence, Her Majesty was forced to withdraw with her companions and go home. Now, said Brougham, what did Madame Demont say, when asked to describe this 'most indecent and disgusting dress' worn by the Queen? All that could be extracted from this far from reticent witness was that the Princess and her companions wore 'ugly masks'. Strange as it might appear, she went to the masquerade in a mask!

Brougham touched on the many occasions when the Princess and Pergami were seen embracing, holding hands, walking with arms entwined, greeting each other or taking leave with kisses: the witnesses of these acts, he said, 'those pure, fastidious and scrupulous witnesses . . . displayed a nicety of moral caution that was exceedingly exemplary'. How odd it was, he commented, that the Princess and her courier had never perpetrated these apparently immoral acts in private, but always, as it appeared, when exposed to the general gaze. 'It would not do that Pergami, on his departure on a journey, should salute her Majesty before the servant entered the room: no, the exhibition of that act was reserved for the presence of a servant to tell it.' And so on. First the audience was summoned, then the performance was given. 'When it is necessary to trace the conduct a step higher in the scale of criminality . . . the act is done . . . in a villa filled with servants, and where hundreds of workmen are at the very time employed; and all this too is done . . . in open day, and exposed to the general gaze.'

Majocchi ('*non mi ricordo*') came in for fierce criticism. 'He would have us believe that the Queen, having free access to Pergami's room, through rooms where no persons slept, chose rather to pass through an occupied room.' The witness, said Brougham, made out at first that there was no other way, but, after much equivocation, admitted that there was . . . and yet, having allowed that the Queen had easy, safe and ready access to the place of guilt . . . she preferred passing through the room where Majocchi slept . . . passing through a room so small that she must have touched the bed—through a room where a fire was burning; and what was most monstrous of all, they were to believe that, to make quite sure that she had been detected, she stopped and looked in the face of Majocchi, to ascertain whether he was asleep. The whole of this story defeated itself.

As for Sacchi's story of the Princess and Pergami asleep in the carriage, Brougham described the evidence as of a nature so disgusting and offensive that he found it difficult even to make the slightest allusion to it. He did, however, appeal to their Lordships' credulity: would they believe that—with the knowledge that a courier was travelling by the side of the carriage, the blinds of which might at any time be raised—the Queen would run the risk of blasting her character, even among the most abandoned of her sex, by going to sleep in the position described by Sacchi? . . . But the credulity of the House must be stretched many degrees; for if it could persuade itself that this had happened once, it would be nothing to what Sacchi had sworn he had been in the constant habit of seeing, again and again. Brougham appealed to their Lordships: whether this story had the smallest appearance of probability, whether such conduct could be accounted for. He was saying nothing of the physical impossibility of the thing, at a time when the carriage was travelling fast over such shocking roads as are found in that part of Italy, with their hands placed across each other while the parties were fast asleep and, of course, without any power over their limbs. To overcome this difficulty, he said, would require the evidence of philosophers.

Brougham considered that their lordships would find the whole story impossible to believe, 'unless the parties are absolutely insane'. Perhaps here he showed something beyond perspicacity. The affair was an extraordinary one, the behaviour of the lovers never quite credible. It is true they kissed and fondled each other, they were constantly together and aroused suspicion by their blatant love-making; they found pleasure in sharing indecent jokes, they often joined each other when half-clad. All this pointed to adultery, yet no one could prove beyond doubt that adultery had been committed. The Princess made no secret of her passion for Pergami; but we have no certain proof that he adored her; indeed, it is often only too clear that he is playing a part, taking full advantage of his success to gain power and wealth.

When, at Calais, they had parted, and the Queen, as she now was, pursued her destiny and set sail for England, she was alone. Pergami, having gained for himself a small fortune, left his patroness to fight her own battles and went back to his comfortable life at Pesaro. As an Italian not subject to English law, he could not be tried for high treason. But if one piece of evidence had been used and proved valid, the Queen might have been spared much humiliation. Pergami did not commit adultery with her because he could not. He was impotent.

In August, when the trial began, Brougham received a letter from a Dr John O'Ryan who had been surgeon on board the *Clorinda*, the frigate in which Caroline and her party sailed from Civita Vecchia to Genoa. He begged leave to state 'that, in various conversations which I had with Mr Pergami [*sic*], he recounted the hardships he suffered in the Russian campaign, and in particular consulted me for pain and debility of back, loins and hips: he felt, as he expressed himself, as if those parts were frozen and rendered him perfectly indifferent to women, in short, that he had lost all desire for the sex ever since his sufferings in the Russian campaign'.[3]

Brougham did not call Dr O'Ryan as a witness: he was evidently keeping this ace up his sleeve. For on 12 September, three weeks before his speech for the Defence opened the second session, Lord Liverpool noted that 'Brougham meant to set up impotency as part of his Defence . . . not original impotency, but impotency in consequence of an operation.' But, 'It is difficult', the Prime Minister added, 'to believe the fact.'

Evidently Brougham, with his unusual insight, did believe it: he saw that Caroline, declaring that she was innocent, believed herself to be so. Sitting sphinx-like in the midst of 250 peers, she betrayed no sign of guilt. She had loved Pergami, she had lavished gifts upon him; everything she had done which was now held up against her, had been done to please him.

Her infatuation, together with an abnormal obsession with sex which she had possessed since puberty, had produced an unnatural relationship in which Pergami, hoping to regain his virility, played his part as a lover, but without satisfaction. The active part in this one-sided affair was played by Caroline. She was lonely, sexually unsatisfied, desperately in need of affection and kindness; and she built up a fantasy in which Pergami obligingly flattered her into believing herself loved and lovely. For a time, at least while on her travels, this dream was enough to make her happy. They both enjoyed dressing up, or dressing each other up, which was mentioned in evidence against them. We hear of the Princess as Columbine, as the Muse of History (in scanty draperies), as a Turkish maiden, a milkmaid, and other pretty fancies, while Pergami was decked out in romantic and colourful garb as her partner. On board ship he lay about in 'a species of Grecian Cloak or toga' and made the Princess laugh by stuffing cushions under it and pretending to be a woman. He loved costly materials, and was seen coming out of Caroline's bedroom 'in a striped silk morning gown' with little underneath. 'He had a surtout made', said another witness, 'according to the Polish fashion, which had some gold lace behind, that reached from the waist down.' This was evidently very striking. He wore earrings, and often exchanged earrings with the Princess. Sometimes they exchanged garments—a red silk cap or a silk cloak. With his abundant curling hair, he was beautiful, and she encouraged his vanity. She bought him a gold chain and herself—like Rosalind—slipped it over his head.

But gradually after the return to Italy the idyll began to grow sour. The pornographic capers of Mahomet the young Turk still caused her delicious sensations, but Pergami was becoming more interested in making money than in making love. He managed the Princess's finances, put a firm curb on her spending, and paid himself lavishly. By the time she came to England he had, according to Joseph Hownam, 'so reduced her finances to his own profit as to have her literally without a shilling'.[4]

Brougham's speech for the Defence ended at half-past twelve on Wednesday 4 October. In two days he had spoken for over eight hours, and wound up in an atmosphere of tense excitement. 'He concluded', said Creevey 'with a most magnificent address to the Lords—an exhortation to them to save themselves—the Church—the Crown—the Country—by their decision in favour of the Queen. This last appeal was made with great passion.'[5] The peers were visibly shaken by Brougham's eloquence: some gathered in groups to confer urgently together: Lord Erskine (who, fourteen years before had presided over the Delicate Investigation), was moved to tears and ran from the House. If the trial had ended on this note, without question the Bill would have been thrown out immediately. As it was, the Defence witnesses had yet to be heard.

'She had two lieutenants of the English Navy with her . . . through most of her journeys. Now, if she does not produce them, as they are both on the spot, she is undone, and all that Majocchi and Demont &c. have sworn must receive universal credit.' This was the opinion of John Wilson Croker, Secretary to the Admiralty and Tory politician—a King's man.

Hownam and Flynn had already been summoned: indeed, Hownam, who since we last met him had married and gone to live in France, was in London awaiting his call to give evidence. Brougham had laid careful plans for the next session, and Lieutenant Flynn—or Captain Fling, as Caroline referred to him—was also ready to appear.

The King was still at Windsor, bilious, gouty and cross. When his ministers waited upon him in the hopes of persuading him to allow the divorce clause to be left out of the Bill, he refused to see them and sent them back to London supperless. Accounts were reaching him of the disconcerting behaviour of the crowds which continued to throng the streets of London and the provincial towns, and demonstrate their partiality for the Queen. He ordered the Home Secretary, Lord Sidmouth, to send him regular reports of the state of the country: he was frightened.

The trial was becoming a political battle. If the Queen won, it would be a victory for the Opposition: if she were to lose and the Bill go through to the Commons, the Government would triumph but Caroline would still have the people's support. 'My feelings will have some small reparation,' the King later told Lord Eldon, 'if the House of Commons agree with the House of Peers, that she really does not deserve consideration as a virtuous and innocent Queen.' And he hoped that the matter would be settled speedily, before the end of the year, 'for I trust in Almighty God that I may be permitted to begin the New Year in peace'.

Meanwhile, the trial went on, the London crowds enjoyed the excitement, and aristocrats were challenged in their carriages.

'I was driving to Bond Street,' wrote Princess Lieven, 'when I met the Queen in a state coach with six horses, being led at a walking pace, and escorted as usual by some hundreds of scallywags. As soon as they saw my carriage they stopped it and ordered my servants to take off their hats, and me to let the window down. Neither I nor my servants obeyed. I was surrounded by people shouting abuse, whistling and booing. Meanwhile the Queen passed by, throwing me a withering glance. I saw two enormous black eyebrows, as big as two of my fingers put together: the contents of two pots of rouge on her cheeks; and a veil over everything.' 'I broke up her escort,' said Princess Lieven, who displayed some courage, surrounded as she was by hostile Londoners. 'They are decent people all the same,' she added; 'they carried off the honours in noise—that was all—and I held the honours in inflexibility.'[6]

At the House of Lords, opinion fluctuated from day to day, from witness to witness. The effect left by Brougham's speech slowly faded as the Defence witnesses failed to convince the Lords that they were speaking the truth: indeed, even '*non mi ricordo*' in its English equivalent was brought into service under the stress of fierce cross-questioning.

When Flynn and Hownam were called to appear, it was expected that after so much dubious evidence from foreigners who had been paid to give it, these British naval officers would provide valuable and truthful support to the Queen's cause. Indeed, this was what the officers themselves planned to do.

Flynn's examination came first, and he was questioned mercilessly by the Solicitor-General, Sir Joseph Copley. 'This cursed Flynn', wrote Creevey '. . . has perjured himself three or four times over, and his evidence and himself are both gone to the devil.' In fact, Flynn's nerve gave way: in his anxiety to please and his desire to aid the Queen, he overdid things; he talked too much, then contradicted himself. 'I knew he was lying,' said

Copley later. 'I looked hard at him. He fainted away and was taken out of Court.'[7]

Hownam, who came next, neither fainted nor feared. Of all her supporters, he was the most loyal, the most eager to fight for the Queen's honour. She was his benefactress, and he had always treated her with respect and gratitude even though he stood up to her when she seemed to him in the wrong. To defend her, he had challenged Count Ompteda to a duel: now with the same attempted chivalry he spoke up on her behalf. His fervent belief in her cause eventually led him into deep water, though the account of his evidence shows that he was straining to be entirely truthful. It must be remembered, though, that in shielding the Princess he was often obliged to shield Pergami, whom he knew to be a blackguard and whom he heartily disliked. Here was the flaw in his carefully prepared evidence: he could not honestly protect the Princess without dishonestly protecting her lover.

He was questioned at length and in detail about the Princess's behaviour on board the polacca.

'I never saw her Royal Highness sitting on a gun with Pergami. I never saw her sitting on a bench with her arms around him. I never saw them kissing each other. I never saw any impropriety or indecency from one towards the other on board . . .'

He was questioned about the Turk, Mahomet, who had joined the party at Jerusalem, and about the much discussed dance. Did he remember this dance? He did. It originated, said Hownam, in a quarrel between Mahomet and the doctor. He was sick on board, and the doctor wanted to give him physic. He afterwards ridiculed the doctor by this dance. 'I had no notion of anything indecent in the dance.'

Asked if he remembered seeing the Princess acting the part of Columbine in the theatre at the Villa d'Este, Hownam 'did not recollect her Royal Highness playing the part of Columbine. Louis Pergami performed there,' he said, 'and all her Royal Highness's household.'

'What part did the Princess perform?'

'I think her Royal Highness performed the part of an automaton. It represented a man who wished to sell an automaton, which was a woman, in fact, that could wind up to anything.' (Great laughter). 'The Princess was the automaton.'

He was then asked where Pergami slept on the return voyage from Jaffa. 'I do not know . . . I heard that he slept under the tent with the Princess, and I believe he did. I do not think, knowing the fact, that it was degrading to the Princess. I think that it was necessary that someone should sleep near her Royal Highness . . . I heard that other persons did also.'

Lord Ellenborough asked if he recollected seeing her Royal Highness under the tent in the day-time.

'Yes. She was asleep, and I closed the tent to protect her from the sun. I can positively say I never recollect to have seen any other person under the tent when it was so closed.'

Lord Grosvenor asked why Her Royal Highness was in such impatience to get ashore on the voyage from Syracuse.

'Her legs were very much swelled, in consequence of her not having been in bed during the voyage.' This aroused interest. Lord Grosvenor enquired when Hownam had seen the Princess's legs.

'I never saw her Royal Highness's legs.'

'Then how did you know that they were swelled?'

'Her Royal Highness told me that they were swelled.'

The Earl of Limerick now asked why Hownam thought it necessary for some person to sleep under the tent with the Princess. 'I beg to ask from what you conceive the necessity to arise?'

'I thought it necessary that somebody should be near her Royal Highness. A woman alone on a ship's deck at sea I should think perfectly authorized in having some person near her.'

'Were any suspicions entertained by you of the crew?'

'None.' (Later he amended this to 'We did not know anything of the crew'.)

'Then it was not from any apprehension of the crew that you conceived it necessary that a man should sleep in the same tent in the dark with the Princess of Wales?'

'When I saw it I looked upon it that way.'

'In what way?'

'That it was not improper that he should sleep there, the Princess being there, on deck, by herself.'

'Then you do not conceive there is any impropriety in a male person sleeping in the same tent with a female, the light being out?'

'From the hatches being open, and all the doors below, I do not. There was no mystery in it whatever.'

'I beg to ask you whether you would like your wife—'

('No, no,' and some laughter.)

'Would you have any objection or conceive it improper that Mrs Hownam should so sleep in a tent with a male person?'

'Every man, I trust, looks at his wife without making any comparison or exception. I never made any comparison.'

'Then you cannot form any opinion on it?'

'I cannot.'

'I beg to know whether you see any impropriety, situated as the tent was, . . . in a male and female so sleeping?'

'I do not conceive there was any impropriety . . . I have seen the Princess in so many situations during her travels that I do not look upon it as improper.'

'What do you mean by saying that you have seen the Princess in so many situations during her travels?'

'I have seen her under a sorry shed at Ephesus, under which we should hardly put a cow in this country, in the midst of horses, mules and Turks. It did not strike me as improper.'

Hownam cannot have known the bad effect that his evidence was having. When, at last, he was dismissed, the relief of the Queen's supporters must have been considerable. Her two naval gentlemen had unwittingly played into the hands of the Prosecution, and, in Greville's opinion, 'all unprejudiced men seem to think the adultery sufficiently proved'.[8]

The Queen's friends rallied round. The Hon. Keppel Craven and Sir William Gell had travelled from Italy on purpose to give evidence, though Gell, was 'quite crippled by the gout' and Craven's appearance before the Lords was 'entirely an act of friendship to Gell' and 'to serve him as another pair of legs'. The Lords were merciful and spared Sir William a long examination.

'Did you ever observe anything in the conduct of the Princess of Wales towards Pergami . . . to induce you to entertain an idea that there was an adulterous intercourse between them?'

'Upon my honour I never saw the Princess speak to Pergami but on matters of business . . .'

'Was there anything in the manners of Pergami which made it disagreeable to you as a gentleman to share with you the duties of chamberlain?'

'Quite on the contrary. He was remarkably attentive to me, and would have handed me downstairs with candles if I would have let him.'*

He was also questioned about Mahomet's dance. He had seen it in Eastern countries, and also in Spain and Portugal. He was asked to describe the dance, but the Lord Chancellor intervened, playfully reminded the Counsel, 'Recollect Mr Williams, that Sir William Gell has the gout.'

Gell was able to defend the Princess's choice of fancy dress in which she appeared before the King of Naples. The much criticized 'Muse of History'

* Fulford describes this as a civility in Italy generally reserved for cardinals and royal persons.

was, in Gell's eyes, perfectly justified. It was copied, he said, from a classical statue in the British Museum.

'Was there anything indecent or indecorous in the style or nature of that dress?'

'The whole world is capable of judging; those statues are very much draped, completely covered.'

The only woman to speak for the Queen was Lady Charlotte Lindsay, who had been with her for a short while in Italy. Lady Charlotte was treated to a merciless cross-examination by Copley—'as if he had been endeavouring to bring out the confession of a murderer at the Old Bailey', she said. Indeed, at one point she was reduced to tears. Brougham sent her a dose of lavender drops, and asked permission for her to sit down. She admitted, after further questioning, that her reason for resigning from the Princess's suite was 'influenced by the degrading reports that had reached me, although I had myself never seen any improprieties in her Majesty's conduct while I was with her in Italy'.[9]

'This answer', said Lady Charlotte, 'seemed to give universal satisfaction. I heard Denman whisper to Mr Brougham, "That was well answered"; and Mr B replied "Perfect! Perfect!"'

On 24 October, forty days after the trial began, Denman, the Queen's Solicitor-General, began his speech summing up the evidence, which went on for two days. Lady Charlotte, concealed behind Sir Thomas Tyrwhitt's red curtain, managed to hear the second part, which she pronounced 'very good—strong—clear and concise'. 'His voice is fine,' she added, 'but not so flexible and pathetic as Brougham's.'[10] Nor did he possess Brougham's sarcastic wit. But he set out to crush the Prosecution's evidence as worthless, and claimed that 'it was most perfectly clear that there was no more ground to suppose that any illicit connexion had taken place before her Royal Highness embarked on board that polacca, than there was for any one of their Lordships to imagine that any female of his family . . . had been guilty of such a crime, merely because she had an opportunity of doing so'. Once aboard, if she had wanted to pass the night in the arms of Pergami she would have found it far safer to do this in her cabin than in a tent on deck.

Denman showed righteous indignation over the more outrageous pieces of evidence which he (Mr Denman) should have thought no husband of the slightest feeling would have permitted to be given against his wife, even if she had deserted his fond and affectionate embraces, much less if he had driven her into guilt by thrusting her from his dwelling . . . This was delicate ground: here, for the first time, the husband's conduct was referred to, and Denman did not pull his punches, speaking of his 'cruelty and profligacy'.

The more imputations he cast upon her, the more he was to be despised for having deserted and abandoned her. Denman could find no example in any history of a Christian king who had thought himself at liberty to divorce his wife for misconduct, when his own misconduct in the first instance was the occasion of her fall.

After this statement had taken effect, Denman gathered himself together for a final outburst which might well have graced the boards of Drury Lane, and which unfortunately led him, carried away as he was, into a disastrous close. 'If your Lordships have been furnished with powers which I might almost say Omniscience itself possesses, to arrive at the secrets of this female, you will think it is your duty to imitate the justice, beneficience and wisdom of that benignant Being, who, not in a case like this where innocence is manifest, but when guilt was detected and vice revealed, said—"If no accuser can come forward to condemn thee, neither do I condemn thee: go, and sin no more."'

It is said that all his life Denman bitterly regretted this ending.

But his speech had had its effect. Once again, as was the way with Caroline, mirth prevailed, and a new comic song was born.

Most gracious Queen, we thee implore,
To go away and sin no more;
Or if that effort be too great,
To go away at any rate.

Sympathy with the Queen's cause began slowly and almost imperceptibly to wane. The trial dragged on into November, and Lord Erskine had a stroke. The Queen issued a statement, which was read for her, and ended: 'She now most deliberately, and before God, asserts that she is wholly innocent of the crime laid to her charge; and she awaits, with unabated confidence, the final result of this unparalleled investigation.'[11]

On Friday 10 November, after the third reading, the vote was taken: 108 in favour and 99 against. The majority had shrunk from twenty-eight to nine, and the Prime Minister decided to throw in his hand.

'The Bill', wrote Creevey, 'is gone, thank God, to the devil.'

Caroline had won.

Chapter Twenty-five

SCENES OF wild excitement broke out after the ending of the trial. 'The lower classes', wrote Lady Erne, 'are under a complete illusion . . . and believe their "poor dear good Queen" acquitted.'[1] So they stuck laurel leaves in their caps and white cockades in their buttonholes—and lost no time in demonstrating their delight. As Caroline was escorted to her carriage the cries and cheers were deafening: but it was remarked that she made no response. She stared ahead of her as if stunned, and as she seated herself those nearest to her saw that she was in tears.

Her long ordeal was ended, but she could feel no joy, only a great weariness. 'No-one, in fact, cares for me,' she wrote afterwards, 'and this business has been more cared for as a political affair than as the cause of a poor forlorn woman.'[2]

The demonstrations went on for three days and nights: there were fireworks, bonfires, dancing in the streets, and illuminations blazed all the way from Piccadilly to Whitechapel. It was a wild, feverish excitement which spread into the provinces and gave cause for uneasiness by its strength of feeling. In the north, rioting, even revolution, was in the air. In London, all the ships in the river glittered mast-high with lights, and processions marched through the city to the music of bands, carrying busts of the Queen with a crown on her head. Windows, of course, were broken. 'The state of the town is beyond everything,' wrote Creevey, who caught the fever himself and 'drank an extra bottle of claret . . . in the midst of our brilliant illuminations at Brooks's'.[3]

On the first Sunday after the finish of the trial, the Queen informed the Dean of St Paul's that she intended to attend a public thanksgiving there on Wednesday 29 November. The Dean was horrified, and begged Lord Sidmouth to advise him what on earth to do; but Sidmouth was not helpful. Apparently, if the Queen wished to attend a service at St Paul's, no one could stop her. And Lord Sidmouth added soothingly that he was convinced that 'no serious disturbance will take place'.[4]

Accordingly, Caroline had her way. She was escorted from Brandenburg

House by a cavalcade of 150 horsemen, and great numbers of people joined the procession as it moved eastwards. At Temple Bar the Queen was met by the Lord Mayor and Sheriffs. The weather was foggy and wet. 'I wish it may pour,' said Lady Erne unkindly . . . 'It would be delightful to have [the Lord Mayor] soaked thro' and thro', as well as the absurd aldermen etc., who attend him.' The same lady wrote a few days later, on 5 December, 'They say she looked very cross . . . and was very much annoyed by their making her open her carriage on her return from the Church; in all that raw fog it must have been disagreeable enough, and rather perilous to her precious health.'[5] 'It was a poor cortège,' added Lady Erne, determined in her disapproval of the whole thing, 'and the cheering was flat.'

Princess Lieven, who had watched the procession as it passed down the Mall, was more charitable. 'There was a crowd of at least 50,000 people. It was beautiful, absurd, frightening, all at once . . . perfect order, enthusiasm and good humour. On the first banner in the procession was written, "The Queen's Guard—the People".'[6] As Caroline's coach passed Carlton House, 'they cheered twice as loud', said Princess Lieven, and added, 'No doubt he was there, hidden in some corner.'

The King was going through a very trying time. While Caroline occupied the centre of the stage, he was obliged to wait in the wings while the great performance in which he himself was the star was in preparation. The coronation had already been postponed once on account of the Queen's trial; and now, in the hope that the violent demonstrations would soon begin to fade, it was fixed for the month of July. Meanwhile, the King consoled himself with his new charmer, Lady Conyngham, and waited impatiently for the moment when he might show himself in public without being booed. His ministers found him impossible to deal with, quarrelling on the slightest excuse. He sought for new ways of dealing with the Queen, and told Wellington that he had papers which would prove to Parliament that she had once shut her daughter, Princess Charlotte, in a closet at Kensington Palace with a Captain Hesse. 'Have you ever heard of such a revolting scheme?' wrote Princess Lieven.[7] And fortunately, this was the opinion of the King's ministers. They had other, more serious, problems connected with the Queen's future. She lay in bed complaining of the English climate and composing letters to Lord Liverpool, setting forth her wishes: she was not happy at Brandenburg House; she demanded a town residence, a palace suitable to her position as Queen, and a household of corresponding size. ('How very audacious!' said Lady Erne.)

She also continued to clamour for her name to be restored to the liturgy. The ministers were resolved, to a man, that this should not happen. 'It would be an insult to all sense of morality and religion to call upon the people of England to do honour to the Queen in the public prayers after such facts have been proved against her.'[8]

By the beginning of 1821, the Queen's popularity showed signs of declining. She and the King were vying with each other for the people's favour, both making carefully planned expeditions to theatres and other public entertainments. 'The Queen is going to try her luck at a concert at the Mansion House this evening,' wrote one Londoner, 'but I really flatter myself that she has sunk considerably lately, and that there is much less interest about her.'[9]

In her lonely state, and without the flattery of Pergami, Caroline did not care a jot about her appearance. For her drives through London she was well provided with befeathered bonnets and pelisses trimmed with fur or lace; but we hear of her visiting Mrs Damer of Twickenham, 'roll'd up in an immense plain, thick shawl with a round hat pulled down over her eyes'. Her spouse, on the other hand, spent a large part of every day preparing himself for public view, and no pains were spared to enhance his impressive appearance. He was enormous: but with care he managed to look every inch a king.

He disguised his shape by 'drawing in his great body with a broad belt, and by close buttoning of a kind of uniform jacket . . . hiding the lower part of his face with a large black neck-cloth, and then swelling out his shoulders and the upper part of his person with tags and embroidery, and covering it with orders, instead of the simple Star and Garter worn by his father; and yet for a man of near sixty he continues to look young by the help of a wig . . .'[10] (Frampton).

His air and manner, we are told, were as graceful as they used to be when he was Prince of Wales—Prince Charming. 'He was', said Wellington, 'the most extraordinary compound of talent, wit, buffoonery, obstinacy and good feeling—in short, a medley of the most opposite qualities, with a great preponderance of good—that I ever saw in any character in my life.'

His wife, unhappily, was never given a glimpse of these good qualities. Their relationship was conducted in a series of avoidances, and so arranged by the King that they never met. This was not for want of trying on Caroline's part: she was only too anxious to meet her husband, and to present him with a petition—for restoration to the liturgy, a decent income, and a London house. But the King, as she might have guessed, refused to meet her: nevertheless, she persisted. She decided that she would attend his first Drawing Room at Buckingham House, and wrote to Lord Liverpool telling him so. The King refused, but she persisted in her proposal. He was in a dilemma: his ministers advised him on no account to refuse her admittance, which would result in a new cause for unpopularity with the public. On the contrary, it was settled that she was to be treated with due honours on her way to Buckingham House, and on arrival there, was to be shown into an apartment downstairs and there told that she could not see the King. This rather cowardly plan succeeded: Caroline made no attempt to pursue the subject, but returned to Brandenburg House to wait for the reassembling of Parliament on 23 January. 'The Ministers,' said Princess Lieven, 'have forced the King to open Parliament himself, which he did not at all want to do, and, further, they are forcing him to name the Queen in his speech—that terrible word which the Ministers went so far out of their way to avoid.'[11]

'The Speash from the Trone,' Caroline told Anacharis, who had returned to Italy, '... was moderate and *conclusive*.' She was pleased with it. 'All further persecutions,' she told him, were at an end; and, carried away by optimism, 'I trust that in the month of *March* next I shall be in Paradis again I mean to say in *Italie*!' Her next announcement was a little too hopeful. 'The Liturgie will now also soon [be] settelled.' She thought that as the ministers were so anxious to remain in office, they would submit 'to give up that paint (point)'. But the ministers, we are told, were 'stout about the Liturgy': the country might pray for its King and all its Princes and Princesses, but never, on any account, for its Queen.

There was also the matter of a London residence. Parliament had not found one for her, so she found one for herself. 'I have bought Marlborough House,' she wrote on 27 January, 'for the somme of 28,000 *guineas* for 14 years to come.' This news was received with horror at Carlton House; but Princess Lieven found the situation amusing. 'It is said that the Queen has bought Prince Leopold's house, which has nothing but a wall to separate it from the gardens of Carlton House. The couple will be able to act the story of Pyramus and Thisbe all over again; it may become quite touching.'[12]

Marlborough House was rented to Prince Leopold of Saxe-Coburg, Caroline's son-in-law. They had never met, but Leopold had made an attempt at a friendly gesture by presenting himself at Brandenburg House. 'He declares', wrote Princess Lieven, 'that in his opinion the proceedings have cleared her; and that he treats her as perfectly pure and innocent; he had judged and decided before the House of Peers had pronounced.'[13] But this rather pompous resolve went unrewarded: the Queen refused to see him. It would be too painful for both, said his mother-in-law. But she still wanted his house. In her next letter to Anacharsis she repeats, 'I have bought Prince Leopold house, namly Malbroug House but there is one great difficulte that he has still Rented for 5 years to come.' Keppel Craven, now acting as her secretary in place of Joseph Hownam* wrote on her behalf a lengthy appeal to his good feelings, begging him to allow her to take over the lease.[14] But her prudent son-in-law, having thought things over, decided that it would be expedient to refuse: he did not wish to fall foul of the King. He gained nothing by his decision: the King disliked him anyway, and turned his back on Leopold at their next meeting. 'The King', said Leopold, in a loud aside to the Duke of York, 'has thought proper at last to take his line and I shall take mine.'[15]

Caroline was undeterred by Leopold's refusal to hand over the lease of Marlborough House, and decided to take Lord Harcourt's house in Cavendish Square. She must have a London house, she said; where she could leave 'some sort of servants' when she returned to Italy. She was already making plans to do this. Parliament had agreed, as soon as her English entourage had been appointed, to pay her an appanage of £50,000 a year; but she had refused to receive it, she told Anacharsis, 'before I ham Restored to the Liturgi' (she still expected this). 'I shall certainly have booth in a few days, Monny and Liturgi . . . And then', she said, 'I mean to fly to my Paradis to Italie.' 'The Coronation', she said, 'is now fixed for the month of May,' and she adds mysteriously, 'Of course I most be gon long before that Period otherwise it will never take place.' But two months later the coronation had still not taken place, and Caroline was still at Brandenburg House, where remnants of the Milan Commission watched and reported upon all comings and goings. 'A new travelling carriage' arrived from the coachmakers and was duly reported on. 'One of the men who came with this coach', wrote the spy, 'told the porter's wife at the Lodge that he thought the carriage was to use abroad, as they had made one simarler [*sic*] in strength sometime back which was sent to France . . .'[16]

But the new coach remained in England. Caroline had evidently decided to stay and see the fun.

On 12 June she wrote, 'The Proclamation for the Coronation for the 19th Juilly has been made,' and she had found out that 'the difference Branches of the Royal Familly which do not go in the Procession will have places at Westminster; for which reason I shall have a consultation to assure what Right Perogatife and Privileges I have on that occasion,' but it is not known what made her resolve to stay in England for the crowning.

Here is the old Caroline: there is a hint that her fighting spirit had returned. Her bouts of illness seem to have left her, and she was able once more to entertain. Although Lady Erne told her daughter that 'the circumstance of her drinking is already becoming pretty generally known', adding,

* Safely managing an iron foundry in France.

'I find that *Brandyburg* is becoming a familiar name for Her Majesty's present residence'—this was one of the more bitchy bits of gossip that circulated during her illness at the end of the trial. She felt well now, and wrote cheerfully, 'Tomorrow evening I shall gave my first Conserte in my Hause in London; Lady Tavistock, Lady Jersey etc., etc.' The aristocracy had decided to accept her invitations and she was given her place in society. The season was in full swing. 'The people are again very much alife,' she wrote; 'at the Lord Mayor's Dinner, at the Opera and the English Theater, the applause have been much in my favour.'[17] She must have felt that she was recognized again as a royal personage: society accepted her invitations, and the Duke of Sussex drove up from Tunbridge Wells to pay his respects.

But though she must still have longed to be back in her 'paradis' there seems to have been a strong reason why she did not go. Did she and Pergami correspond? It is hard to believe that they did not. What happened, one wonders, to keep her so resolutely parted from him? Or did they, in fact, meet? The last time we saw him was at Calais, where, presumably at Caroline's command, he left her and went back to Pesaro. On 3 April 1821, Sir Charles Stuart (of the Milan Commission) wrote to the Earl of Clanwilliam, Lord Castlereagh's private secretary, 'I think it necessary to lose no time in acquainting you that Pergami left Paris yesterday on his way to England. He arrived [in Paris] the preceding night, and slept at the Hotel de Bourbon. I cannot find that he communicated with any person during his short stay.'[18] Did he communicate with anyone in London? The spies who hung about Brandenburg House made no mention of him in their meticulous, ill-spelled reports of the comings and goings. Pergami's sister, the Countess Oldi, was still in the Queen's service, and had 'a house in the neighbourhood'.[19] There were quarrels between the Countess and Lady Anne Hamilton: 'jealousy . . . the cause of this on both sides', reported the spy, and it seems likely. But Caroline, in her letters to Sir William Gell, makes no mention of Pergami. If he did visit her in England, it was on business: he had his family to support, and they were all living in her house at Pesaro, where eight years later William Austin visited them. Whatever the rights and wrongs of her association with Pergami, Caroline had given generously all that he demanded. It seems likely that the affair had ended. She gives one clue which points to this possibility: 'Italie is lost for me at least for a long Period, and if I should go upon the Continent *I should go to a different and new atmosphere*!'[20]

A small army of carpenters, painters, upholsterers and carpet-layers had for some time been at work, both at Westminster Abbey and in Westminster Hall, where the coronation banquet was to be held after the ceremony. The date was settled at last: the King would be crowned on 19 July. The delays had made him nervy and irritable: he had enjoyed making the elaborate arrangements, spending lavishly on the splendour with which he hoped to capture the admiration, if not the love, of his subjects. 'The show', wrote one spectator afterwards, 'was all that Oriental pomp, feudal ceremonial and British wealth could unite.'[21]

But as the day drew near the King began to dread some mistake or interruption in the elaborate ceremony: he was terrified of what might happen if the Queen succeeded in making an appearance. However careful the plans to exclude her, he believed that she might, in her cunning way, find some means to inflame the populace against him and create pandemonium. For the past four months she had pestered him with petitions and appeals: to appear at his Drawing Room, to have her name restored to the liturgy, and finally, to attend the coronation—'one of her rights and privileges which her Majesty is resolved ever to maintain'.[22] She even asked him 'to name such ladies which will be required to bear her Majesty's Train on that day', and begged him to inform her 'in what Dresse the King wishes the Queen to appear in on that day, at the Coronation'.[23] She was fanatical, and her meaning was clear: she intended to be crowned, and she believed that she had every right to be.

He had asked for reports to be given to him on all the Queen's activities, and learned with disquiet that she had been visiting all the smaller theatres, 'by way of bringing herself to the recollection of the mob, and preparing a stir at the Coronation'.[24] This confirmed his fears. He was determined that at all costs Caroline must be kept out of Westminster Abbey; and he ordered an extra contingent of guards.

They were needed. Mrs Richard Trench, who attended the coronation, witnessed the incredible scenes outside the Abbey. She had been up since a quarter to four, and, coiffed, befeathered and robed in white satin, she arrived at Westminster at six 'after various difficulties occasioned by the dulness of doorkeepers, and some danger from the circumstance of my being within a few yards of the gate at the very instant the guards were called out to oppose the Queen'.[25]

Evidently the doorkeepers, intent on keeping out the Queen, were confused and uncertain of their orders. 'Tired to death', wrote this eye-witness, 'at having been sent backwards and forwards by doorkeepers, I was at last near the right entrance, when I heard loud shouts, a few faint hisses, and a cry of "Close the doors!" The Guards are called out, the Battle-axes rushed in, and absolutely carried me in amongst them.' The great door closed behind her—'closed', she said dramatically, 'against a woman—and a Queen'.

Caroline had arrived. Ignoring the pleas of her advisers, she drove to the Abbey, determined that she would get in or create havoc. She had been confident that with the help of the crowds, her supporters, she would succeed in doing one or the other.

When the doorkeeper refused to admit her, her Chamberlain, Lord Hood, told him that she was the Queen. This made no impression: the man said that his orders were that no one was to be admitted without a peer's ticket. Lord Hood immediately produced a ticket signed 'Wellington'. The doorkeeper grudgingly accepted it, but pointed out that it only admitted one person. Caroline was accompanied by Lady Anne Hamilton and Lady Hood and insisted that, as Queen, she could not enter the Abbey unattended. The doorkeeper regretted that he could not admit three persons on one ticket. By this time the Guards had closed their ranks, waiting for the Queen's next move. As they expected, she decided to try another door; but whichever way she turned, her way was barred. She quietly re-entered her carriage, and gave orders to drive back home.

She was defeated. The crowds who had been her friends, on whose support she had so confidently relied, hardly noticed her departure: the pageantry and splendour of the coronation was beginning to manifest itself as the doors were flung open again and more and more carriages drove up. Jewels flashed, feathers waved, and the sun played on the scarlet and gold of uniforms and peers' robes. The bells of Westminster rang out as, red-faced, dumpy, expressionless, the Queen drove away westwards to Brandenburg House.

But she refused to accept defeat. That same day she wrote to the King. 'The Queen must trust that after the Public insult her Majesty has received this morning, the King will grant her just Right to be crowned next Monday, and that his Majesty will command the Arch-Bishop of Canterbury to fulfil the Queen's Particular desire to confer upon her that sacred and August Ceremony.'[26]

Meanwhile the Archbishop of York, in his coronation sermon, was astonishing the congregation at the Abbey by assuring them that 'judging of the future by the past, we had reason to expect a reign of extraordinary virtue'.[27] The King, magnificent in his coronation robes, went through the whole exhausting ceremony with faultless grace and dignity, and occasional draughts of sal volatile. It was an unforgettable scene. 'The way in which the King bowed', wrote one spectator, 'was really royal.' At last, after the years of waiting, he was crowned King, invested with the potency of David and Solomon and the insignia which he had inherited from generations of kings.

Caroline, barred from the sight of His Majesty, was obliged to while away the empty day and decided to go to the theatre. She invited a few of her household to join her and hoped to forget the morning's humiliations by visiting Drury Lane, where she watched Mr Robert Elliston in 'a magnificent pageant of the coronation' with himself impersonating the King so well it was 'like a portrait'.

During the performance she felt unwell, but insisted upon staying to the end, when she rose and curtsied to the pit, galleries and boxes, and it was noticed that she looked wild and haggard.

She was ill, but she tried to ignore it, dosing herself with large quantities of calomel laced with laudanum to ease the pain.

Henry Holland, who had been her physician during her travels, called at Brandenburg House after witnessing her expulsion from Westminster. For the first time, he reported, her spirit had given way. Holland was shocked by the change in her appearance: the illness he diagnosed at once as acute inflammation of the bowels. It had gone on, he said, for more than two days without even attempt at relief. 'Seeing at once the urgent danger of the Queen's state, I sent instantly for other medical aid from town . . .'

The doctors prescribed their drastic remedies. She was blooded, losing, said Creevey, 64 oz of blood in one night; and heavily dosed with calomel topped up with 'a quantity of castor oil that would have turned the stomach of a horse'.[28]

But in spite of these remedies she made a partial recovery, and was able to receive Brougham. He brought her will and some deeds for her to sign, and asked if it was her pleasure to execute them, 'to which she said, "Yes, Mr Brougham," in the tone of a person in perfect health.'[29] Denman, her solicitor, and other legal gentlemen were called in; and 'the will and papers being read to her, she put her hand out of bed and signed her name four different times in the steadiest manner possible'.

She then announced 'with great firmness', 'I am going to die, Mr Brougham, but it does not signify.'

Brougham said, 'Your Majesty's physicians are of quite a different opinion.' 'Ah,' she said, 'I know better than them. I tell you I shall die, but I don't mind it.' Next day, after a sleepless night with appalling pain, she told Lord Hood, '*Je ne mourrais pas sans douleur, mais je mourrai sans regret.*'

Without regret. She had lived fearlessly, fiercely, grasping short-lived pleasures, but bestowing all that she had to give ungrudgingly. It was her tragedy that she was never loved; but there were a few who saw her as she was and pitied her, a sad woman who tried to overcome her failures by playing the clown.

References

ABBREVIATIONS: Asp/Charlotte = Aspinall, A., ed., Letters of the Princess Charlotte, Home and Van Thal, 1949.

Asp/Geo. IV = Aspinall, A., ed., The Letters of King George IV, 1812–30, 3 vols., Cambridge University Press, 1938.

Asp/P.O.W. = Aspinall, A., ed., The Correspondence of George, Prince of Wales, 1770–1812, 8 vols., Cassell, 1963–71.

Brougham = Brougham, Henry, The Life and Times of Henry, Lord Brougham, 3 vols., Blackwood, 1871.

Bury = Campbell, Lady Charlotte (afterwards Bury), the Diary of a Lady-in-Waiting, 2 vols., John Lane, The Bodley Head, 1908.

Gell = Letters between Princess Caroline and Sir William Gell. Private Collection.

Glenbervie = Douglas, Sylvester, Lord Glenbervie. Diaries, 2 vols., Constable, 1928.

Gower = Leveson Gower, Granville, Private Correspondence, 1781–1821, 2 vols., John Murray, 1916.

Harris = Harris, James, Earl of Malmesbury, Diaries and Correspondence of James Harris, 1st Earl of Malmesbury, 4 vols., R. Bentley, 1844.

Hownam = Hownam, Joseph, Diary. Private collection.

Huish = Huish, Robert, Memoirs of Caroline, Queen of Great Britain, 2 vols., T. Kelly, 1821.

See Bibliography for full details of other books mentioned.

CHAPTER ONE

1. Stanley, Maria J., The Early married life of Maria Josepha, Lady Stanley, p. 24.
2. —— p. 23.
3. Trench, Mrs. Melesina, The Remains of the late Mrs. Richard Trench, p. 44.
4. Stanley, p. 20.
5. Huish, I, p. 9.
6. Asp/P.O.W./III, p. 9.

CHAPTER TWO

1. Brooke, John, King George III, p. 347.
2. Harris, III, p. 153.
3. —— III, p. 156.
4. —— III, p. 160.
5. Asp/P.O.W./II, p. 503.
6. —— II, p. 508n.
7. —— II, p. 509.
8. Harris, III, p. 166.
9. —— III, p. 168.
10. —— III, p. 170 (translated).
11. —— III, p. 179.
12. —— III, p. 180.
13. —— III, p. 184.
14. —— III, p. 189.

CHAPTER THREE

1. Harris, III, p. 187.
2. —— III, p. 191.
3. —— III, p. 195.
4. —— III, p. 193.
5. —— III, p. 233.
6. —— III, p. 197.
7. —— III, p. 211.
8. Melville, L., An Injured Queen, p. 47.
9. Harris, III, p. 211.
10. —— III, p. 208.
11. —— III, p. 215.
12. —— III, p. 215.
13. —— III, p. 215.
14. Frampton, Mary, Journal, p. 84.
15. Harris, III, p. 218.
16. —— III, p. 219.

CHAPTER FOUR

1. Asp/P.O.W./I, p. 231.
2. —— I, p. 302.
3. —— I, p. 289.
4. —— I, p. 293.
5. —— II, p. 443n.
6. —— III, p. 16.
7. Gower, I, p. 221.
8. Asp/P.O.W./III, p. 11.
9. —— III, p. 44.
10. —— III, p. 50.
11. —— III, p. 51n.
12. —— III, p. 13.
13. —— III, p. 3.
14. Jerningham, Frances, The Jerningham Letters, I, p. 75.

CHAPTER FIVE

1. Asp/P.O.W./III, p. 55.
2. Keppel, George T., Fifty years of my life, I, p. 271.
3. Stuart Dorothy, Daughters of George III, p. 193.
4. Asp/P.O.W./III, p. 64.
5. —— III, p. 122.
6. —— III, p. 65.
7. —— III, p. 69.
8. —— III, p. 70.
9. —— III, p. 70.
10. —— III, p. 75.
11. —— III, p. 79.
12. —— III, p. 79.
13. —— III, p. 84.
14. —— III, p. 98n.
15. —— III, p. 106.
16. —— III, p. 108.
17. —— III, p. 108.
18. —— III, p. 131.
19. —— III, p. 130.
20. —— III, p. 133.
21. —— III, p. 132–8.

CHAPTER SIX

1. Asp/P.O.W./III, p. 141.
2. Greenwood, Alice, Lives of the Hanoverian Queens of England, II, p. 260.
3. Gower, Iris L., The Face without a Frown, p. 205.
4. British Museum MSS. 23582.
5. Asp/P.O.W./III, p. 159.
6. —— III, p. 161.
7. —— III, p. 168 (translated).
8. —— III, p. 168.
9. —— III, p. 171.
10. —— III, p. 179.
11. —— III, p. 197.
12. —— III, p. 198.
13. —— III, p. 198.
14. —— III, p. 233.
15. —— III, p. 239.
16. —— III, p. 193.

CHAPTER SEVEN

1. *The Times*, 29 Sept. 1796.
2. Asp/P.O.W./III, p. 258.
3. —— III, p. 281.
4. —— III, p. 283.
5. —— III, p. 194.
6. —— III, p. 379.
7. —— III, p. 497.
8. Glenbervie, I, p. 71.
9. Asp/P.O.W./III, p. 471.
10. Stuart, Dorothy, Daughter of England, p. 13.
11. Asp/P.O.W./III, p. 374.

CHAPTER EIGHT

1. Elliot, Sir Gilbert, Life and Letters, III, p. 36.
2. Grosvenor, C. and Wortley, C., The First Lady Wharnecliffe, I, pp. 150–1.
3. Murray, Amelia, Recollections from 1803–1837, p. 47.
4. Glenbervie, I, p. 215.
5. —— II, p. 87.
6. —— I, pp. 224–5.
7. —— I, p. 225.
8. —— II, p. 87.
9. Brooke, John, King George III, p. 370.
10. Lord Essex to Lord Lowther, Lonsdale MSS.
11. Asp/P.O.W./V, p. 77.
12. —— V, p. 84.
13. —— V, p. 93.
14. Gower, I, p. 473.
15. Asp/P.O.W./V, pp. 88–93.
16. —— V, pp. 112–18.
17. —— V, p. 126.

CHAPTER NINE

1. Stanhope, Lady Hester, Memoirs, I, p. 310.
2. Glenbervie, II, pp. 91–2.
3. Gower, I, p. 255.

4. Glenbervie, I, p. 260.
5. —— I, p. 260.
6. Caetani, Vittoria, The Locks of Norbury, p. 222.
7. —— p. 230.
8. Stuart, Dorothy, Daughter of England, pp. 33–4.
9. Huish, I, p. 135.
10. —— I, p. 153.

CHAPTER TEN

1. Huish, I, p. 104.
2. —— I, p. 114.
3. Asp/P.O.W./V, p. 396n.
4. Huish, I, p. 154.
5. Bury, I, p. 185.
6. Gower, II, p. 204.
7. —— II, p. 204.
8. Huish, I, p. 131.
9. —— I, p. 177.
10. Asp/P.O.W./VI, p. 127.
11. Huish, I, p. 402.
12. Stuart, Dorothy, Daughter of England, p. 51.
13. Gower, II, p. 432.

CHAPTER ELEVEN

1. Asp/Charlotte, p.x.
2. Tremayne Collection.
3. Richardson, Joanna, The Disastrous Marriage, pp. 65–6.
4. Harris, IV, p. 357.
5. Asp/P.O.W./V, pp. 431–2.
6. —— VI, p. 77.
7. —— VI, pp. 82–3.
8. —— VI, p. 511.
9. —— VI, p. 196.
10. —— VI, p. 194.
11. Gower, II, p. 266.
12. Asp/P.O.W./VI, p. 194.
13. Bury, I, p. 9.
14. —— I, p. 16.
15. —— I, p. 42.
16. —— I, p. 2[illegible].
17. Glenbervie, II, p. 61.
18. Bury, I, p. 46.
19. —— I, p. 73.
20. —— II, p. 283.
21. Asp/P.O.W./VIII, p. 49.

CHAPTER TWELVE

1. Asp/Charlotte, p. 16.
2. Glenbervie, II, p. 105.
3. —— II, p. 106.
4. Creston, Dormer, The Regent and his daughter, p. 125.
5. Shelley, Percy Bysshe, Letters, I, p. 86.
6. Bury, I, p. 158.
7. —— I, p. 79.

8. Bury, I, p. 13.
9. Calvert, Frances, An Irish Beauty of the Regency, p. 102.
10. Bury, I, p. 102.
11. —— I, p. 95.
12. Asp/Geo. IV/I, p. 116.
13. Bury, I, p. 80.

CHAPTER THIRTEEN

1. Knight, E. Cornelia, Autobiography, p. 113.
2. Asp/Charlotte, p. 17.
3. Asp/P.O.W./VIII, p. 30.
4. Asp/Geo. IV/I, pp. 518, 521.
5. —— I, p. 519.
6. Asp/Charlotte, p. 100.
7. Asp/Geo. IV/I, p. 376.
8. Brougham, II, p. 160.
9. —— II, p. 161.
10. Asp/Geo. IV/I, p. 204.
11. Asp/Charlotte, p. 47.
12. Bury, I, p. 116.
13. Asp/Charlotte, p. 49.
14. —— p. 58.
15. —— p. 48.
16. Knight, E. Cornelia, Autobiography, p. 120.
17. Asp/Charlotte, p. 52.
18. —— p. 53.

CHAPTER FOURTEEN

1. Knight, E. Cornelia, Autobiography, p. 124.
2. Asp/Charlotte, p. 54.
3. —— p. 53.
4. —— p. 55.
5. Ogilvy, Mabell, In Whig Society, 1775–1818, p. 159.
6. Asp/Geo. IV/I, p. 228.
7. Berry, Mary, Extracts of the Journals and Correspondence of Miss Berry, II, p. 533.
8. Asp/Charlotte, p. 59.
9. Hedley, Olwen, Queen Charlotte, p. 267.
10. Jerningham, Frances, The Jerningham Letters, II, p. 5.
11. Bury, I, p. 156.
12. —— I, p. 184.
13. —— I, p. 186.
14. —— I, p. 186.
15. —— I, p. 163.

CHAPTER FIFTEEN

1. Asp/Charlotte, p. 102.
2. Knight, E. Cornelia, Autobiography, p. 140.
3. Asp/Charlotte, p. 72.
4. —— p. 92.
5. —— p. 93.
6. —— p. 97.

CHAPTER SIXTEEN

1. Asp/Charlotte, p. 100.
2. —— p. 100.
3. —— p. 102.
4. —— p. 101.
5. Bury, I, p. 197.
6. —— I, p. 193.
7. Asp/Geo. IV/I, p. 419.
8. *The Times*, 22 April 1814.
9. Bury, I, p. 203.
10. —— I, p. 199.
11. Brougham, II, p. 216.
12. —— II, p. 222.
13. —— II, p. 223.

CHAPTER SEVENTEEN

1. Asp/Charlotte, p. 139.
2. Creston, Dormer, The Regent and his Daughter, pp. 228–9.
3. Brougham, II, p. 229.
4. —— II, p. 230.
5. Asp/Charlotte, p. 128.
6. —— pp. 137–8.
7. Brougham, II, p. 254–5.

CHAPTER EIGHTEEN

1. Bury, I, p. 184.
2. Clerici, G., A Queen of Indiscretions, p. 41.
3. Stoeckl, Agnes de, Four Years an Empress, p. 228.
4. Gower, II, p. 516.
5. —— II, p. 535.
6. —— II, p. 535.
7. Melville, Lewis, An Injured Queen, pp. 359–60.
8. Asp/Geo. IV/I, p. 522.
9. Gower, II, p. 516–17.
10. Holland, Sir Henry, Recollections of a Past Life, p. 137.
11. Gell, June 1815.
12. Hownam, p. 26.
13. —— p. 35.
14. —— p. 37.
15. Gell, 14 April 1815.
16. Hownam, p. 36.

CHAPTER NINETEEN

1. Hownam, pp. 41–2.
2. Clerici, G., A Queen of Indiscretions, p. 63.
3. Hownam, p. 48.
4. Gell, 30 July 1815.
5. Hownam, p. 48.
6. Gell, 30 July 1815.
7. —— 20 October 1815.
8. Hownam, p. 73.
9. —— p. 72.
10. Clerici, G., A Queen of Indiscretions, p. 92.

CHAPTER TWENTY

1. Hownam, p. 81.
2. —— p. 100.
3. —— p. 102.
4. —— p. 107.
5. Gell, 21 April 1816.
6. —— 21 April 1816.
7. Hownam, p. 114.
8. Gell, 21 April 1816.
9. Hownam, p. 140.
10. —— p. 141.
11. —— pp. 147–8.
12. —— p. 148.
13. —— p. 151.
14. —— p. 152.
15. —— p. 167.
16. —— p. 168.
17. —— p. 171

CHAPTER TWENTY-ONE

1. Hownam, p. 173.
2. —— p. 187.
3. —— p. 193.
4. Gell, 18 January 1817.
5. Clerici, G., A Queen of Indiscretions, p. 60.
6. Gell, 20 November 1816.
7. Asp/Geo. IV/II, p. 351.
8. Gell, 20 November 1816.
9. Hownam, p. 195.
10. Gell, June (?) 1817.
11. —— undated.
12. —— 10 August, probably 1816.
13. —— 29 October 1817.
14. Hownam, pp. 210–12.
15. Brougham, II, p. 332.
16. Hownam, p. 212.
17. —— p. 212.

CHAPTER TWENTY-TWO

1. Asp/Geo. IV/II, p. 273.
2. Gell, 25 February 1818.
3. Asp/Geo. IV/II, p. 279.
4. Gell, 1818.
5. Creevey, Thomas, The Creevey Papers, p. 180.
6. Gell, 15 September 1819.
7. —— 13 April 1820.
8. Greville, Charles, The Greville Memoirs, I, p. 94.
9. Creevey, Thomas, The Creevey Papers, p. 179.
10. Hibbert, Christopher, George IV, p. 163.
11. Arbuthnot, Harriet, Journal, I, p. 25.
12. Grosvenor, C. & Wortley, C., The First Lady Wharncliffe, I, pp. 268–9.
13. Crocker, John W., The Croker Papers, I, p. 159.
14. Gell, 13 April 1830.
15. Creevey, Thomas, The Creevey Papers, p. 187.
16. —— p. 188.

17. Creevey, Thomas, The Creevey Papers, p. 189.
18. Melville, Lewis, An Injured Queen, p. 472.

CHAPTER TWENTY-THREE

1. Fulford, Roger, The Trial of Queen Caroline, p. 86.
2. —— p. 90.
3. —— p. 114.
4. Creevey, Thomas, The Creevey Papers, p. 191.
5. —— p. 191.
6. —— p. 192.

CHAPTER TWENTY-FOUR

1. Greville, Charles, The Greville Memoirs, I, p. 105.
2. Creevey, Thomas, The Creevey Papers, p. 192.
3. Asp/Geo. IV/II, p. 357.
4. Hownam, p. 223.
5. Creevey, Thomas, The Creevey Papers, pp. 192–3.
6. Lieven, Princess, Letters to Prince Metternich, p. 91.
7. New, Chester W., The Life of Henry Brougham, p. 257.
8. Greville, Charles, The Greville Memoirs, I, p. 106.
9. Berry, Mary, Extracts of the Journals, III, p. 256.
10. —— III, pp. 257–8.
11. Fulford, Roger, The Trial of Queen Caroline, p. 240.

CHAPTER TWENTY-FIVE

1. Grosvenor, C. & Wortley, C., The First Lady Wharnecliffe, I, p. 286.
2. Croker, John Wilson, The Croker Papers, I, p. 165.
3. Creevey, Thomas, The Creevey Papers, p. 201.
4. Melville, Lewis, An Injured Queen, pp. 515–16.
5. Grosvenor, C. & Wortley, C., The First Lady Wharnecliffe, I, p. 289.
6. Lieven, Princess, Letters to Prince Metternich, p. 96.
7. —— p. 97.
8. Mr. Wortley to Lord Liverpool, 18 December 1820. In Yonge, Charles D., Life and Administration of Robert Banks Jenkinson, 2nd Earl of Liverpool, 1868, III, p. 117.
9. Frampton, Mary, Journal, p. 321.
10. —— p. 322.
11. Lieven, Princess, Letters to Prince Metternich, p. 106.
12. —— p. 106.
13. Melville, Lewis, An Injured Queen, p. 528.
14. Gell, 11 February 1821.
15. Melville, Lewis, An Injured Queen, p. 528.
16. Asp/Geo. IV/II, p. 417.
17. Gell, 12 June 1821.
18. Asp/Geo. IV/II, p. 425.
19. —— p. 418.
20. Gell, 12 June 1821.
21. Trench, Mrs. Melesina, The Remains of the Late Mrs. Richard Trench, p. 451.
22. Melville, Lewis, An Injured Queen, p. 543.
23. —— p. 543.
24. Frampton, Mary, Journal, p. 323.
25. Trench, Mrs. Melesina, The Remains of the Late Mrs. Richard Trench, pp. 450–1.
26. Melville, Lewis, An Injured Queen, p. 545.
27. Trench, Mrs. Melesina, The Remains of the Late Mrs. Richard Trench, pp. 451–2.
28. Creevey, Thomas, The Creevey Papers, p. 214.
29. —— p. 214.

Bibliography

Collections of royal letters compiled and edited by the late Professor A. Aspinall, C.V.O., M.A., D.Litt.:

Letters of the Princess Charlotte, 1811–1817, Home & Van Thal, 1949.

The Correspondence of George, Prince of Wales, 1770–1812, 8 vols., Cassell, 1963–71.

The Letters of King George IV, 1812–1830, 3 vols., Cambridge University Press, 1938.

Arbuthnot, Harriet, *The Journal of Mrs. Arbuthnot, 1820–1832*, eds. Francis Bamford and the Duke of Wellington, 2 vols., Macmillan, 1950.

Berry, Mary, *Extracts of the Journals and Correspondence of Miss Berry from the year 1783–1852*, ed. Lady Theresa Lewis, 3 vols., Longmans, 1865.

Brooke, John, *King George III*, Constable, 1972.

Brougham, Henry, *Memoirs of the Life and Times of Henry, Lord Brougham*, 3 vols., Blackwood, 1871.

Caetani, Vittoria, Duchess of Sermoneta, *The Locks of Norbury*, John Murray, 1940.

Calvert, Frances, *An Irish Beauty of the Regency*, John Lane, 1911.

Campbell, Lady Charlotte (afterwards Bury), *The Diary of a Lady-in-Waiting*, 2 vols., John Lane, The Bodley Head, 1908.

Clerici, Graziano, *A Queen of Indiscretions, the tragedy of Caroline of Brunswick, Queen of England*, translated by Frederic Chapman, John Lane, 1907.

Coxe, Howard, *The Stranger in the House—A life of Caroline of Brunswick*, Chatto & Windus, 1939.

Craven, Elizabeth, *The Beautiful Lady Craven*, eds. A. M. Bradley and Lewis Melville, 2 vols., John Lane, 1914.

Creevey, Thomas, *The Creevey Papers*, selected and re-edited by John Gore, John Murray, 1948.

Creston, Dormer, *The Regent and his Daughter*, Thornton Butterworth, 1932.

Croker, John Wilson, *The Croker Papers*, ed. Lewis Jennings, 3 vols., John Murray, 1884. Also 2 vol. edition published by Charles Scribners Sons, New York, 1884.

Douglas, Sylvester, Lord Glenbervie, *The Diaries of Sylvester Douglas, Lord Glenbervie*, ed. Francis Bickley, 2 vols., Constable, 1928.

Elliot, Sir Gilbert, 1st Earl of Minto, *Life and Letters from 1751–1806*, ed. Countess of Minto, 3 vols., Longman, 1874.

Frampton, Mary, *The Journal of Mary Frampton from 1779–1846*, Sampson Low, 1885.

Fulford, Roger, *The Trial of Queen Caroline*, Batsford, 1967.

Gower, Granville Leveson, 1st Earl Granville, *Private Correspondence, 1781–1821*, ed. Castalia, Countess Granville, 2 vols., John Murray, 1916.

Gower, Iris Leveson, *The Face without a Frown: Georgiana, Duchess of Devonshire*, Frederick Muller, 1944.

Greenwood, Alice, *Lives of the Hanoverian Queens of England*, 2 vols., George Bell, 1909–11.

Grenville, Richard, Duke of Buckingham and Chandos, *Memoirs of the Court of George IV*, 2 vols., London, 1859.

Greville, Charles, *The Greville Memoirs, 1814–1860*, ed. Lytton Strachey & Roger Fulford, 8 vols., Macmillan, 1938.

Grosvenor, Caroline & Wortley, Charles, *The First Lady Wharncliffe and her Family*, 1779–1856, 2 vols., Heinemann, 1927.

Hamilton, Lady Anne, *Secret History of the Court of England*, 2 vols., W. H. Stevenson, 1832.

Harris, James, Earl of Malmesbury, *Diaries and correspondence of James Harris, 1st Earl of Malmesbury*, 4 vols., R. Bentley, 1844.
Hedley, Olwen, *Queen Charlotte*, John Murray, 1975.
Hibbert, Christopher, *George, Prince of Wales*, Longmans, 1972.
—— *George IV, Regent and King*, Allen Lane, 1973.
Holland, Sir Henry, *Recollections of a Past Life*, London, 1872.
Huish, Robert, *Memoirs of Caroline, Queen of Great Britain, etc.*, 2 vols., T. Kelly, 1821.
—— *Memoirs of George IV*, 2 vols., 1830.
Jerningham, Frances, *The Jerningham Letters, 1780–1843*, ed. with notes by Egerton Castle, 2 vols., R. Bentley, 1896.
Keppel, George T., Earl of Albermarle, *Fifty Years of my Life*, 2 vols., London, 1876.
Knight, Ellis Cornelia, *Autobiography of Miss Knight, lady companion to Princess Charlotte*, ed. Roger Fulford, Kimber, 1960.
Leslie, Shane, *Mrs. Fitzherbert*, 2 vols., Burns & Oates, 1939.
Lieven, Doroteya, Princess, *The Private letters of Princess Lieven to Prince Metternich, 1820–1826*, ed. Peter Quennell & Dilys Powell, John Murray, 1948.
Melville, Lewis, *An Injured Queen*, Hutchinson, 1912.
Murray, Hon. Amelia, *Recollections from 1803–1837*, London, 1868.
New, Chester W., *The Life of Henry Brougham to 1830*, Clarendon Press, 1961.
Nicolson, Harold, *Bènjamin Constant*, Constable, 1949.
Nightingale, Joseph, *Memoirs of the Public and Private Life of her most Gracious Majesty Caroline, Queen of Great Britain*, J. Robins, 1820.
Ogilvy, Mabell, Countess of Airlie, *In Whig Society, 1775–1818*, Hodder & Stoughton, 1921.
Parry, Sir Edward, *Queen Caroline*, Benn, 1970.
Ponsonby, Henrietta, *Countess of Bessborough, Lady Bessborough and her family circle* (Journals and Correspondence) ed. Earl of Bessborough in collaboration with A. Aspinall, John Murray, 1940.
Richardson, Joanna, *The Disastrous Marriage*, Jonathan Cape, 1960.
Shelley, Percy Bysshe, *Letters of Percy Bysshe Shelley*, ed. Frederick L. Jones, 2 vols., Oxford University Press, 1964.
Stanhope, Lady Hester, *Memoirs of Lady Hester Stanhope*, 3 vols., London, 1845.
Stanley, Maria Josepha, Baroness Stanley of Alderley, *The Early Married Life of Maria Josepha, Lady Stanley* (selections from her correspondence), with extracts from Sir John Stanley's 'Praeterita', ed. Jane Adeane, Longmans, 1899.
Stoeckl, Agnes de, *Four Years an Empress, Marie-Louise, second wife of Napoleon*, John Murray, 1962.
Stuart, Dorothy M., *The Daughters of George III*, Macmillan, 1939.
—— *Daughter of England*, Macmillan, 1951.
Tisdall, E.E.P., *The Wanton Queen*, Stanley Paul, 1939.
Trench, Mrs Melesina, *The Remains of the late Mrs. Richard Trench, being selections from her journals, letters and other papers*, edited by her son, the Dean of Westminster, Parker, Son & Brown, 1862.
Turnbull, Patrick, *Napoleon's Second Empress*, Michael Joseph, 1971.
Wellesley, Gerald, Duke of Wellington, *Wellington and his friends. Letters of the first Duke of Wellington, as selected and edited by the 7th Duke of Wellington*, John Murray, 1965.
Yonge, Charles D., *Life and administration of Robert Banks Jenkinson, 2nd Earl of Liverpool*, 3 vols, London, 1868.

Index

Acre (St. Jean d'Acre), 72, 171–2
Adolphus, Prince, *see* Cambridge, Duke of
Albemarle, Lord, 34
Alexander I, Tsar, 134–7; in England, 139–41
Amelia, Princess, 107; illness and death, 94
Ancona, 182
Antalte, Marquis, 183
Aston, Mrs Hervey, 21, 22
Angerstein, Amelia, 71, 122
Angerstein, John Julius, 70–1, 122
Ansbach, Margravine of, 196
Aristodemo, Pacitta's opera, 140
Auerstadt, battle of, 88
August, Prince, *see* Friedrich August
Augusta, near Catania, 166, 168
Augusta, Princess, daughter of George III, 90, 107n, 129
Augusta, royal yacht, 21
Augustus, Prince, *see* Sussex, Duke of
Austin, Sophie, 76–7, 82
Austin, William, 68, 75–8, 87, 88, 97, 123, 223; birth and parentage, 76, 82; taken to Montague House, 76, 82; stays in the house, 77, 78; Caroline besotted with him, 78; leaves England with her, 150; in her entourage, 164, 172, 173, 188; with her in London, 192

Baden, Maria of (Duchess of Brunswick), 91
Batti, Italian architect, 177
Bayreuth, Margravine of, 179
Bayswater, Caroline's cottages in, 103, 104, 123
Beerbohm, Max, 23
Bellingham, John, assassin of Perceval, 103
Bentinck, Lord William, 153 and n.
Berne, 152, 154
Berry, Agnes, 99 and n., 119
Berry, Mary, 70, 99 and n., 102, 119, 154
Bessborough, Lady, 27, 44, 65, 153, 158
Bethlehem, 173
Bidgood, Robert, Caroline's page, 80, 81, 88
Bill of Pains and Penalties, 192, 194, 206, 217
Birollo, Francisco, 201
Blackheath, Caroline lives at, 58–60, 64, 68–70, 72, 73, 89, 91, 92, 97, 117, 124, 145, 156, 191; Woodlands, 70 and n., 71. *See also* Montague House
Bonaparte, Lucien, 182
Book, The, Caroline's defence, 83, 117; withdrawn by royal command, 83
Borgia, Count, 170–1
Bower, Mrs, wet nurse, 38, 51
Brandenburg House, Fulham, 196, 205, 218–19, 221–3, 225, 226
Bridgeman, Orlando (Lord Bradford), 24, 30
Briggs, Captain, commander of *Leviathan*, 164
Brighton, 25, 26, 35, 37, 38, 44, 47, 103, 105, 206; Pavilion, 26
Brougham, Henry, 122, 126, 137, 177, 189; and Caroline, 106, 107, 111, 117, 121, 122, 125, 139; edits her letter to the Prince, 110, 129; supports establishment for Charlotte, 111–13; and the Orange betrothal, 137; and Charlotte's escape to her mother's, 145–9; tries to stop Caroline leaving England 148; and the 'Venice Forgery', 183; Hownam's visit to him, 187; sends his brother to Pesaro, 187; meets Caroline at St. Omer, 190; advice to her, 191; at Caroline's trial, 195–7, 216; cross-examines Majocchi, 198–201; and Sacchi, 204; obtains adjournment, 204–5; opens the defence, 207–12; and Dr. O'Ryan, 210; at Caroline's deathbed, 226
Brougham, James, 183 and n., his mission to Italy, 187–9; deceived by Pergami, 187–8; on relations between Caroline and Pergami, 188
Browne, Colonel, 199
Brunswick, 2–3, 7, 150; Court of, 1–3; occupied by the French, 89; Caroline's return to, 151
Brunswick, Augusta, Duchess of, Caroline's mother, 3–5, 7, 93, 94, 118; and Caroline's marriage, 7–10, 13; dislike of Queen Charlotte, 8, 9, 12; accompanies Caroline on first stage of journey, 15–20; on Princess Charlotte's birth, 43; escapes to England from the French, 89–91, 119; pensioned by George III, 91; lives in Hanover Square, 92, 93, 119; and the exiled French court,

Brunswick, Augusta—*cont.*
93–4; illness and death, 119–20; buried at Windsor, 120
Brunswick, Caroline, Princess of, *see* Caroline
Brunswick, Charles William Frederick, father of Caroline, 1–4, 6, 12–15, 18–20, 37, 89; wife and mistresses, 3–4; and Caroline's marriage, 7–8; instructions and advice to her, 11, 23; declares war on Napoleon, 88; wounded in battle, 88; death, 88–9
Brunswick, Charlotte Augusta, sister of Caroline, marriage to Prince of Wurtemberg, 1, 4; unfaithfulness, 4; imprisoned at Castle Lode, 4, 5, 44; mysterious death, 4–5, 14
Brunswick, Dowager Duchess of, Caroline's grandmother, 3
Brunswick, Frederick William, Duke of, brother of Caroline, 4, 89, 180; exiled in England, 91–2; death of his wife, 91; meeting with Caroline, 161n; killed at Quatre Bras, 4, 151n., 162
Buccleuch, Duchess of, 59
Buckingham House, 220, 221
Buckinghamshire, Lady, 122
Burney, Fanny, 114
Burt, Rev. Robert, 24
Bury, Lady Charlotte, lady-in-waiting to Caroline, 2, 5, 33–5, 68, 72
Byron, Lord, 59, 154, 193

Calais, 190, 191, 209, 223
Camara, Caroline's courier, 175, 201
Cambridge, Duke of (Prince Adolphus), 30, 114
Campbell, Mrs. Alicia, 148; sub-governess to Princess Charlotte, 86–7, 148
Campbell, Lady Charlotte, lady-in-waiting to Caroline, 32, 58, 85–6, 91, 92, 99, 102, 104, 112, 119, 122–4, 134, 140, 156, 178; and Princess Charlotte, 122, 131–2; in Italy with Caroline, 157, 159, 161; and Pergami, 160
Campe, Herr, 58, 59, 67
Canning, George, 54, 56, 122, 180, 181; admiration for Caroline, 68–9, 193
Canterbury, Archbishop of, *see* Manners-Sutton *and* Moore
Carlton House, 25, 26, 31, 32, 34, 38, 44, 49, 51, 53, 54, 56–8, 65, 66, 74, 93, 96, 97, 103, 105, 111, 115, 135, 139, 143, 144, 146–8, 156, 192, 193, 219, 221; Princess Charlotte born at, 39; transformed into palace, 42, gardens and furniture, 42; rooms of Prince and Princess, 42–3; fête at, 98–100; thrown open to the public, 100; breakfast to celebrate Wellington's victories, 125; Prince of Orange at, 127–8; Assembly for Allied Sovereigns, 141–2
Caroline, Princess of Brunswick (Princess of Wales) (Queen Caroline), upbringing, 1–5; rumours of love affairs, 5–6; and Prince Louis Ferdinand of Prussia, 6; and Malmesbury's mission, 7–17; receives Prince of Wales's portrait, 9–10; formal betrothal, 10; Treaty of Marriage, 10; and Queen Charlotte, 10, 12; and Lady Jersey, 11, 13, 14, 22, 23, 27, 34, 35, 37
journey from Brunswick, 17–21; arrival in the Thames, 21; meeting with the Prince, 22–3, 30; plans for the wedding, 28; the wedding, 30–2; wedding night at Carlton House, 32, 35; 'honeymoon' at Kempshot Park, 34–5; at Brighton, 35, 37, 38; pregnancy, 35–9; birth of Charlotte, 39; and the Prince's will, 48; loneliness and unhappiness, 45, denounces Lady Jersey to the Prince, 46–8; he proposes separation, 47; letter to the King on reconciliation, 48; Lady Jersey's resignation, 49
household arrangements, 51; interview with the Prince, 52; enemies and partisans, 53–4, 56; leaves Carlton House, 57; lives at Charlton, 57, 58; moves to Montague House, Blackheath, 58–60; declines to return to Carlton House, 59; visits the King, 61, 62; received by him at Kew, 64–5
conducts orphanage, 67–8; her income, 68; and Sir Thomas Lawrence, 71–2; his portrait of her, 71–2; and Sir Sidney Smith, 72, 83; and Lady Douglas, 73–5, 77; and William Austin, 75–8, 87–8; anonymous letter to Sir John Douglas, 77, 78 and n.; the Delicate Investigation, 74–82, 85, 88; draws up *The Book*, 83; at Court for the King's birthday, 83–4
no part in Charlotte's upbringing, 85; lack of interest in her, 87; her father's death, 89, arrival of her mother, 90, 92, 93; her brother and his family, 92; breach with Duke of Cumberland, 97; her husband's power as Regent, 98; and the Regent's fête, 99; and Lady Hertford, 99–100; the Regent's illness, 101; her appearance and temperament, 102; and the Sapio family, 102–4, 106, 110, 122–4; buys cottages in Bayswater, 103, 104, 123; restrictions on Charlotte's visits, 104, 105
campaign to liberate Charlotte, 106, 110, 115, 121; and Charlotte's affair with Hesse, 108–10, 142, 143; sends letter edited by Brougham to Carlton House, 110–11, 129; loyal addresses to her, 111, 118–19, 121; and separate establishment for Charlotte, 112–13
the Prince's abuse of her, 116; and Privy Councillors' inquiry, 117–19; bizarre way

of life, 122–4; experiments with witchcraft, 123–4; sells Montague House, 124; moves to Connaught Place, 124; and Wellington's victories, 125; ostracized, 125–6; and Charlotte's confirmation, 129; and the Orange betrothal, 137, 142, 143; and the Allied Sovereigns, 138–9; appearance at the opera, 140; the Tsar fails to visit her, 140–1

and Charlotte's escape to her house, 145–8; leaves England, 149–51; farewell visit from Charlotte, 149; meets her brother in Brunswick, 151 and n.; moves to Switzerland, 151–2; in Italy, 152–3; meets Marie-Louise, 152, 154; and the Pope, 154, 157–8; sketching, 155; received by Murat in Naples, 155; reorganizes her entourage in Rome, 156; establishes herself in Genoa, 157–8; and Joseph Hownam, 156–65; and Ompteda, 158; and Pergami, 159–66; leaves for Milan, 161; ostracized by English there, 161, 164; watched by the Regent's agents, 161–2; death of her brother, 162

voyage in *Leviathan*, 164; in Napoleon's former house on Elba, 164; in Sicily, 164–6; portrait painted as Venus, 165–6; buys estate near Catania, 166; buys a polacca, 167–8;

sails for Tunis, 168; Tunis and the Bey, 168–70; and Charlotte's marriage, 170, 184; and Count Borgia, 170–1; sails for Palestine, 171; in Jerusalem, 172–4; and dubbing of Knights of the High Order, 173; establishes Order of St. Caroline, 174; return voyage to Sicily, 174; obtains permission to proceed to Rome, 175; received by the Pope, 176; at Villa d'Este on Lake Como, 177–8; her debts, 177, 180, 183–4; buys Villa Barone for Pergami, 177; seeks Order of Malta for him, 178; arrival of the Sapios, 178; visits in Italy and Germany, 178–9; in Vienna, 179–80; at Lucien Bonaparte's villa, 182; settles at Pesaro, 182; and the 'Venice Forgery', 183; in touch with her daughter again, 184; learns of Charlotte's death, 184–6, 188

sends Hownam with letter to Brougham, 187; James Brougham's visit, 187–9; learns of George III's death, 189–90; finds herself Queen, 190; meets Brougham at St. Omer, 190; proceeds to Calais, 190–1; reception in Dover and London, 191–2; proposals for her trial, 192, 194; adultery with Pergami alleged, 192, 197, 198, 200–4, 208–9, 214–16; supporters and opponents, 192–3; question of the liturgy, 193, 219–22

the trial, 194–217; her arrival in House of Lords, 194; Italian witnesses, 197–201, 203–4; other prosecution witnesses, 202–3; adjournment, 204, 206; crowds and demonstrations, 205, 212; caricatures, posters and broad-sheets, 205–6; Brougham opens the defence, 207–12; and question of Pergami's impotence, 210–11; defence witnesses, 212–16; her statement read, 217; third reading passed by only nine votes, 217; proceedings dropped, 217

demonstrations for her, 218; attends thanksgiving in St. Paul's, 218–19; signs of declining popularity, 220; public appearances, 220; buys Marlborough House, 221; and Prince Leopold, 221; he refuses to give up lease of Marlborough House, 221–2; still spied on, 222, 223; and the coronation, 222–3; excluded from it, 224; fails to gain admission to Abbey, 224–5; letter to the King, 225; taken ill at Drury Lane Theatre, 226; seriously ill, 226; makes her will, 226; death, 226

Carthage, 169

Castelfranco, 165

Castlereagh, Lord, 193, 196, 223

Catania, 165–7, 178

Catherine the Great, Empress, 4

Charles I, opening of his coffin, 120–1

Charlotte, Princess, daughter of Caroline, 4, 33, 43, 44, 49, 51, 55, 56, 65, 66, 81, 86–8, 107. 121, 136, 140, 148–9, 155; conception, 32; birth, 39; and the Prince of Wales' will, 41; plans for her entertainment, 55–6; and George III, 63–5; her disposition, 63; at Carlton House, 63; at Shooter's Hill, 64; and William Austin, 78, 87–8

her upbringing, 85–8; and the Duchess of Brunswick, 90–3; and George III's illness, 95; weekly dinners with her mother, 100–1; virtual prisoner at Windsor, 103; restrictions on visits to her mother, 104, 105, 107; and Captain George FitzClarence, 107, 118; affair with Captain Hesse, 107–11, 126, 151, 219

seeks to obtain an establishment, 111–13; letter to her father, 111; inquisition at Windsor, 112–13; and Miss Knight, 113–15; at Carlton House ball, 113–15; forbidden to see her mother, 115; interview with her father, 116–17; and Privy Councillors' enquiry, 117; gossip about her, 117–18; relations with her parents, 121–2, 125–6

plans for her marriage, 126–8; and the Prince of Orange, 126–30, 132–3, 137, 141; her confirmation, 129; shortened visit to her mother, 131–2; at Assembly for Allied Sovereigns, 141; in love with Prince August, 142–4, 147; engagement to Prince of Orange broken off, 142, 143; and Prince Leopold of Saxe-Coburg, 144; her father's plans for her,

Charlotte, Princess—*cont.*
144; escapes to her mother's house, 144–7; states her terms, 146, 147; agrees to go to Carlton House, 147–8; smuggles out letters, 148; sent to Cranbourne Lodge, 148; complains of her treatment, 148; and her mother's departure abroad, 149
marriage to Prince Leopold, 170, 184; in touch with her mother again, 184; dies after giving birth to stillborn son, 184, 188; grief in England at her death, 185
Charlotte, Queen, 8, 9, 11, 15, 18, 23, 24, 29, 32, 38, 43, 44, 47–9, 51, 52, 54, 60, 61, 63–5, 84, 90, 92, 96–8, 110, 112–15, 120, 121, 134, 142, 144; and Caroline's reputation, 6, 12; and her marriage, 6, 7 and n.; and Mrs. Fitzherbert, 27; and clothes for Caroline, 28; and the wedding, 30, 31; hostility to Caroline, 33, 38; and domestic details, 35–8; preparations for Caroline's baby, 37–9; and the King's health, 61–3, 94–5; and Princess Charlotte, 107; and Duchess of Brunswick's death, 119; suffers from dropsy, 129; and Princess Charlotte's proposed marriage, 130; and the Allied Sovereigns, 138, 139
Charlton, Caroline lives at, 57, 58
Chiswick House, 126
Cholmondeley, Earl and Countess of, 52
Cholmondeley, Miss, killed in carriage accident, 71
Clanwilliam, Earl of, 223
Claremont, 184
Clarence, Duke of (William IV), 30, 31, 36, 107n., 115, 121; and Princess Charlotte's birth, 40; on the Prince of Wales, 54; and the Duchess of Brunswick, 89–90; on his father's insanity, 98
Clarke, Mary Ann, 195
Clerici, Graziano Paolo, 166, 174
Clermont, Earl of, 21, 22
Clorinda, HMS, frigate, 167, 210
Clyde, HMS, frigate, 89
Cole, William, 81
Como, 162, 164, 203; Villa d'Este, 162, 177–83, 200, 201, 213; Villa Barone, 177, 203
Connaught Place, Bayswater, Caroline lives at, 124, 131, 138, 144, 147, 149, 156
Consalvi, Cardinal, 175, 176, 182
Conway, Field-Marshal, and Conway House, 51
Conyngham, Lady, 192, 219
Copley, Sir John (Solicitor General), 195, 199, 200, 205, 207, 212–13, 216
Coutts, Messrs, bankers, 177, 182
Coutts, Thomas, 183
Cranbourne Lodge, Windsor Forest, 144; Charlotte at, 148
Craven, Hon. Richard Keppel, Chamberlain to Caroline, 151, 153–7, 191, 194; his sketches, 155; supports Caroline at her trial, 196, 215; acts as her secretary, 221–2
Crede, Maurice, Caroline's outrider, 180–1
Creevey, Thomas, 125, 126, 141, 189, 193, 218; at Caroline's trial, 194–6, 203–5, 207, 211, 212, 226
Croker, John Wilson, 194, 205, 211
Cumberland, Duke of (Prince Ernest), 7n., 27, 31, 37, 61, 114; visits to Caroline, 60; influence over Prince Regent, 96–7
Cuxhaven, 20, 150

Damer, Mrs., 220
D'Angoulême, Duc, 115
D'Angoulême, Madame, 93, 94
Darlington, Lord, 206
D'Artois (Charles), 115n.
Dashwood, Lady, head governess, 38, 43; death, 51
Davoust, Marshal, 88
De Clifford, Dowager Baroness head governess to Princess Charlotte, 85–6, 100, 105–7, 112, 113; and Charlotte's affair with Hesse, 108; resignation, 111, 113
Delicate Investigation, the, 79–83, 85, 88–90, 110, 116, 117, 122, 146, 192, 211; Caroline cleared of adultery, 82; criticism of her, 82
Demont, Louise, Caroline's maid, 189, 194; evidence at Caroline's trial, 202–3, 207, 208, 211
Denman, Thomas, 193; at Caroline's trial, 196, 197, 216; speech for the defence, 216–217; at Caroline's deathbed, 226
De Stael, Madame, 164
Devonshire, Duchess of, 44
Devonshire, Duke of, 138; and Princess Charlotte, 126
Devonshire House, 138
Dorset, Duke and Duchess of, 31
Douglas, Sir John, 72–4, 146; anonymous letter to him, 77; and the Delicate Investigation, 79
Douglas, Lady, 72–80, 146; and Sir Sidney Smith, 72, 77; Caroline's violent friendship with her, 73–5; acts as lady-in-waiting, 73; spreads reports about Caroline, 77; Caroline banishes her, 77; her statements, 78–80, 82
Drummond, Sir William, 100–1
Duncan, Lord, 200

Edmeades, Dr. Thomas, 76; and the Delicate Investigation, 81–2
Edward, Prince, *see* Kent, Duke of
Elba, 138, 151, 156, 164
Eldon, Lord, 65, 83, 104, 112, 145, 147, 212, 215; inquisition of Princess Charlotte, 112, 113, 116; at Caroline's trial, 194, 195, 201, 203, 212

Elgin, Martha, Countess of, governess to Princess Charlotte, 55 and n., 63–5, resignation, 85
Elizabeth, Princess, 29, 36, 38, 39, 90, 91, 107n., 111, 129; on the Prince of Wales and Caroline, 34; and Caroline's pregnancy, 36, and Princess Charlotte's birth, 40
Ellenborough, Lord, 79, 145, 147, 200, 214
Elliston, Robert, 226
Elphinstone, Miss Mercer, friend of Princess Charlotte, 103, 126–9, 132, 133, 144, 146; correspondence with her stopped, 103, clandestine correspondence, 105, 106, 111–113, 115, 117; and Charlotte's affair with Hesse, 109–10; ban on her lifted, 122; and Prince August, 142; smuggled letter from Charlotte, 148
Erne, Lady, 218, 219, 222
Errington, Henry, 224
Erskine, Lord, 79, 211, 217
Exmouth, Lord, 159, 164, 170, 192

Fisher, Bishop John, in charge of Princess Charlotte's education, 85–7, 101, 143, 145
FitzClarence, Captain George, 107, 118
FitzGerald, Lord Henry, 69, 102
Fitzherbert, Mrs. Maria, 22, 30, 44, 48, 54; marriage to Prince of Wales, 24–6; he leaves her, 26–7; and his marriage to Caroline, 30; and his will, 40–1; re-united to him, 70; withdraws from his life, 98–9
Fitzroy, Georgiana, 127
Flynn, Lieutenant, RN: joins Caroline's entourage, 167; commands the polacca, 168–70; evidence at Caroline's trial, 211–13
Forbes, Lady Elizabeth, 151, 208
Fox, Charles James, 49, 65, 96; and Mrs. Fitzherbert's marriage, 25
Frederick, Prince of Wales, 18, 28n.
Frederick, William III, King of Prussia, 134; in England, 140
French Revolution, 1, 48, 56
Friedrich August of Prussia, Prince, and Princess Charlotte, 142–4, 147
Fulford, Roger, 215n.

Gandersheim, Abbess of, 9, 13
Garth, Frances, sub-governess to Princess Charlotte, 43, 51, 55, 58, 73, 81
Gell, Sir William, 138; Chamberlain to Caroline, 151, 154–6, 194, 196; resignation, 154; travels and scholarship, 154, 155; sketches, 155; letters from Caroline, 150, 159, 161, 162, 164, 169–70, 172, 177, 178, 181–4, 189, 191, 221–3; evidence at her trial, 215–16
Genoa, 153, 157–9, 164; Palazzo Durazza, 157, 158
George III, King, 3, 9, 10, 17, 18, 23, 28 and n., 29–30, 33, 36, 42, 48, 54, 55, 60, 82–4, 87, 92, 96, 98, 106, 113, 120, 146, 161–2, 222; and the Prince of Wales's marriage, 7; sends Malmesbury to Brunswick, 7, 45; family life, 24; and the Prince of Wales's debts, 25–6; and the wedding, 30, 31; learns of Princess Charlotte's birth, 39–40; and the Prince of Wales's will, 41; Princess Charlotte's christening, 44; refuses to grant Prince legal separation, 52; fondness for Princess Charlotte, 55, 63; illness, 60; state of his mind, 60–3, 65–6; visits to Caroline, 61, 62; receives her at Kew 64–5; in charge of Princess Charlotte, 66; and the Delicate Investigation, 78–9; and Princess Charlotte's education, 85; and Duchess of Brunswick's escape to England, 89–90; reunion with his sister, 90–1; provides pension for her, 91, 119; and death of Princess Amelia, 94; his Jubilee, 94; relapses into insanity, 94–5; pronounced incurable, 102; death, 189–90
George, Prince of Wales (Prince Regent) (George IV), 7, 8, 12, 13, 15, 17, 20, 47–50, 62, 64, 68, 74, 84, 87, 92, 93, 106, 107, 142, 168, 182, 187, 188, 195, 212, 221, 226; decision to marry Caroline, 6, impatience at delays, 9–10; and Lady Jersey, 11, 13, 20, 26–9, 31, 34, 35, 37, 53, 54; meeting with Caroline, 22–3, 30; and Mrs. Fitzherbert, 22, 24–7, 30
his debts, 25–6, 28; plans for his wedding, 28; the King refuses to make him General, 29–30; his wedding, 30–2; wedding night at Carlton House, 32, 35; early married life, 33–4; 'honeymoon' at Kempshot Park, 34–5; settlement of his money affairs, 35; birth of his daughter, 39
and Carlton House, 42–3; and the royal nursery, 43, 55; takes pains not to meet his wife, 44, 46; proposes separation, 47, 52, 53; interviews with Caroline, 53–4; lack of attention to his daughter, 55–6, 85; and her place of residence, 66; re-united with Mrs. Fitzherbert, 70; and Sir John Douglas's allegations, 77, 78n.; and William Austin, 78, 87; and the Delicate Investigation, 79, 80; possible new proceedings, 82, 83; and death of the Duke of Brunswick, 89
sworn in as Regent, 96; retains Tories in power, 96, 103, 106; and Lady Hertford, 96; 98, 99, 136, 192; and the Duke of Cumberland, 96–7; fête at Carlton House, 98–100; Mrs. Fitzherbert's withdrawal, 98–9; his debts and expenditure, 100; illness, 101; drink and drugs, 101; full powers as Regent (1812), 102; and Charlotte's affair with Hesse, 109; letter from her, 111–13; his behaviour to her, 112, 113, 115, and Miss Knight

George, Prince of Wales—*cont.*
114–15; on Charlotte and her mother, 114–15; interview with Charlotte, 116–17; and Privy Councillors' inquiry, 117–18; and opening of Charles I's coffin, 120–1; plans for Charlotte's marriage, 126–8; and the Prince of Orange, 126–30, 132–3
and Louis XVIII, 134–5; and Grand Duchess Catherine of Oldenburg, 135–7, 139; visit of Allied Sovereigns, 139–42; and the Tsar, 139–41; and Charlotte's broken engagement, 143; dismisses Miss Knight, 144; and Charlotte's escape to her mother's house, 145, 146; visits Charlotte at Cranbourne Lodge, 148–9
and Caroline's departure from England, 149, 150; and Ompteda, 160, 162; the Milan Commission, 161–2; seeks grounds for divorce, 162; death of his father, 189; proclaimed King, 189; serious illness, 189; retires to Windsor on Caroline's arrival in London, 192; and Lady Conyngham, 192, 219; and proposals for Caroline's trial, 192; at Brighton and Windsor during trial, 206, 211; refuses to omit divorce clause from Bill, 211; postponement of coronation, 219; seeks new ways of dealing with Caroline, 219; public appearances, 220; contrives not to meet Caroline, 220; and Prince Leopold, 222; the coronation, 224–5; exclusion of Caroline, 224
Gifford, Sir Robert (Attorney General), 195, 196, 199, 202, 206
Gillray, James, 77
Gizziliere, Count, 159, 178; agent for the Regent, 162
Glenbervie, Lady, 151, 157, 159; lady-in-waiting to Caroline, 68, 93, 97, 99
Glenbervie, Lord, 59–61, 80, 81, 97, 98, 101, 102, 157, 159
Gloucester, Duke of, 61, 126
Godfrey, Rev. Philip, 204
Goldsworthy, Miss, governess to the Princesses, 51, 114, 121
Grassini, Madame, 140
Greenwich, 21, 58, 127, 191; Park, 59, 62, 123, 151
Grenville, Lord, 78, 79, 83, 89
Greville, Charles, 191–2, 207, 215
Greville, Hon. Fulke, 21
Grey, Earl, 137, 143, 148, 200, 201
Grimm, Herr von, 202
Grosvenor, Lord, 214

Haeckle, Mme. de, Duchess of Brunswick's lady-in-waiting, 92, 93
Halford, Sir Henry, 96, 133, 137; and opening of Charles I's coffin, 120
Hamilton, Lady Anne, 156, 191, 192, 194, 223n, 225
Hamilton, Lord Archibald, 194
Hanover, 15, 18–20, 67
Hanover Square, Duchess of Brunswick lives in, 92, 93, 97, 119
Harcourt, Lord, 27, 222
Harcourt, Mrs., lady-in-waiting to Caroline, 19, 58
Hayman, Miss 72, 73, 81, 97, 98, 119; sub-governess to Princess Charlotte, 55–8; dismissed, 57 and n.; Keeper of Caroline's Privy Purse, 57, 68–70; resignation, 103, 104
Hayter, Sir George, painting of Caroline's trial, 203
Hertford, Lady, 96, 98–100, 136, 192
Hertzfeldt, Mlle., Duke of Brunswick's mistress, 3, 9, 12, 23, 85
Hervey, Misses, 118
Hesse, Captain Charles: affair with Princess Charlotte, 107–11, 126, 142, 143, 219; supposed son of Duke of York, 107; equerry to Caroline, 151, 156, 157
Hieronymous, John, 180
Holland, Henry, architect, 42
Holland, Dr. Henry, Caroline's physician, 151, 157, 161, 226
Holroyd, Maria (Lady Stanley of Alderley), 44–5
Hood, Lady, 225
Hood, Lord, Caroline's Chamberlain, 225, 226
Hownam, Lieutenant Joseph: travels with Caroline, 156–65, 170–2, 174–6, 178, 179; deals with her correspondence and business, 157; and the Pope, 158; and Pergami, 159–60, 162–4, 213; in Sicily, 164–5, 167; in Tunis, 168–70; negotiations with British Fleet, 170; in Palestine, 172–4; and Caroline's debts, 177; at Villa d'Este, 177–8, 182; and Ompteda, 181, 213; and the 'Venice Forgery', 183; and news of Charlotte's death, 184–6; sent to England with letters for Brougham, 187; marries and settles in France, 211, 222 and n.; evidence at Caroline's trial, 211–15
Huish, Robert, 5–6, 31, 32, 80
Hutchinson, Lord, 190, 191

Ilchester, Lady, 148

Jaffa, 171, 174, 213
Jason, HMS, frigate, 135, 150
Jena, battle of, 6, 88
Jerningham, Lady, 25, 120
Jersey, 4th Earl of, 27, 39, 51
Jersey, Frances, Countess of, 11, 13, 14, 20, 23, 26–9, 31, 34, 35, 37, 44, 53–6, 193; Lady of the Bedchamber to Caroline, 21–2, 27, 34; and Caroline's reception, 21–2, 27; Caroline

denounces her to the Prince, 46–8; resigns her post, 49, 51
Jersey, Sarah, Countess of, 193, 223
Jerusalem, 164, 170, 171, 213; Caroline's visit, 172–4; Knights of the High Order, 173–4
Jordan, Mrs. Dorothea, 36, 107n.
Jupiter, HMS, frigate, 20, 21, 29

Keith, Lord, 109, 110
Kempshot Park, 34–5
Kensington Palace, 59, 91, 93, 97, 98, 102, 104, 107, 108, 118, 157, 187, 219
Kent, Duke of (Prince Edward), 30, 89, 101, 121, 134; visits to Caroline, 60, 73; and Douglas's allegations, 77–8
Kent, William, 42
Kew, 62–4
Knight, Cornelia, 91, 107, 113; assistant governess to Princess Charlotte, 113–15; Lady Companion, 114, 118, 119, 121, 126, 127, 129, 132, 137, 143, 146, 147; and Prince Regent's interview with Charlotte, 116–17; and the Orange betrothal, 133; and Prince August, 142; dismissed by the Regent, 144
Knight, Sir Joseph, 114
Kress, Barbara, 202

Lausanne, 152
Lawrence, Sir Thomas, 71–2, 140; and the Delicate Investigation, 80–1
Leach, John, 145
Leeds, Duchess of, governess to Princess Charlotte, 113, 118, 127–8; asked to resign, 143–4
Leeds, Duke of, 31, 47
Lennox, Lady Sarah, 24
Leopold of Saxe-Coburg, Prince, 144, 221; marries Princess Charlotte, 170, 184; tells Caroline of Charlotte's death, 184–5; rents Marlborough House, 221; refuses to give up lease to Caroline, 222; and George IV, 222
Letters from the Baltic (Rigby), 5
Leveson-Gower, Granville, 69
Leviathan, HMS, battleship, 164, 167, 168
Lieven, Count, 136, 139
Lieven, Princess, 135, 136, 192, 212, 219, 221
Limerick, Earl of, 214
Lindsay, Lady Charlotte, lady-in-waiting to Caroline, 99, 105, 123, 140, 151, 191, 208; evidence at her trial, 216
Liverpool, Lord, 103, 115, 116, 210, 217, 219, 220; and the Orange betrothal, 137
Lloyd, Frances, Caroline's coffee woman, 77, 80, 81
Lock family, 70–1
Louis XVIII, 93; restoration, 134–5; reception to him, 134
Louis, Mrs., Charlotte's maid, 86, 147
Lyttelton, Lord, 196

Maasdam, Baron Van der Duyn Van, 132
McMahon, Colonel, 53–5, 65
Mahomet the Turk, 211, 213, 215
Majocchi, Theodore, Caroline's postillion, 175; evidence at her trial, 197–201, 208–9, 211
Malmesbury, James Harris, first Earl of, 45; mission to Brunswick, 7–17, 58, 67, 70, 88; and formal betrothal and Treaty of Marriage, 10; advice to Caroline, 11–13, 16, 18–21; journey from Brunswick, 15–21; and meeting between Prince of Wales and Caroline, 22–3
Mamoodh Bashaw, Bey of Tunis, 154, 168–70, 174, 198
Manby, Captain, RN: named as Caroline's lover, 77; and the Delicate Investigation, 80, 81
Manners-Sutton, Archbishop Charles, 192, 225
Marie-Louise, Empress, and Caroline, 152, 154, 178
Marietti, Messrs., Italian bankers, 177, 182, 183
Marlborough House, 221–2
Marmont, Marshal, 125
Mary, Princess, 107n., 112, 115
Mecklenburg-Strelitz, Prince Charles of, 130
Melbourne, Lady, 117
Meneval, Baron, 152
Messina, 165, 167, 174
Metternich, Prince, 135, 140, 180
Milan, 159, 161, 164, 166, 181, 182
Milan Commission, 161–2, 178, 180n., 181, 189, 199, 202, 207; money offered to Caroline's servants, 189; its findings, 192; members continue to spy on Caroline, 222, 223
Minto, Lord, 35, 57, 59
Mirabeau, Comte de, 2, 3
Montague House, Blackheath, 58, 59, 67, 69–73, 76–8, 81, 82, 91, 97, 124, 162
Montjoye, Count, aide-de-camp to Duke of Brunswick, 88, 89
Moore, Archbishop John, 31, 43
Morning Chronicle, 39, 114; publishes Caroline's, letter to the Prince, 111
Munich, 179, 181
Munster, Count, 162; and the Milan Commission, 180n.
Murat, Joachim, King of Naples, 155–6, 180
Murray, Hon. Amelia, 60

Naples, 155–8, 167, 184, 198, 200, 203, 207, 208
Napoleon I, Emperor, 4, 72, 89, 92, 125, 152, 153, 155, 156n., 157 and n., 164, 171; campaign in Germany, 7, 15, 16 and n.; abdication, 134; banished to Elba, 138; escape from Elba, 151, 156

Nazareth, 172
Northumberland, Duke of, 65
Nott, Dr., tutor to Princess Charlotte, 86–7

Oglander, British Consul in Tunis, 168
Oldenburg, Grand Duchess Catherine of, 135–7, 139–41
Oldi, Countess (Angelina Pergami), 161, 164, 188; continues in Caroline's service, 223
Ompteda, Baron (Count) Friedrich de, the Regent's agent, 158, 160, 162, 163, 180 and n., 181, 200; challenged by Hownam to duel, 181, 213; banished from Milan, 181
Orange, Frederick, Prince of, 143
Orange, William, Hereditary Prince of: as suitor for Princess Charlotte, 126–30, 132–3, 137, 141; in England, 127–9; betrothal announced in Holland, 132; the engagement broken, 142, 143
O'Ryan, Dr. John, 210
Osnabruck, 15–17

Palermo, 164
Palliser, Admiral Sir Hugh, 21
Palmerston, Lord, 92
Parma, 154, 178
Payne, Commodore Jack, 17, 20, 27, 29
Peace of Paris, 151
Pembroke, Countess of, 65 and n.
Perceval, Spencer, 83, 96, 98, 117; assassinated, 103, 106
Pergami, Bartolomeo, 159–68, 171, 172, 175–6, 178–80, 182, 183, 185–8, 190, 197, 213, 222, 223; engaged by Caroline as courier, 159; claims noble birth, 160; brings his family with the party, 160–1; Caroline calls him her Chamberlain, 163; given title of Baron, 166; Knight of the High Order of Jerusalem, 173; Grand Master of the Order of St. Caroline, 174; Caroline buys Villa Barone for him, 177; adultery with Caroline alleged, 192, 197, 198, 200–4, 208–9, 211–12; caricatures of him, 205; returns to Pesaro, 209, 223; said to be impotent, 209–11; handling of Caroline's finances, 211
Pergami, Signora Livia, 160, 188
Pergami, Luigi, 160, 188, 213
Pergami, Vittorina, 160, 164, 174, 177, 188
Pergami, Voloti, 160–1
Pesaro, 182, 184, 185, 187, 209, 223; Villa Vittoria, 188
Pitt, William, 35, 36, 60, 68
Pius VII, Pope, 154, 175, 178, 181, 182, 188; visits Caroline in Genoa, 157–8; receives her at Monte Cavallo, 176
Portland, Duke of, 10
Privy Councillors' inquiry (1813), 117–19
Pulteney's Hotel, Piccadilly, 135, 138–40

Quatre Bras, battle of, 4, 151n., 162

Ramsay, Allan, 63
Robinson, 'Perdita', 25
Rome, 155, 156, 175–6, 178, 180, 181, 184, 189
Rosebery, Lord, 200
Rosenweit, Mlle., 15
Rosslyn, Lady, 148
Royal Marriages Act (1772), 24, 26
Royal, Princess (Princess of Wurtemberg), 56, 90
Rutland, Duchess of, 31

Sacchi, Giuseppe, 203–4, 209
Sackville, Lord, 60
St. Caroline, Order of, 174
St. Helens, Lord, 17 and n.
St. Leger, Colonel, 151
St. Omer, 190
St. Paul's Cathedral, Caroline's thanksgiving service at, 218–19
Sapio family, 102–4, 106, 110, 122–4, 188; arrival at Villa d'Este, 178
Sardinia, King and Queen of, 178
Saurau, Count, Governor of Milan, 181
Scaramonger, Turkish firm, owed money by Caroline, 177
Schiavini, Count Michele: in Caroline's entourage, 164; Knight of the High Order of Jerusalem, 173
Scott, Sir Walter, 193
Seymour, Lady Rose, 30
Seymour, Lord Hugh, 27
Sheffield, Lady, 71
Shelley, Frances, Lady, 140
Shelley, Percy Bysshe, 100
Shrewsbury House, Shooter's Hill, 64
Sicily, 164–6, 174
Sidi Hassan, son of the Bey of Tunis, 170
Sidmouth, Lord, 211, 218
Simmons, Dr., 94
Smith, Admiral Sir Sidney 72; defence of Acre, 72, 171; allegations against him, 77, 80, 81, 83
Smythe, John, 24
Snape, Andrew, 59
Sophia, Princess, 93, 97, 107n.
Soult, Marshal, 125
Spencer, Lord, 79
Stade, 19, 20
Stafford, Lady, 27
Stanhope, Lady Hester, 68, 171
Stanley, John (Lord Stanley of Alderley), 1–2
Stanley of Alderley, Lady, *see* Holroyd, Maria
Starkie, Charlotte's dancing master, 148
Stikeman, Thomas, Caroline's page, 67, 76
Stuart, Lady Maria, 31, 32
Stuart, Lord Charles, 179–80

Stuart-Wortley, Lady Caroline, 59–60
Sussex, Duke of (Prince Augustus), 31, 72, 134, 143, 148, 195, 223; and Lady Douglas, 77; and the Orange betrothal, 137; and Charlotte's escape to her mother's house, 145, 146
Syracuse, 165, 174, 214

Tavistock, Lady, 223
Taylor, Ann and Jane, 63
Terracina, 175
Thomas, Colonel, 47
Thurlow, Lord, 78
Tierney, George, 106
Times, The, 37, 47, 48, 51, 140, 191
Tomassio, Chevalier, 183n.
Tooke, Horne, 49
Topography of Greece and Ithaca (Gell), 154
Townshend, Lady, Caroline's Mistress of the Wardrobe, 39, 87–8, 123
Tramezzani, Signor, 140
Trench, Mrs. Richard, 224
Tunis, 164, 171; Caroline's visit, 168–70; threatened bombardment by British Fleet, 170; and abolition of slavery, 170
Tyrwhitt, Sir Thomas, 194, 195, 216

Udney, Mrs., sub-governess to Princess Charlotte, 86
Underwood, Dr. Michael, *accoucheur*, 37–9

Vauxhall, 92; Gardens, 125
'Venice Forgery', the, 183
Vernon Harcourt, Archbishop, 225
Victoria, Queen, 73
Vienna, 179–80, 199

Wales, Prince of, *see* George, Prince of Wales
Walmoden, Countess, 18
Walpole, Horace, 42, 99n.
Warwick House, Princess Charlotte lives at, 66, 105, 114, 115, 118, 122, 129, 131, 136, 142–4, 146, 147
Wellesley, Lord, 103
Wellington, Duke of, 106, 125, 127, 192, 193, 219, 220, 225
West, Benjamin, 71
Westminster Abbey, 224–5
Westminster election (1796), 49
Weymouth, 37, 38, 64–6; Gloucester Lodge, 38
Whitbread, Samuel, 106, 119, 122, 123, 137
Wilberforce, William, 193
Willis, Rev. Dr. Francis, 62
Wilson, Mary Ann, Caroline's housemaid, 81
Wilson, Mrs. Selina, 33
Windsor, and Windsor Castle, 33, 37, 39, 40, 64, 90, 92, 97, 98, 101, 103–5, 107, 108, 110, 112, 115, 118, 127, 129, 211; Lower Lodge, 66, 105; St. George's Chapel, 120
Wolfenbüttel, 1
Wood, Alderman (Sir) Matthew, 192, 195; arranges Caroline's reception at Dover, 191; offers her board and lodging, 191
Wraxall, Sir Nathanael, 27, 31

York, Archbishop of, *see* Vernon Harcourt
York, Cardinal (Henry Benedict Stewart), 121
York, Duchess of, 194
York, Frederick, Duke of, 9, 29, 30, 54, 96, 107, 114, 130, 145, 147–8, 189, 222; and the Regency, 137; at Caroline's trial, 195, 196; and Mary Ann Clarke, 195

THEA HOLME

Born in London in 1903, Thea Holme attended the Central School of Drama and toured with Sir Philip Ben Greet's company in France and the United States. She subsequently made her debut on the London stage with Sir Nigel Playfair. At the outbreak of the Second World War, she was engaged by the BBC as a member of their first repertory company, and has written and acted in many radio programs. Thea Holme is the author of a book about the Carlyles, a history of Chelsea, and a biography of the future George IV's daughter, Princess Charlotte.